# Disembedded Markets

AF835114

This book offers a sociological analysis of globalised capitalist markets, advancing the notion of 'disembedded markets' to challenge the idea of 'social embeddedness' common in economic sociology. Avoiding an exclusive focus on institutions, networks and trust relationships surrounding markets, the author concentrates on private property as the key institution of markets, in order to emphasise the historical origins of modern capitalism and the free market narrative, and to develop a socio-historical analysis of the disembedding process together with an account of the built-in contradictions and limits of market universalisation. Through an analysis of their encompassing character, this volume demonstrates that disembedded markets do not fit standard theoretical accounts of sociality – a problem taken up not only by Karl Marx, but also by Friedrich August von Hayek and Niklas Luhmann – and questions the attempts of the emerging approach known as 'economic theology' to draw parallels between the practices that arise from disembedded markets and from forms of religious experience and ritual. A rigorous examination of the phenomenon of disembedded markets and the claims to which they give rise concerning the equivalences between religion and capitalism, this book will appeal to scholars of sociology and economics with interests in capitalism, social theory and global markets.

**Christoph Deutschmann** is Professor Emeritus and former Chair of Sociology at the University of Tübingen, Germany. He has worked as a research fellow at the Institute for Social Research in Frankfurt/M, at Tohoku University in Sendai, Japan, and at the WZB Berlin Social Science Center. His research interests and publications are in the fields of economic sociology, the sociology of work, and social theory.

## Classical and contemporary social theory

**Series Editor:** Stjepan G. Mestrovic, Texas A&M University, USA

Classical and Contemporary Social Theory publishes rigorous scholarly work that re-discovers the relevance of social theory for contemporary times, demonstrating the enduring importance of theory for modern social issues. The series covers social theory in a broad sense, inviting contributions on both 'classical' and modern theory, thus encompassing sociology, without being confined to a single discipline. As such, work from across the social sciences is welcome, provided that volumes address the social context of particular issues, subjects, or figures and offer new understandings of social reality and the contribution of a theorist or school to our understanding of it.

The series considers significant new appraisals of established thinkers or schools, comparative works or contributions that discuss a particular social issue or phenomenon in relation to the work of specific theorists or theoretical approaches. Contributions are welcome that assess broad strands of thought within certain schools or across the work of a number of thinkers, but always with an eye toward contributing to contemporary understandings of social issues and contexts.

**Urban Walls**
Political and Cultural Meanings of Vertical Structures and Surfaces
*Edited by Andrea Mubi Brighenti and Mattias Kärrholm*

**Updating Charles H. Cooley**
Contemporary Perspectives on a Sociological Classic
*Natalia Ruiz-Junco and Baptiste Brossard*

**Freud as a Social and Cultural Theorist**
On Human Nature and the Civilizing Process
*Howard L. Kaye*

**From the Peaceable to the Barbaric**
Thorstein Veblen and the Charro Cowboy
*Beatriz Aldana Marquez*

For more information about this series, please visit: https://www.routledge.com/sociology/series/ASHSER1383

# Disembedded Markets

## Economic Theology and Global Capitalism

**Christoph Deutschmann**

Routledge
Taylor & Francis Group
LONDON AND NEW YORK

First published 2019
by Routledge
4 Park Square, Milton Park, Abingdon, Oxon OX14 4RN
605 Third Avenue, New York, NY 10017

*Routledge is an imprint of the Taylor & Francis Group, an informa business*

First issued in paperback 2020



*British Library Cataloguing in Publication Data*
A catalogue record for this book is available from the British Library.

*Library of Congress Cataloging-in-Publication Data*
A catalog record has been requested for this book.

ISBN: 978-1-138-61402-4 (hbk)
ISBN: 978-0-367-66116-8 (pbk)

Typeset in Times New Roman
by Taylor & Francis Books

# Contents

# Acknowledgements

The pre-history of this book goes back to my studies and seminars on the sociology of money, particularly those on the work of Karl Marx and Georg Simmel, which I started more than twenty-five years ago in Tübingen. What I gradually learnt from these classic authors, as well as from the debates with my students and colleagues, was to understand money as a relational phenomenon, that is, as something that is primarily relevant not due to its inherent qualities, but to the social relationships and opportunity contexts which it constitutes. Exploring these relationships and contexts, however, became a long journey, one without a clear destination and full of – not always productive – detours. And I am afraid that even this book may mark only a preliminary end of the journey, and not a definitive one.

What helped me greatly to keep orientation were several research stays at the Max Planck Institute for the Study of Societies in Cologne, first as a scholar-in-residence in 2008 and then again in 2011 and 2015. Jens Beckert, Wolfgang Streeck, Sascha Münnich and many other colleagues at the institute encouraged me to continue my project, and gave me many valuable comments and much useful advice. Martijn Konings played a key role in pushing me to start writing this book. Moreover, I have to thank Paul Windolf for extended intellectual exchanges on financial markets and money, and Stefan Schwarzkopf, Uwe Schimank and Axel Paul for reading early versions of the manuscript and for giving me important feedback. Scott Stelle not only helped me correct the linguistic deficiencies of the manuscript, but he also gave me productive comments; moreover I have to thank Michael Helfield for his excellent work in editing the manuscript. Last, but not least, I am grateful to SAGE Publications, to the Max Planck Institute for the Study of Societies, and to Leipziger Universitätsverlag for granting me permission to reprint in this book parts of some of my earlier publications:

## References

Deutschmann, Christoph (2012a). 'Capitalism, Religion and the Idea of the Demonic', MPIfG Discussion Paper, February, Köln: Max Planck Institute for the Study of Societies.

Deutschmann, Christoph (2015). 'Disembedded Markets as a Mirror of Society: Blind Spots of Social Theory'. *European Journal of Social Theory* 18(4), 368–389.

Deutschmann, Christoph (2016b). 'Multiple Futures or One Future? The Capitalist Growth Imperative'. *Comparativ: Zeitschrift für Globalgeschichte und vergleichende Gesellschaftsforschung* 26(2), 17–28.

# 1 Introduction

## Economic theology as a challenge to economic theory

Political theology is an approach well known in political science, going back to Carl Schmitt's controversial enquiry into the theological foundations of state sovereignty (Schmitt 1934).[1] In comparison to this approach, economic theology is of much more recent origin, and is still relatively unknown. This study aims to clarify it and to review it from the perspectives of economic sociology and a social theory.

What is economic theology? Above all, it is something very different from what one might first guess, such as a theological ethic of economic action, which of course is not new, but a discipline deeply anchored in the traditions of theological thinking. Most religions have instituted ethical norms to guide the economic practices of their believers concerning, for example, the responsible handling of money and wealth, restrictions on charging interest, the giving of charity to the poor, and fairness and honesty in business transactions. A theological ethic is based on the religious distinction between a transcendent sphere and the profane world; it aims to transform revelation-based knowledge into practically relevant principles of moral conduct (for an overview, see Wilson 1997). Economic theology does not contradict the distinction of the transcendent and the profane. What it rejects, however, is the exclusive attribution of the economy to the profane world. To be precise, we are not talking about the economy in general, but of the economy of present-day global capitalism.

Global capitalism has emerged from a process which economic sociologists – following Karl Polanyi – characterise as a 'disembedding' of markets. 'Disembedding' refers to the expansion of markets across given territorial, institutional and social confines starting in the early nineteenth century and resulting in the historical formation of capitalism as a global system. As an encompassing social system, disembedded markets give rise to the very epistemological problem that is associated with any idea of society as a 'totality': in becoming total, markets cannot become an object to any observer, but are experienced as a 'horizon', framing actions and observations in an involuntary way and being accessible only from the perspective of a participant. While Carl Schmitt concentrates on the implications of politics becoming total, economic theology focuses on markets, which, by virtue of their disembeddedness, take on an encompassing character and cannot be known as a totality by anyone – and liberal economists (in particular Friedrich August von Hayek) have emphasised this point. As an encompassing social reality, markets and money (as their medium) possess enigmatic and even numinous qualities that traditionally have been attributed to religious experience. No longer is capitalism being interpreted as a system merely 'influenced' by religious traditions, as Max Weber (1978) did in his studies of the Protestant ethic. Rather, economic theology follows Walter Benjamin (1985), who in his famous fragment defined capitalism *as* a religion. This is a departure from conventional economic thought and its view of the economy as a profane reality governed by nothing but utilitarian rationalism and materialism. Economic science, in this view, has been confronted with a historically new world of contingencies, which, though being man-made, are reminiscent of religious transcendence due to their encompassing and existential character. To deal with these contingencies in practice, action patterns showing formal parallels with religious rituals have evolved. From such a viewpoint, it may become understandable why some authors, such as Alexander Rüstow (2001) and Robert Nelson (2001), have diagnosed a latent proximity between theology and economic theory.

How can such an unorthodox approach be justified? In the recent debate, three lines of discussion have developed. The first debate concerns the theological genealogy of the term 'economy' itself. *Oikonomia* in the original ancient Greek, as coined by Aristotle, can be translated as 'management' or 'housekeeping'. The concept marked the domestic sphere of reproduction, to be distinguished from the public realm (the *polis* or city-state). As Giorgio Agamben (2011) has shown, the concept's original profane meaning underwent a change in the course of its reception by Christian theologians. Paul and the Church Fathers in the first centuries CE used the concept of *oikonomia* in order to circumscribe the governance of mundane life by God. Christian teaching emphasised the idea of one God; it rejected the Gnostic dual world-view with its distinction between the superior being and an inferior creator God (the 'demiurge'). The Trinitarian formula was introduced to settle the problem of how God as a transcendent being could nevertheless enter into mundane history and reign over the human world. *Oikonomia* now referred to the management of the world by God through his three-fold presence as father, son and Holy Spirit (Agamben 2001: 17–18.). At the same time, the Church followed the Aristotelian conception of the mundane economy as a big household being organised as a self-sufficient sub-unit of a hierarchically structured cosmos and as something that is not compatible with chrematistic practices of making more money with money. William of Auxerre (1160–1229) condemned interest as a sinful human intervention into the sovereignty of God over time; Thomas Aquinas (1225–1274) followed Aristotle in denouncing interest and usury as unnatural and evil. Despite the gradual rise of markets, commerce and banking during the Middle Ages, the condemnation of usury by the Church became even harsher. Only after the Reformation did the interpretation of divine providence change. It shifted from the perception of God as an omnipresent ruler to that of a legislator, leaving men the freedom to regulate their own affairs within the natural laws that he had instituted.

As a consequence, the economy could no longer be conceptualised as an entity purposively organised by God; rather, it was interpreted – such as in the work of Thomas Hobbes and Bernard de Mandeville – as a 'machine' coordinated by natural laws. Still in the physiocratic school of the eighteenth century (most famously represented by Anne Robert Jacques Turgot and François Quesnay), economic governance was understood as the application of metaphysically based 'laws of nature' to human reproduction (Koslowski 1998: 32–33; Priddat 2013: 51–52). Gradually, however, the focus shifted from natural laws to human interests and to the modern idea of the economy as an order not instituted by God but as a phenomenon emerging spontaneously from free market forces.

And it this concept that leads us to the second debate, which has to do with open and hidden references to theology within modern economic theory. Adam Smith's 'invisible hand',[2] that is, his concept of an emergent self-regulation of market transactions providing social welfare in an unintentional way, has remained a core piece of economic theory up to the present day. Different from later economic theorists, Smith never presented any rigorous theoretical explication of the concept, but confined himself to a variety of ad hoc illustrations. And the scientific character of Smith's conception continues to be contested.[3] While most economists view Smith as the founder of modern, scientific economics, Lisa Hill (2001) made a strong point that such an interpretation cannot be upheld without reservations upon closer examination of Smith's philosophical and theological background. Although he found little attractive in Christianity, Smith shared the deist belief in a benevolent divine 'Providence' that was widespread amongst the intellectuals of his time: 'God exists, the world is the product of design, and the observable order of regularity in human affairs is a direct result of his design and purpose in nature' (Hill 2001: 5). As Hill argues, these assumptions were basic to the argument set out in *The Theory of Moral Sentiments* (Smith 1991 [1759]) as well as in *The Wealth of Nations* (Smith 1999 [1776]). In this sense, Smith's work is 'manifestly theological' (Hill 2001: 1). Smith conceptualised the economy as a two-tiered model, with the first tier representing the individual action level and the second tier representing the social system level designed by divine Providence. This distinction of levels allowed him to follow the Stoic justification of apparently vicious human desires and actions as indirectly beneficial. Even intentionally immoral individual actions can have positive consequences for society as a whole in a way that is transparent not to limited human reason, but only to the divine creator. In this sense, the old concept of *oikonomia* as divine governance of profane human affairs continues to be present in Smith's apparently secular concept of the invisible hand (see also Viner 1972; Viner 1998: 37–38; Agamben 2011: 277–278; Priddat 2013; and Binswanger 2015).

Even if one concedes theological influences on Smith's thinking, one could argue that this is irrelevant for modern economics, since there has been no lack of later attempts to establish equilibrium theory on a truly 'scientific' basis. The milestones here were, as it is well known, the general equilibrium models of Leon Walras (1954) and, much later, that of Kenneth Arrow and Gerard Debreu (Arrow and Debreu 1954). The 'scientific' reconstruction of the invisible hand here meant its *mathematical* explication as an overall constellation of goods and factor prices that would satisfy the condition of Pareto optimality. 'General equilibrium' referred to an ideal stage of the total system, in which no rational actor would have reasons to change their disposition; it was a model which was designed to serve as a tool with which to reconstruct the actual working of market forces. As many critics have noted, however, the mathematical demonstration of general equilibrium was possible only under extremely restrictive assumptions, assumptions that were far away from empirical evidence such as the perfect rationality of actors, perfect knowledge and competition, given and concave preferences, given technologies, constant returns of scale, the absence of external effects, and the neutrality of money. This meant eliminating the uncertainty of markets on the level of analytical premises and assuming everything away that could give rise to empirical doubts about the possibility of a general equilibrium being reached. General equilibrium analysis is empirically void, as Friedrich Hayek noted:

> What is the problem we wish to solve when we try to construct a rational economic order? On certain familiar assumptions the answer is simple enough. *If* we possess all relevant information, *if* we can start out from a given system of preferences and *if* we command complete knowledge of available means, the problem, which remains, is purely one of logic. That is, the answer to the question of what is the best use of the available means is implicit in our assumptions.
>
> (Hayek 1945: 519)

The real problem of economic analysis does not lie in mathematics, but in the fact that the knowledge required to implement general equilibrium theory is 'not given to anyone in its totality' (Hayek 1945: 520). The price for reconstructing the invisible hand idea in mathematical terms is its empirical irrelevance. The theory ends up in the tautology that the working of free market forces culminates in the welfare optimum, the latter in turn being defined as the very result of free market forces.

Hayek's critique of neoclassical equilibrium theory is clear and concise. The intellectual provocation lies in the conclusions he draws from it. The most plausible conclusion would have been a concept of markets as a black box, a field of contingencies, where almost everything can happen. Price signals may induce a positive, welfare-enhancing feedback effect on individual actions, but likewise may produce contradictory impulses,[4] or may induce self-reinforcing disequilibria and bubbles, as is often the case in real estate and financial markets. Markets are an arena providing ample opportunities for actors to phish and cheat each other (Akerlof and Shiller 2015). Market transactions may produce negative externalities at the cost of third parties instead of enhancing the general welfare. Competition in the markets tends to undermine itself by reinforcing power asymmetries and giving rise to monopolies. Instead of such a black box concept, Hayek ends up with a euphemistic portrait of markets as spontaneous processes generating a higher level of human evolution. Since markets are able to process a level of complexity that surpasses anything individual human reason can grasp, there is no chance to assess the 'rationality' of price signals. Nevertheless, we have to accept them, as Hayek argues, not only as a matter of fact, but with 'humility', because they represent a 'higher' order of human affairs transcending the power of individual reasoning. 'True' individualism, in contrast to 'false' rationalist individualism, qualifies itself by its 'consciousness of the limitations of the individual mind which induces an attitude of humility toward the impersonal and anonymous processes by which individuals help to create things greater than they know' (Hayek 1948: 8). Hayek's apology of free markets not only brushes away management and organisation as fundamental issues of economic practice and theory, but also appears to be self-contradictory: Hayek criticises individual reason in the name of an allegedly superior collective reason incorporated into the evolutionary process. However, how should the latter be accessible without recourse to the former? What Hayek is offering is not a scientific theory, but a eulogy for market-driven evolutionary progress, and its in-built superior reason, which not by chance is reminiscent of theological thought. Smith's divine providence appears again, albeit not in an explicit theological language but in that of higher evolutionary 'reason' (for a discussion and critique of Hayek, see Kley 1992; Brodbeck 2001; Backhaus 2005; Vogl 2010; and Fleischmann 2010).

A further tradition of economic thinking, where theological heritage is also influential, albeit less in the sense of economic theology and more in the sense of conventional theological ethics, is the German school of ordoliberalism. This school, which had a strong programmatic influence on the reconstruction of the West German economy after 1949, constituted itself in Freiburg and Cologne in the 1920s and early 1930s; its leading members were Walter Eucken, Alexander Rüstow, Wilhelm Röpke, Franz Böhm and Alfred Müller-Armack (for an overview, see Koslowski 2000: 93–274). The term 'ordoliberalism' denotes precisely the difference between this school and the Anglo-Saxon liberal tradition of Adam Smith, David Ricardo and Jeremy Bentham: what is advocated here is not a 'genuine' liberalism, relying on the welfare-producing effects of spontaneous market forces, but a market economy that is embedded into a strong institutional and moral order. It was the common conviction of the ordoliberals that the traditional free market concept, which they termed derogatorily as 'paleo-liberalism', had become outdated due to the crises of the early twentieth century. Alexander Rüstow (2001) even warned of the belief in free markets becoming a 'religion' in a dangerous and fatal sense. This did not mean that the ordoliberals deemed religion to be irrelevant for the governance of markets. However, as they argued, the genuine locus of religion should not be the market process itself, but the institutional and normative order framing it. Such an institutional frame was considered vital to preventing the rise of monopolies and excessive social inequalities, to enforcing the rules of fair competition, and to securing the equality of social chances. It was not the market itself, but only a strong state that could contain excesses of self-interest and guarantee the smooth and beneficial working of the market mechanisms. The role of government was not confined to setting up general rules, a point that had been vital for Hayek. Discretionary interventions to regulate competition were considered legitimate to some degree too; Müller-Armack even advocated collective bargaining and social policy interventions to protect the market position of the poor, though there were profound disagreements on these issues within the circle of the ordoliberals (Hien and Joerges 2017). The state, in turn, could be strong and superior to particular interests only under the condition of founding its legitimacy not on secular, democratic values, but on higher, transcendent ones. As Philip Manow (2001) has shown, the theorists of ordoliberalism did not develop their position from a liberal background, but from a strong commitment to Protestant theology. Eucken, Böhm, Röpke and Müller-Armack were deeply concerned about the decay of Christian values in modern, secularised mass society, and their concept of a 'social' market economy was intended to set a counterpoint against this tendency (Holthaus 2015; concerning Röpke, see also Horn 2011). They did not see the state primarily as an institution of free citizens laying down the rules of the market, but as an agency of moral education, fighting not only market monopolies, but also greed, egoism and consumerism. The key responsibility of economic policy should not only lie in promoting wealth and economic efficiency, but in managing competition and individual motivation in a way that is conductive to superior moral values.

This interventionist conception of the state revealed profound differences between ordoliberalism and the Anglo-Saxon tradition of liberalism. For the Anglo-Saxon liberals, including Smith, Ricardo, John Stuart Mill, Bentham and Hayek, markets constituted the very core of a free and universal civil society, with the state performing only an instrumental role for citizens to regulate their proper affairs. For the ordoliberals, on the contrary, the state was an agency *superior* to markets. As an agency instituted by God to contain the sinful nature of man, the state, not markets, represented the true and ultimate nexus of society. Ordoliberalism, thus, is at odds with the universalistic impetus of Hayekian liberalism. What it offers instead is a national container model of the economy, which plays down the transnational scope of markets in contemporary capitalism.

A third debate where economic theology is present has evolved around the interpretation of modern capitalism as a 'secularised' form of Christian eschatology. One of the leading authors here is Robert Nelson with his interpretation of economics *as* a religion (Nelson 2001). Being educated as a professional economist and drawing largely on the historical work of Jacob Viner (1972, 1978), Nelson reviews the history of modern economic thought, aiming to detect hidden normative foundations in apparently 'technical' and 'scientific' discourses. His special focus is on a 'theological' reconstruction of the teachings in Harvard (Paul Samuelson) and Chicago (Frank Knight, Milton Friedman, George Stigler) as the two dominant schools of economics in the United States. He then goes on to consider the approaches of 'institutional economics'. Nelson's point is that modern economists, contrary to their self-understanding as scientists, actually are taking the role of preachers: 'Beneath the surface of their formal economic theorizing, economists are engaged in an act of delivering religious messages. Correctly understood, these messages are seen to be promises of the true path of salvation in this world – to a new heaven on earth' (Nelson 2001: xx). He then continues: 'Startling as the thought must be to most current economists, it may be that their most important social role has been preachers of a religion with the special character that it acts to uphold the normative foundation required for a rapidly growing economy' (Nelson 2001: 8). Economic 'theology' is preaching the values of rationality and efficiency as a means to attain a state of material abundance, which would put an end to the evils of this world and establish a paradise on earth. Its main task is to solve what Nelson calls the 'market paradox': encouraging self-interested and profit-maximising action while at the same time upholding the social virtues of markets, such as adherence to contracts; honesty and trust in business transactions; and commitment to the greater public good. Nelson views the economic profession as a new priestly class preaching the new gospel of this-worldly salvation by seeking never-ending material progress. What still had been considered merely as a *symptom* of religious salvation in the Protestant tradition – capital profit – inadvertently became its very substance.

A point that has remained ambiguous in Nelson's approach is the question of the genuine object and level of his analysis. Does he focus only on the alleged transformation of the economic profession into a preaching class, or does he actually talk about larger, structural transformations of society and religion? Theology as a reflexive discourse on religion should not be mixed up with religion itself. Religion is based on primary experiences of revelation – consider, for instance, Moses' encounter with God on Mount Sinai – and sacred texts and rituals passing on these experiences and keeping them alive. Theology comes into play only in a second step, if a religious belief becomes institutionalised and, hence, needs to be explicated, interpreted and applied to concrete social situations. Parallel to this, one would have to observe the difference between primary economic practice and the experiences arising from it and economics as a scientific reflection of practical experiences. Thus, even if one accepts Nelson's thesis of an inner affinity between economics and religion, it would have been more adequate to characterise economics as a kind of 'theology' of economic practice, not as a 'religion', as Nelson does. Beyond Nelson's perspective on the economic profession, a separate analysis of the modern capitalist economy itself, its historical context, and its original icons, rituals and legends would have been required to make his case, and such an analysis is lacking in his writings.

Birger Priddat's interpretation of capitalism as a secularised version of Christian eschatology (Priddat 2013, 2015) is not free from the inclination to mix up immanent reconstructions of economic and social thought with historical context analysis either. Taking Smith's theorem of the invisible hand as a starting point, Priddat interprets modern capitalism as a system where the transcendent dimension of the old theological *oikonomia* has been replaced by the concept of an open earthly future for mankind. As he argues, Smith's position in the history of economic thought is central, because his theory marks the transition point between the old, theological and the new, capitalist *oikonomia*. While Smith attributed the working of the invisible hand still to God's providence, the benefits resulting from it no longer flow to the redeemed, but to the lesser mortals. The new capitalist *oikonomia* is embodied in the credit system and the capital form of money. As capital, money no longer is a mere medium of circulation, but is bound to be invested into projects that will pay off (or not) in an uncertain future. With the capitalisation of money, the organisation of social time changes, as it no longer follows the cyclical logic of a traditional, stationary economy. The new mundane 'religion' of capitalism is governed by an imperative of growth, transforming time into a dynamic, linear, future-oriented flow. The growth imperative corresponds to an imperative of credit and debt, which Priddat interprets as a 'secularisation' of the biblical concept of sin (Priddat 2015: 154). Again the question remains open: how does a change in the level of *ideas* about money and credit give rise to a new 'religion'? If something like a new religion actually were to emerge, this would presuppose a social transformation much larger than a merely conceptual one. What is lacking in Priddat, as well as in Nelson, is a thorough analysis of the structural changes of society itself that give rise to the alleged 'new religion'.

As a first step towards a more comprehensive analysis, the changes in the role of economic science highlighted by Nelson and Priddat should be located in the context of the larger debate on secularisation, which began between philosophers and historians after the Second World War. Karl Löwith's analyses of the theological background of modern ideas of mundane progress are instructive as a starting point (Löwith 2004). The big European revolutions in the new age – the political ones of the seventeenth and eighteenth centuries as well as the industrial revolution of the nineteenth century – were accompanied by sweeping visions about a new human civilisation to come. Despite their vast differences, these visions – Löwith comments on the conceptions of Giambattista Vico, Nicolas de Condorcet, Turgot, Voltaire, Pierre-Joseph Proudhon, Auguste Comte, Georg Wilhelm Friedrich Hegel and Marx – coincided in their critique of traditional theological interpretations of history. History no longer was interpreted as a process governed by divine providence, but as one that is, whether consciously or not, made by man himself. The common point of the enlightened proclamations was their confidence in humans being capable of building a new society, which would be much more peaceful, just and affluent than the existing aristocratic order. Modernity would provide freedom for the individual by having society coincide with the freedom of all. Even more so, some theoreticians (Hegel, Comte, Marx) postulated 'laws' of reason governing history from within and leading mankind, even without intention, to ever higher levels of global civilisation.

Löwith's critique of the idealistic philosophy of history focuses on two points. First, drawing on Jacob Burckhardt he argues that there is no scientific justification for any 'laws' of history and for predicting its course on their basis. The future, let alone the 'end of history', cannot be known by anyone. The very assumption of humans being the subjects of their own history is incompatible with the parallel assumption of a 'higher' logic of human progress governing history. If men really were masters of their own history, the future would be contingent solely on their own action, and thus would be completely open and indeterminable for any non-participant observer. As rational justifications can be ruled out, the only possible explanation for the idealistic belief into progress and human emancipation lies in its implicit reference to the idea of salvation anchored in the Christian legacy. Indeed, the idealist philosophy of history came down to a 'secularisation' of Christian faith as the vision of salvation got applied to the earthly fate of men and transformed into a programme for mundane progress.

Löwith's second point is that this notion rests on a fundamental misunderstanding of the original biblical doctrine. As he argues, the term 'salvation', as coined by Paul and then later Augustine, referred to the redemption of man from sinful earthly existence, and it had nothing to do with any idea of mundane improvement. Löwith concedes that Christian teaching, with its message about the birth, death and coming return of Jesus Christ, introduced an entirely new understanding of time as a linear, future-oriented movement differing from the cyclical time conceptions of Greek cosmology. However, the new order of time had no historical meaning except for its reference to the historical events of the arrival and 're-arrival' of Jesus Christ. Beyond that, historical time was interpreted as a period for the believers to wait for the return of Christ, with no inherent determination as to earthly progress. The philosophers of enlightenment, however, developed the idea that humans should no longer content themselves to wait for the return of Christ, but should rather take their destination into their own hands (see Koselleck 2003: 177–178). In Löwith's view, this secular turn in Christian eschatology meant a thorough misinterpretation of the original doctrine of salvation. Its legitimacy was ambiguous, as it depended factually on the very same theological heritage which was the target of its critique.

Löwith's interpretation did not remain uncontested. Prominent critics of it were Hans Blumenberg (1996 [1966]: 35–36) and Jürgen Habermas (1971), both insisting on the genuine character of the legitimacy of modern secular philosophies of history, albeit arguing from different premises. Blumenberg interpreted secularisation as a legitimate self-defence of reason against the agnostic and disorganising consequences of theological 'absolutism', which he located in the advance of the nominalist school and its view of God as an absolutely sovereign and transcendent ruler in the early new age (see Blumenberg 1996 [1966]: 401–402). Habermas took recourse to the built-in rationality of communicative action, which he interpreted as the driving force of the modern secularisation of Christian faith. For lack of space, I do not go deeper into this debate here, but it suffice it to say that the critics have shown that Löwith's analysis leaves open a key question: if the legitimacy of the secular turn of Christian eschatology is so doubtful, how could it nevertheless become so overwhelmingly successful?

An influential recent attempt to reconstruct the rise of secular society from an encompassing perspective is Charles Taylor's *A Secular Age* (Taylor 2007). Taylor's analysis of secularisation focuses on three key characteristics: the first characteristic of secularised societies is that in such societies religions have lost their former dominance in the public arena. The self-evident ever-presence of God in public life in pre-modern societies has given way to a plurality of different social spheres, each of them being governed no longer by religious principles but by their own norms. Moreover, the religious sphere itself is characterised by a colourful pluralism of beliefs. The second characteristic is the manifest decay of church life as it reveals itself in declining commitment to religious customs and decreasing attendance at church services, both of which can be observed at least in many Western countries. The third, and perhaps most important, characteristic is the perception of religious belief not as a self-evident and uncontested tradition but as a personal option that may be chosen. Thus, even societies showing no visible decline, or even an upswing, in religious activities (e.g. the United States) can be called 'secular' if church affiliation is no longer obligatory for everybody, but is instead based on personal choice and commitment. The optionality of the belief in God, in turn, depends on what Taylor calls the 'immanent frame' (Taylor 2007: 539–540), which is a cultural identity that is no longer open to the experience of transcendence, but which is centred instead on the mundane well-being of man and on the principle that each individual is responsible for seeking their own destinies. To characterise this frame, Taylor also introduces the term 'exclusive humanism' (2007: 19).

The first part of Taylor's voluminous study is devoted to a historical and philological reconstruction of the rise of exclusive humanism during the Modern Age in Europe. Following Max Weber's (1972, 1978) and Richard Tawney's (1926) analyses, Taylor argues that the reformatory move to make evangelical prescriptions obligatory for ordinary believers had the unintended effect of giving rise to a 'disciplinary society' focusing on thorough control of daily social life. Moreover, he points to Hugo Grotius' and John Locke's ideas about a 'natural' moral order based on the institutions of possessive individualism and to the concept of civil society emerging at the time. The modern market 'imaginary' of individuals meeting freely for exchange and seeking their personal gain is a cornerstone of Taylor's concept of exclusive humanism (2007: 159–160). So far, Taylor's analysis marks a counterpoint to economic theology, since in his view it is just the development of the economic institutions of private property and civil society that contributed to the rise of a 'secularised' society buffering itself against the experience of transcendence (2007: 176–177). Following Weber once again, he characterises the transition from pre-modern societies open to God and cosmological forces to modern enlightened humanism as a process of 'disenchantment'. Interestingly, Taylor also uses the term 'disembedding' to describe the same process, thereby unintentionally reminding us of Karl Polanyi's analysis, which I will come to below (2007: 146–147). Up to this point, there seems to be no room for any 'economic theology' in Taylor's approach.

However, Taylor is clearly aware that such an interpretation alone would not suffice. He distances himself from 'subtraction stories' of secularisation, and describes it as a process by which society frees itself from the ballast of religious superstition and concentrates its energies on the rational mastery of mundane life. Of course, he also knows that the fathers of the idea of civil society, Hugo Grotius, John Locke, Adam Ferguson, and Adam Smith, were anything else but hostile towards the idea of a divine creator instituting the rules of society. Even Smith's theory did not imply a complete departure from theology, though Smith's idea of God reduced itself largely to the rationalised constructions of Deism.

Religion and civil society are not necessarily antagonistic to each other. Had the idea of the 'buffered', self-controlled and self-sufficient individual actor really been the last word of exclusive humanism, it could not have challenged the Christian heritage so profoundly. To bring exclusive humanism into the position of a genuine alternative to religion, additional forces must first have come into play. Secular humanism had to offer also new ways to explore the 'fullness' of life, as Taylor puts it – that is, to open new dimensions of moral and spiritual experience. Indeed, this is what happened, as Taylor tries to show in his voluminous chapter about the 'nova effect' of new spiritual, aesthetic, religious, and anti-religious movements that have emerged since the late eighteenth century. Moreover, in the twentieth century the nova effect continued, penetrating popular cultures and creating a generalised culture of 'authenticity' and expressive individualism (Taylor 2007: 299–300).

As critics have noted, the problem with Taylor's approach, besides its one-sided focus on the Western and Christian tradition, lies in its culturalist bias (Koenig 2011). This applies in particular to the second and third steps of his analysis, the reconstruction of the Romantic counter-movements against enlightened humanism and of their repercussions in the twentieth century. While Taylor's analysis of the rise of the humanist alternative to Christian faith still takes account of hard-core economic and institutional changes – in particular of the regimes of private property and natural law – such references are lacking almost completely in the subsequent parts of his study. There, Taylor focuses almost exclusively on the dimensions of cultural, moral, spiritual and aesthetic experience, while playing down economic, institutional and political change.

## Key questions of the study

The perspective of this study is not a theological but a sociological one. My aim is to develop a deeper understanding of the manifest or latent proximity between theology and key traditions of economic theory by taking a third perspective, that of social theory. The study refers to the questions left open by Taylor, Nelson and Priddat. I will argue that the case for a 'theological' perspective on the economy first of all depends on a clear methodological distinction between social practice and the intellectual reflection of this practice. If there is something like a 'religious' quality to the economy, it first needs to be identified on the level of social practice and social institutions, the 'theological' reflection of practice coming into view only in a second step. A broad sociological view of the institutional transformations underlying the rise of modern capitalism, beyond a culturally biased account like Taylor's, is required to understand the influence of theological thought on economic science. The focus of the socio-historical analysis which I am suggesting will be on the process which economic sociologists describe as the 'disembedding' of markets. The term is understood here as a negative counterpart to Karl Polanyi's concept of the social 'embeddedness' of markets (Polanyi 1944). Polanyi himself characterised the rise of modern industrial capitalism – the 'Great Transformation', as he called it – as a process where markets became 'disembedded' from their traditional institutional framework, and that this process gave rise to global capitalism as a system of 'self-regulated' markets.

As we have seen above, Taylor employs the same term, albeit in a very different sense. In Taylor's account, the concept of 'disembedding' denotes the transition from an enchanted world, open to supra-natural forces, spirits and demons, to the coherent and rational order of modern civil society (Taylor 2007: 146–147). The key point of the present study will be that this is not the whole story and that the continuation of the story is different from what Taylor suggests it is. We have to distinguish the first move of disembedding, as described by Taylor, from a second move of disembedding, that is, the disembedding of markets from their politically and religiously legitimated institutional framework in the sense first described by of Polanyi. The second move refers to the transition of institutionally embedded civil society, as it had evolved in the eighteenth century, to the global system of capitalism emerging in the nineteenth century. As I will explain in detail below, the disembedding of markets includes a spatial (or territorial) dimension, as well as a social, material and temporal one; in other words, it covers all dimensions of human existence. The result is not, as I will argue, the transformation of society into Weber's often cited 'iron cage' of instrumental rationality. To the contrary, the second move results in a re-enchantment of the economy and society, which, in some sense, comes down to a reversal of the first move of disembedding. As Martijn Konings puts it: 'Far from being characterized by a growing externality of economy and sociality, capitalism operates through their imbrication: morality, faith, power and emotion, the distinctive qualities of human association, are interiorized into the logic of the economy" (Konings 2015: 2). In a similar vein, Jens Beckert speaks of an 'enchanted world of capitalism' (Beckert 2016: 269).

The disembedding of markets refers to a spectacular expansion of the property options of money in all four dimensions cited above. Pushed by the promises of an ever-present market narrative, the reach of markets and money did not only expand territorially, as the well-known concept of 'globalisation' suggests. The commodification of social relations intensified too; moreover, the scope of marketable objects was enlarged due to the extension of the market nexus from finished products and services to the conditions of production (land, means of production, labour). The capital form of money, which had formerly been confined to the sphere of commerce, spread into the sphere of production. Money was no longer an entitlement for merely what *had been produced*, but also for what *could be produced* via the organised exploitation of the creative potential of labour, and this opened the economy up to the dimension of time. The economic process detached itself from nature-based and cyclical forms of time, and developed its own linear and future-oriented logic; dreams, technological visions and 'imagined futures' (Beckert 2016) became vital to keeping the system moving. Society indeed found itself faced with vast promises of earthly progress and welfare; however, it also found itself faced with hitherto unknown social polarisations and threats. Above all, there is the polarisation between those owning capital and wealth and those owning little or nothing and finding themselves positioned on the debt side of wealth. The capitalist universalisation of markets gave rise to the social dichotomy of capital and labour, which laid the ground for intense processes of social emulation, whose consequences were not only destructive, as Mishra (2017) argues,[5] but also productive. With the commodification of labour, capitalist entrepreneurship and a dynamic mode of social reproduction emerged. One industrial revolution followed another, and continuously emerging technical utopias and inventions gave rise to processes of 'creative destruction', to cite Joseph Schumpeter's well-known term. Nevertheless, the integrative potential of markets and money clearly has its limits and cannot always prevent the turn from productive to destructive modes of emulation. Capitalism has always tended to evoke more dreams and aspirations than it could fulfil. Thus, men find themselves again in a world of existential uncertainty, of unheard of promises, and of abysses: a kind of uncertainty, however, which this time does not go back to supra-natural spirits but to none other than humans and their own 'demonic' drives (Tillich 1988, 1989).

Markets are a calculable and profane reality only as long as they continue to be embedded in an institutional order based on political or religious values – this being not only Polanyi's point, but also that of the above-discussed theories of economic ordoliberalism. With their disembeddedness, markets no longer constitute a mere economic sub-system *within society*, but the most encompassing of all social systems, governing individual actors not only via external constraints, but also via framing their 'inner worlds', their thoughts and their perceptions.[6] As an encompassing system, it is indeed a 'black box' that, as a whole, is inaccessible to any observer because the observer would have to be more intelligent than the very sum of human intelligence operating in the system itself. Observations are social acts being possible only *within* society and relative to the particular social position of the observer, and not from any 'external' standpoint. Even economic science meets its limits here, and can ignore these limits only at the expense of either being empirically void, or of ending up as a morally laden, highly speculative discourse (Foley 2006). The only way out of this dilemma would be to renounce the holistic pretensions of economic theory and to concentrate on empirically verifiable but historically contextualised partial analyses, as many economists are in fact doing. This, however, is not compatible with their moral role as experts of the common good, a role which economists nevertheless still have their eyes on, as Nelson had noted (see above). Today, there is a growing awareness even amongst economists that economics cannot take the role of an 'oikodicee' for society, as Joseph Vogl (2010) has put it.[7] As an encompassing social system, disembedded markets are an opaque reality, impervious to coherent rational explanations. When nevertheless proposing the 'heuristic fiction' of rational and efficient markets (Beckert 2016: 256), economic theory does not follow scientific reason in the first instance, but the practical needs of a society having to cope with the real contingencies of markets. What is relevant is not whether theories are true or false, but whether they are credible and capable of guiding economic action and political decisions. From this viewpoint, the social role of economic theory resembles that of theology, which is to endeavour to translate the superior intelligence of God in a way that is accessible for human reason and practice. Though differently from theology, economics is not in a position to have recourse to holy scripts revealing God's intentions.

The epistemological puzzle coming into view here is not only one of economics, but also one of sociology and of the social sciences in general. It arises as soon as 'society' as a whole is taken as an object of scientific analysis,[8] and it applies to markets too in the case of the latter becoming an encompassing social reality due to the disembedding process. The only thing that social scientists can do is take the position of a second-order observer – that is, not taking society as a direct object of observation, but reconstructing the ways in which social actors *imagine* their collective identity and their environment. How do actors cope with an environment which they perceive as opaque and uncertain? The classic field where sociologists have followed such kinds of questions is the sociology of religion. It is neither necessary nor possible here to recapitulate the sheer variety of sociological approaches to the study of religion.[9] For the present purposes, it is sufficient to remind you, the reader, of two influential conceptualisations, which in fact – as we shall see later more in detail – are intertwined with each other. The first one, going back partly to Max Weber and taken up recently by Martin Riesebrodt, focuses on the problem of contingency. It defines religion as a system of beliefs in supernatural powers which are deemed to control conditions of mundane life outside of human influence. These beliefs, as 'premises' of religion, are combined with practices that are designed to communicate with the supernatural powers: 'Religious practices, as a rule, aim to establish contact with or access to these powers with means that are culturally given' (Riesebrodt 2007: 113, my translation). Religion is interpreted as a social system helping the followers to manage existential contingencies by entering into a communicative relationship with the superior powers, and trying to influence their will in a way that is beneficial to the followers (and to humans more generally). By establishing a relationship with the gods or one single god (or God), the believers constitute a social order amongst themselves in an indirect way. This is the point of the second type of conceptualisation, which goes back to Emile Durkheim and Georg Simmel and their emphasis on the 'social' character of the religious imagination: 'A religion is a unified system of beliefs and practices relative to sacred things, that is to say, things set apart and forbidden – beliefs and practices which unite into one single moral community called a Church, all those who adhere them' (Durkheim 1995 [1912]: 44). This definition focuses on the capacity of religions to constitute overarching forms of moral communities. Different from particular communities like families or ethnic groups, the religious community is the most encompassing one and, hence, a singular one; in this sense, religion is constitutive of 'society' (Durkheim 1995 [1912]: 421). In a similar vein, Simmel interpreted religion as a special type of social relationship, distinguishing itself by its unconditional and encompassing character (Simmel 1992 [1898], see Joas 1997: 110).

The sociology of religion is not theology; it cannot provide information about superhuman powers via the interpretation of holy scripts, testimonies and other sources of revelation. What it can do, however, is analyse the *practical* consequences of human action being guided by the belief in superhuman powers, or by the collective nexus of a church. What is relevant for sociology is not the question of the 'inner truth' of the religious imagination, but rather its impact on social action. This is the programme that Max Weber followed in his studies on world religions and the programme that I will follow here too, albeit only in a methodological sense and not in a substantial sense. In contemporary global capitalism, the management of uncertainty is clearly no longer the exclusive domain of traditional religions; instead, disembedded markets have evolved as a key field of existential contingencies. As I will argue in this study, markets have become a powerful competitor to the world's religions in at least two respects. First, markets have become a truly global social nexus, surpassing even the universality of the traditional world religions and religion-based civilisations.[10] Second, markets can no longer be characterised as a profane area of mere 'material' reproduction and utilitarian action, as the usual economic argument goes. Instead, markets have become a social system, which, like the religions, opens ways to experience the unknown and permeates social and individual life in an encompassing way. If we follow Durkheim in characterising religion as the utmost universal form of sociality, then it is capitalism and not any of the historical world religions which constitutes the genuine religion of modernity. What I am developing here is an approach to analysing the *practical* conditions, implications and consequences of individuals and collectives being guided no longer by the superhuman power of the gods, but by the forces of disembedded markets.

## Overview

The plan of the book is as follows: Chapters 2, 3 and 4 concentrate on the issue of disembedded markets from a historical point of view, starting with a discussion of the ambiguities and deficiencies in Polanyi's work (Chapter 2). My suggestion is to read Polanyi against the grain, that is, not as a theorist of economic embeddedness, but as one of disembedding. I will point to the modifications to and corrections of his analysis that appear to be necessary from such a perspective. Chapter 3 defends the liberal conception of private property as a universal *social* system against the critical denunciations of markets as a system of merely utilitarian or instrumental action. Moreover, I will highlight the role of the liberal market narrative in promoting the historical process of disembedding. Chapter 4 presents a stylised historical analysis of the disembedding process in its territorial, social, material and temporal dimensions, and of its built-in countervailing forces. Again, my intention here is to elaborate Polanyi's double-movement theorem and to correct its asymmetries and analytical deficiencies.

Chapter 5 turns to social theory, and it discusses the issues of functional differentiation and of the place of disembedded markets in a functionally differentiated society. As I will argue, the common system-theoretical description of modern markets as a core of a functionally defined 'economic' sub-system appears deficient, since it does not account for the disembedded character of modern, globalised markets. The universal character of markets suggests a comparative discussion of religion and its place in society. Recapitulating a broad consensus amongst sociologists of religion, I argue that religion in stratified societies has become a way for these societies to represent themselves in the double sense of marking the most encompassing level of collective identity and constituting the interface between society and its extra-social environments. Chapter 6 turns to global capitalism and the relationship between modernity, capitalism and religion, starting with a critical review of the return of religion thesis. In Chapter 7, I will discuss the key question of whether capitalism can do without a supreme value system reflecting the collective identity of society (as the theory of functional differentiation pretends). Here, I will focus critically on Niklas Luhmann's system-theoretical approach and his analysis of the inherent epistemological paradoxes of the concept of modern society. Though Luhmann offers a clear discussion of these paradoxes, I argue that his concept of societal 'self-descriptions' remains deficient; although he played with the idea, he did not consider the possibility of interpreting disembedded markets as the functional equivalent of religious self-descriptions. Chapter 8 offers a critical examination of the functional equivalence thesis, focusing on social universality and contingency management as the key dimensions of functional equivalence. As I will argue, the thesis of a functional equivalence between capitalism and religion can be followed only with major reservations. I will emphasise the limits of disembedding, and the vicious feedback evolving in the globalisation of markets, as well as in the processes of capitalist growth and 'creative destruction'. Chapter 9 deepens the issue of contingency management by developing a multi-level sociological model of capitalist dynamics, focusing on the macro–micro interactions in the process of capitalist growth. This will bring additional light to the analysis of the vicious circles inherent in the logic of creative destruction. The findings will be related to the actual debate on the phenomenon of 'financialisation'. The conclusion (Chapter 10) brings together the various threads laid out in the previous chapters, culminating in the thesis that the capitalist dream of absolute wealth is destroying itself, just as it is coming close to being a 'religion' of mankind.

## Notes

1 For a thorough commentary on Schmitt's position, see Meier 2012.
2 Smith first introduces the famous term in *The Theory of Moral Sentiments* (1759; Part IV, Chapter 1). In *The Wealth of Nations*, it appears only once (1776; Book IV, Chapter 2).
3 As Duncan Foley puts it: 'Neither Smith nor any of his successors has been able to demonstrate rigorously and robustly how private selfishness turns into public altruism' (Foley 2006: 3).
4 For example in the case of the 'Veblen Effect', where the high price of a good is valued intrinsically due to its social status implications.
5 Referring to René Girard, Mishra speaks of 'appropriative mimicry' (Mishra 2017: 62).
6 Michel Foucault's well-known term *gouvernementalité* circumscribes this comprehensive mode of domination.
7 With his term 'oikodicee', Vogl reminds us of parallels of the neoclassical market model with the concept of 'theodicee' coined by the German philosopher Gottfried Wilhelm Leibnitz, who was one of the pioneers of the philosophy of enlightenment in the eighteenth century. According to Leibnitz, all that happens in the world, whether apparently just or unjust, goes back to the superior wisdom of a divine creator. Thus, the existing world can be justified as 'the best of all possible worlds' – a theory which was mocked by Voltaire in his satirical novel *Candide*.

8 This is what sociologists, despite Theodor Adorno's and Niklas Luhmann's well-known warnings, have been doing up to the present day when producing ever new phrases such as 'risk society' (Beck 1986), 'post-industrial society' (Bell 1974), 'experience society' (*Erlebnisgesellschaft*; Schulze 1993), or, most recently, 'externalization society' (*Externalisierungsgesellschaft*; Lessenich 2016). The very inflation of such formulas is an indication of the epistemological problem that I am pointing to here.

9 According to Detlef Pollack (1995: 163), there have been 'hundreds' of attempts to define religion.

10 This is also the point in Shmuel Eisenstadt's and Wolfgang Schluchter's interpretations of capitalist modernity as a historical successor to the 'axial' civilisations (Eisenstadt 1986, 2000; Schluchter 2016).

# 2 Disembedded markets and society

## Ambiguities in Polanyi's analysis

The central issue of this book is the nature of disembedded markets and their impact on society. Thus, it appears appropriate to start with a discussion of Karl Polanyi's work, which initiated the debate on the 'social embeddedness' of markets. Needless to say, Karl Polanyi is an author, whose research has stimulated key debates in a variety of disciplines in the social sciences, including economic history, social anthropology, sociology and economic sociology, and it is still doing so. However, what Polanyi has left behind is not a closed theoretical system, but an analysis of capitalism that is open to very different interpretations. My aim here is to go somewhat deeper into some of the ambiguities in Polanyi's analysis, since such a discussion may reveal insights still hidden in Polanyi's thinking.

Let me start immediately with one central ambiguity that runs across Polanyi's entire analysis and has given rise to extended controversies (i.e. Lie 1991; Krippner et al. 2004; Hann and Hart 2009; and Go 2012). On the one hand, Polanyi in his work aims to make a historical and anthropological critique of classical and neoclassical economic thinking. Referring to a broad background of empirical evidence about markets and economic practices in primitive and stratified societies, Polanyi points to the fictitious character of neoclassical assumptions about 'economic man' (*homo economicus*). When securing the needs of their material reproduction, people in pre-modern societies did not act as isolated individuals; nor were their actions governed by the motive of material gain. Rather, economic actions were 'submerged' (Polanyi 1944: 46) into non-economic relationships securing social order, cohesion and trust, which Polanyi classifies along with his well-known typology of reciprocity, redistribution and household. In many cases, markets as a separated social sphere did not exist at all, and, where they did exist, markets were encapsulated into a dense network of political and social institutions. Markets, thus, had no overarching social importance: 'Though the institution of the market was fairly common since the later Stone Age, its role was no more than incidental to economic life' (Polanyi 1944: 43). On the other hand, for Polanyi there is one big exception from these apparently sound 'anthropological' findings, namely, modern capitalism. Here, the constellation between markets and society, as described before, gets turned upside down. Polanyi views modern capitalism as a society governed by 'self-regulating' markets, with markets no longer being embedded in social institutions and society becoming a mere 'adjunct to the market. Instead of economy being embedded in social relations, social relations are embedded into the economic system' (Polanyi 1944: 57). Contrary to his own emphasis on embeddedness, Polanyi interprets the neo-classical fiction of 'economic man' as a realistic description of capitalism. How is such a sudden intellectual turn possible, and how does Polanyi justify it? Here is where the opinions of the interpreters of his work diverge. For Fred Block (2003; see also Block and Somers 2014: 73–74), the inconsistency in Polanyi's argument goes back to the biographical circumstance that Polanyi's shift from his earlier Marxist position to his later anthropological insights was still under way when he was finishing *The Great Transformation*. As Block argues, it was only in the process of writing *The Great Transformation* that Polanyi developed his key concepts of embeddedness and fictitious commodities. The conclusion of the latter would have been 'the concept of the always embedded economy – that market societies must construct elaborate rules and institutional structures to limit the individual pursuit of gain or risk degenerating into a Hobbesian war of all against all' (Block 2003: 297). According to Block, Polanyi felt pressed to publish the manuscript before the end of the war and did not allow himself enough time to revise the manuscript accordingly. Block's interpretation, however, has been met with many critical comments. Most recently, Kari Polanyi-Levitt criticised Block for discarding the idea of the disembedded economy and for 'moving Polanyi into the mainstream of economic discourse' (Polanyi-Levitt 2013: 102). According to Polanyi-Levitt, Polanyi aimed to point to the 'existential contradiction between the market economy and a viable society' (2013: 102). In her view, Polanyi's position was in line with the Marxian critique of capitalist commodification and alienation.

So, should we read Polanyi as an anthropologist (Block) or as a Marxist (Polanyi-Levitt)? The usual answer, surely also the answer that Polanyi would have given himself, would consist in pointing to his concept of a 'double movement' of capitalism. To put it in Polanyi's own words:

> For a century, the dynamics of modern society was governed by a double movement: the market expanded continuously, but this movement was met by a countermovement checking the expansion in definite directions. Vital though such a countermovement was for the protection of society, in the final analysis it was incompatible with the self-regulation of the market, and thus with the market system itself.
>
> (Polanyi 1944: 130)

For Polanyi, the emergence of a system of self-regulated markets meant a break with fundamental conditions of human existence. As he saw it, the experiences of the British industrial revolution clearly revealed the disastrous social and ecological effects of the commodification of land, labour and money. The inclusion of those 'fictitious' commodities into the market system necessarily produced political counter-movements to re-embed and regulate those markets, which Polanyi analysed in the second part of the book. However, by hampering the forces of market self-regulation, these counter-measures did not really help to settle the crisis; to the contrary, they created further instability, thus 'forcing the development of the market economy into a definite groove' (Polanyi 1944: 4).

On closer inspection, Polanyi's concept of a 'double movement' contains not one but two ambiguities. First, if the roots of the crises of capitalist societies lie in the emergence of a self-regulated market economy, how can it happen that efforts to contain the self-regulating logic of markets do not settle the crisis but have the effect of aggravating it? Again, Fred Block's comments are instructive here. As he argues, it was Polanyi's point that the destabilising impact of the counter-movements was not due to their anti-market impetus *as such* but to their internal inconsistency. Protective interventions into agrarian and labour markets, for example, were incompatible with the parallel maintenance (or re-introduction) of the gold standard system; a similar inconsistency was characteristic of the Speenhamland system in early-nineteenth-century England. According to Polanyi, the functioning of the market system was based on the premise of a coherent interaction of the market forces: 'The three tenets – competitive labor market, automatic gold standard, and international free trade – formed one whole' (Polanyi 1944: 138). Thus, the socially disruptive consequences of the counter-movements were due to the fact that they were orchestrated in an inconsistent and conflicting way.

However, even if one follows this interpretation, a second and even more basic ambiguity in Polanyi's concept remains: given the strong anthropological foundation for the social embeddedness of economic action, which Polanyi insists upon, how is it possible at all for a self-regulating economy to emerge out of an embedded economy? As it appears, the design of Polanyi's double-movement theorem is highly asymmetric and biased in favour of the second sequence, the reaction of society to the unfettering of market forces. Polanyi puts all his emphasis on demonstrating why a system of self-regulating markets, once established, cannot sustain and must provoke social and political counter-movements. However, what about the first sequence, that is, the rise of the market economy itself? What Polanyi is offering here are ad hoc hypotheses at best. Sometimes, he seems to explain the rise of the market economy from the ideological influence of the laissez-faire doctrine. He characterises the economic liberalism of the 1830s as a 'militant creed' (Polanyi 1944: 137) that took possession of the minds of the political and economic elites. Here, Polanyi suddenly seems to switch from the perspective of social anthropology to that of the sociology of knowledge without any attempt to justify and elaborate this turn. In other passages of the text, Polanyi insinuates that the invention of industrial machinery could have stimulated the rise of a self-regulating market: 'We do not intend to assert that the machine caused that which happened, but we insist that once elaborate machines and plant were used for production in a commercial society, the idea of a self-regulating market was bound to take shape' (Polanyi 1944: 40). Again, there is no attempt to elaborate this hypothesis any further – a hypothesis which in the light of well-known contemporary sociological criticisms of technological determinism appears controversial and seems to mix up causes and consequences of the commodification of industrial labour.

Some authors (e.g. Peck 2013) have tried to impute a 'dialectical' logic to Polanyi's double-movement theorem: market forces give rise to social countermovements, the latter in turn will lead to a revival of market forces, and so on. Such interpretations are hardly convincing, as Polanyi's argument is clearly not dialectical, but anthropological in the sense that it refers to fundamental aspects of the human condition. Fred Block's interpretation, too, cannot help us any further at this point. As Block (2003) argues, even an extremely liberalised market economy can never be completely 'non-embedded'. The self-regulation of markets does not come about spontaneously, as Block emphasises in line with Polanyi, but requires detailed political interventions to secure property rights and the freedom of competition. In this way, markets are always embedded into a political and institutional context, albeit of a kind different from pre-modern societies. What Block (not Polanyi himself) seems to overlook here is an elementary point: market regulations are, despite international trade agreements, largely bound to the frame of the nation-state; the market system itself, by contrast, is transnational and global. Block's thesis of the 'always embedded economy' certainly holds true in the sense that markets even in their pure, 'disembedded' form are clearly a *social* system based on the institution of private property. The neoclassical 'economic man' model indeed is deeply misleading (I will come back to this point below in Chapter 3). However, this does not mean that markets are subject to one global *political* authority. The markets are self-regulating *just because* they are a superior, universal system beyond the nationally (or regionally, as in the case of the European Union) bounded reach of states. Transnational firms and globally mobile investors can easily circumvent and hollow out national regulations, choosing the locations of taxation and investments according to their preferences. Even more, they can threaten the political sovereignty of nation-states by making them compete for their favour and comply with their demands; an example is the 'race to the bottom' that could be observed in the area of corporate taxes and taxes on high income between 1985 and 2009 (Genschel and Schwarz 2011). As Polanyi himself had remarked, states and local social orders in their turn are 'embedded' into the larger system of transnational markets, which they cannot control as a whole. As Wolfgang Streeck has put it: 'While politics may operate as a countermovement to the capitalist market, and sometimes even as a successful one, the market moves on its own generating the movement to which the countermovement must try to respond' (Streeck 2012: 315).

The problem we are encountering here has consequences concerning the applicability of Polanyi's concepts to contemporary global capitalism. Polanyi characterised nineteenth-century market liberalism as a 'stark utopia'. He was convinced that the market system emerging from that utopia could not survive the social crises and catastrophes that it produced: 'In retrospect our age will be credited with having seen the end of the self-regulating market' (Polanyi 1944: 142). Polanyi interpreted the rise of nineteenth-century global capitalism as a kind of historical 'accident' that was extremely unlikely to be repeated. Today, we know that his predictions were premature. With the liberalisation of global capital markets after the fall of the Bretton Woods system in 1973, and even more after the fall of the socialist system, global capitalism has experienced a powerful revival. With globalisation, liberalisation and deregulation, the 'crisis-proneness' of capitalism has revived too. To interpret these developments, it appeared natural for political economists and critical theorists of capitalism (e.g. Fred Block, Colin Crouch, Jürgen Habermas, Axel Honneth, Bob Jessop, Claus Offe, Wolfgang Streeck) to turn to Polanyi's double-movement concept once again.[1] The re-discovery of Polanyi's work that has gone on since the late 1970s can be explained largely from that background. However, is it really possible to lift out Polanyi's theory from its original historical context of the nineteenth and early twentieth centuries, and to apply it to the development of capitalism a second time? A theory that concentrates exclusively on the second phase of the 'double movement', but that has almost nothing to say about the first phase – to repeat myself – is certainly not a good theory. The global deregulation of markets after 1973 cannot again be brushed aside as a historical 'accident'. It is at odds with a theory that defines the social embeddedness of markets as an 'anthropological fact'.

The task of elaborating Polanyi's double-movement concept thus appears sufficiently clear. What is needed are efforts to correct the one-sided 'anthropology' of Polanyi's position, which tends to exclude the social universality of markets from the human condition. Further historical and empirical investigations are necessary to clarify the historical forces giving rise to the first phase of the double movement (the missing link in Polanyi's analysis). How could a global system of disembedded markets emerge out of the context of an embedded economy? This is a big question, which obviously will require a complex answer. As a first step, it is important to recapitulate Polanyi's own historical analyses of the spread of the market system. What I am suggesting, then, is to read Polanyi against the grain, that is, not as a theorist of embedding but one of disembedding, less as an anthropologist and more as a Marxist, without sacrificing his anthropological findings.

The basic points are well known: Polanyi interprets modern capitalism as the outcome of the European 'Great Transformation' of the eighteenth century. The Great Transformation is defined as a process where markets expanded beyond their traditional institutional and political framings. This meant that society came to be dominated by self-regulating markets, which Polanyi, following the neoclassical view, interprets as an asocial system governed by egoistic material interests. Still under the mercantilist rule of the eighteenth century, markets were not left to themselves, but market access, prices, product quantities, quality standards and many other issues were strictly regulated by the local and national political authorities. Then, the liberal governments in the nineteenth century followed the idea of 'laissez faire' and concentrated their interventions on guaranteeing private property rights and the principles of free competition. Given these conditions, the markets were allowed to regulate themselves according to the signals of prices, costs and profits.

For a systematic review of Polanyi's statements concerning the universalisation of markets, it appears helpful to distinguish between territorial, social, material and temporal dimensions of disembedding. The territorial dimension refers to the *spatial extension and integration of markets*; the social dimension refers to the *degree of inclusion of the population* in the market nexus; the material dimension refers to the *scope of objects* entering into market transactions; and the temporal dimension refers to the *time horizon* of transactions. The advantage of a reconstruction of Polanyi's statements along these four dimensions is that it allows for a systematic assessment of the strengths and weaknesses of Polanyi's analysis. As I want to show, Polanyi's analysis focuses on the territorial and social dimensions of the universalisation process. What he dealt with insufficiently were the material and temporal dimensions of disembedding. I will conclude with some critical comments concerning Polanyi's basic understanding of universalised markets as a social order. I agree with John Lie (1991) that Polanyi did not sufficiently distinguish between disembedded markets as an empirical and historical reality and the description of that reality by classical and neoclassical economics.

Concerning the territorial dimension of the extension of markets (see Polanyi 1944: 56–57), I can confine myself here to a brief summary. Polanyi distinguishes between three types of markets: external, local and national. He shows that the evolution of markets did not follow the pattern imagined 'naïvely' by the economists of the eighteenth and nineteenth centuries, with market exchange starting at the local level and then spreading successively to the national and international levels. Rather, the sequence of the argument should be 'almost reversed' in the light of actual knowledge, as Polanyi argues. The true starting point had been long-distance trade, developing not *within* ethnic communities, but emerging from encounters *between* communities and often taking on not the character of barter but of 'adventure, exploration, hunting, piracy and war' (Polanyi 1944: 59). With growing division of labour and centralisation of political authority, local markets developed; however, due not only to political barriers, but also to the poor technical conditions of communication and transport, they remained separated from each other and from external trade. The politics of European mercantilism in the seventeenth and eighteenth centuries strove to remove the barriers between the local trade markets and to create a national market while keeping up and even tightening the barriers between national and international markets. The breakthrough in the disembedding process that occurred in the nineteenth century, thus, did not come from a gradual expansion of local markets, but from the removal of national and regional customs barriers, which resulted in an overall integration of markets and a spectacular growth in trade. With annual increases of 4.18 percent between 1820 and 1870 and 3.40 percent between 1870 and 1913, the volume of world trade increased at a pace many times higher than that of any earlier historical age (Osterhammel 2009: 1033). And one could add that the integration of markets was greatly facilitated by technical innovations in the world's transport and communication systems, such as the steamship, the railway, the telegraph and the telephone. Though still being shaped by a 'euro-centric' perspective and needing corresponding elaboration, Polanyi's account so far seems to be largely in line with later historical research.

Social disembedding in the broadest sense refers to the progressive inclusion of the population in the market nexus and the parallel elimination of rural and household-based subsistence economies. This process leads to the intensive expansion of the commodity form in society in contrast to the extensive, territorial form, as the commodity form would now permeate social relationships within a *given* territory. The basic step here is what Marx called 'primitive accumulation', that is, the expropriation of peasants from their land. This process did not only take place in the distant past, but continues up to the present in a large variety of forms (Perelman 2000). As it is well known, Polanyi's analysis confines itself to one episode of that process, the institution and demise of the English Speenhamland system between 1795 and 1834. Polanyi characterises it as an attempt to prevent the rise of a self-regulated labour market, which, given the parallel progression of the Industrial Revolution and the rise of an industrial labour market, led to severe dysfunctionalities and finally had to be abandoned. Polanyi interprets the abolition of the Speenhamland system as a key step in the surmounting of local subsistence economies in order to promote the commercialisation of labour and to integrate the population into the market nexus, which became the dominant source of its existence. Again, Polanyi's principal point about the early nineteenth century as the key transition period from slavery and serfdom to free labour seems uncontroversial,[2] though the perspective of his analysis appears limited and should be extended with regard to the temporal horizon as well as to the regional scope of the change. Later researchers, in particular Maurice Dobb and Edward P. Thompson, have delivered more detailed and precise accounts of the commercialisation of labour in England. While starting long before the institution of the Speenhamland Law, the inclusion of labour into the market developed, as Thompson shows, in a more gradual and more complex way than that suggested by Polanyi. In the 1830s, for example, a large working class indeed had developed; however, still at this time the majority of workers were artisans, masters, journeymen, homeworkers, and being employed for the most part in small shops and not in factories (Thompson 1963: 234–235). What they were selling were their products and not their labour power. The social construction of labour power as a commodity indeed was based on 'fictitious' premises, as Polanyi had emphasised. In fact, labour power cannot be divorced from the person of the worker himself or herself, and human beings are not born for the sake of selling their capacities at a market. It took a long time for this fiction to become institutionalised and for the labour market to become established in England, let alone in the rest of Europe. This was a complex transition, developing in nationally and culturally divergent forms, a fact which was reflected in persisting differences in the interpretation of the work contract between Germany and England: 'German owners and workers viewed employment as the timed appropriation of worker's labor power and disposition over worker's activity. In contrast, British owners and workers saw employment as the appropriation of worker's materialized labor via its products' (Biernacki 1995: 12). As Richard Biernacki shows, this resulted in very different regimes of management, control and remuneration in both countries; I will come back to this point below (Chapter 4).

The social dimension of disembedding should be distinguished from the material dimension, which is the extension of the scope of objects to be included in the market nexus. Polanyi's analysis of material disembedding exhausts itself largely in his theory of the 'fictitious commodities' of land, labour and money, which, though being treated as commodities, are not actually commodities. Here we are arriving at a controversial point in Polanyi's analysis. As he argues, land, labour and money are resources that are essential for the reproduction of society. Their commodification meant that society was confronted with hitherto unknown existential threats, such as environmental pollution, poverty, social disorganisation and unrest, and excessive market fluctuations. Polanyi connotes the uncertainty created by the extension of the market nexus to land, labour and money almost exclusively in negative terms; only in passing does he note that the self-regulating market has also produced an 'unheard-of material welfare' (Polanyi 1944: 3). With regard to the commodification of labour, for example, he emphasises the social and material risks of workers when being exposed to labour markets. While Polanyi's gloomy descriptions may be largely justified with regard to the early phases of the Industrial Revolution, his conceptualisations fail to meet the full complexity of social arrangements between capital and labour that developed in the later stages of 'intensified' capitalist accumulation. The standardisation and shortening of working hours, for example, did not only have the effect of 'protecting' workers against the pressure of markets, as Polanyi argues in his double-movement concept; rather, they also enabled workers to identify with the rhythm of the intensified capitalist labour process and to become more productive and committed (Stearns 1975, Deutschmann 1985).

The freedom of workers in labour markets had a positive double effect, and not only a negative one, something which Marx – differently from Polanyi – had always emphasised: workers were released not only from their means of subsistence, but also from relationships of personal dependence. Marx's distinction between labour and labour power remains vital and cannot be treated as a mere formality, as Polanyi seems to do. It is not the person, but their labour power that is getting 'commodified', though – of course – both cannot factually be separated from each other. What free workers are selling are not their products but their capacities to produce, and, different from the slave, they have a personal interest in doing so. This – to emphasise the point again – is a complex social arrangement, which took a long time to become institutionalised. The cooperative arrangements between capital and labour, such as the development of industrial relations and internal labour markets, did not simply protect people against markets, as Polanyi assumes. Rather, they resulted in a spectacular enlargement of the innovative capacities of firms and, hence, of the options embodied in money. Money now became a private property title on the creative and innovative capacities of labour; as such, it was no longer just money but capital. Different from the material 'factors of production', humans are endowed with the ability to generate something new. While the capacities of machines, plants, technical systems, and even computers are basically calculable, it is impossible to give an exhausting definition to the capacities of free labour, since such a definition would have to include not only all inventions of the past and present, but also of the future. With the extension of markets to labour and the other factors of production, money became an entitlement not only on what actually *had been produced*, but also on *what could be produced* via the organised employment of labour.

Mobilising the creative capacities of labour – of course – is not possible by force, but depends on the active cooperation and commitment of workers. Finding the right balance between controls, sanctions and incentives here became a key challenge for capitalist entrepreneurs and managers. The final success of these efforts is documented by the fact that the commodification of labour in the course of the Great Transformation resulted in an unprecedented explosion of economic growth. Between 1820 and the present, the world economy grew at a pace many times higher than it had in any period during the last two thousand years. Growth instead of stationary reproduction became the regular pattern of economic development (Maddison 2001, Broadberry and O'Rourke 2010). What is vital for capitalist growth is not simply higher productivity in the sense of an increasing per capita output of a *given* set of products and/or services, but in the sense of *innovation* (Baumol 2002), which enhances the *value* of production. Capitalist growth is based on the continuous invention of new products, services, technologies, and logistic concepts and the concomitant elimination of conventional ones. As Schumpeter and later researchers (Freeman and Louca 2001) have shown, the capitalist process of creative destruction does not develop continuously, but in cycles and waves, producing ever-new industrial revolutions. The invention of machinery was a result of that process, not a factor coming from the outside, as Polanyi seems to assume.

For Marx, the extension of the power of money to the potential of free labour had been the key point of his definition of capital. By mobilising the creative capacities of labour, money itself takes on the character of a 'capacity' (*Vermögen* in German) that is bound to grow and accumulate. As the creativity of labour is basically indefinable, the property claim embodied in the capital form of money can never be ultimately redeemed, but only continues on in a never-ending process of capital accumulation. Since money in its capital form is determined to grow, the need for a complementary increase in the supply of money and credit arises too. This requires the commodification of money as the third 'fictitious' commodity in Polanyi's list. Thus, the commodification of labour and that of money can be interpreted as being two sides of the same coin.

Again, however, Polanyi's analysis of the commodification of money and credit appears fragmentary and bound to the experience of his time. For Polanyi, the gold standard represented the cornerstone of the self-regulation of money and of the market system as a whole. Consequently, he interprets the failure of the gold standard in the early 1930s as 'the final failure of the market economy' (Polanyi 1944: 200). As Polanyi argues, in line with the contemporary liberal consensus, the gold standard was vital to securing the stability of international trade, as it set limits to discretionary political intervention and made foreign exchange calculable. To counter the negative repercussions of external trade imbalances on the domestic economy, national central banking systems were developed, whose interventions, however, were often inconsistent with the rules of the gold standard and contributed to the erosion of the market system. While the trade-off between the key goals of national economic policy – the often-cited 'magic triangle' of employment, price stability and external trade equilibrium – has remained a recurrent issue up to the present day, Polanyi's interpretation of the gold standard as the cornerstone of the self-regulation of the market system has clearly become anachronistic. Even in the time of its institutionalisation, the gold standard was much more politicised than the liberal narrative of gold as a 'neutral' anchor of value would have one believe (Knafo 2013). When introducing the gold standard in 1821, the British government was not guided only by liberal motives, but also by their intention to tighten national political control over money and the banking system, as Samuel Knafo has shown. In practice, the gold standard regime turned out to be much more open to discretionary monetary policies than the official legend pretended. The gradual abrogation of the gold standard in the twentieth century did not mean the end of the market economy, but aimed to avoid the dysfunctional consequences of the gold standard for the market process itself, which became evident in the Great Depression of the 1930s. Many of the deflationary and slow-growth problems after the First World War could have been avoided if the 'golden brake' of the financial system would have been removed earlier, as Milton Friedman and Anna Schwartz – as the key authorities on liberal monetarism in the 1960s – have argued (Friedman and Schwartz 1963). A possible return to some form of gold standard is deemed to be unrealistic and anachronistic by the majority of experts today, even after the global financial crisis of 2008–2009 (Knafo 2013). Thus, Polanyi was clearly premature in proclaiming the end of the market system after the end of the gold standard. The spectacular expansion of world trade even after the abolition of the gold base of the dollar in 1971 gives abundant evidence for the dispensability of the gold anchor as a mechanism to stabilise globalised markets.

So far, I have referred to Polanyi's analysis of the territorial, social and material dimensions of the disembedding of markets. However, there is still a fourth dimension of disembedding hardly touched by Polanyi, the temporal one. Modern sociological interpretations of time, following the theories of Emile Durkheim, Robert Merton, Pitirim Sorokin, George Mead, Alfred Schütz and Niklas Luhmann, have emphasised the character of time as a social emergent: time is understood not as an external standard, coordinating social activities from the outside, but something that is generated within the social process (for an overview of this idea, see Bergmann 1992). Simple societies develop 'natural' patterns of time that reflect the dependence of agrarian production on nature and the limited social horizon of small, self-sufficient communities. Complex societies, by contrast, depend on abstract forms of time calculation, bridging a large variety of different social roles, and mediating complex divisions of labour, with modern 'world time' as a final stage (Luhmann 1975). A parallel distinction is that between cyclical and linear forms of time. Where the reproductive activities of a society follow a stationary pattern, this tends to reflect itself in a cyclical organisation of time with no clear differentiation between the present, the past and the future (Bergmann 1992: 102). Thus, as pre-modern societies are embedded in traditional institutions, they are embedded in cyclical and organic time structures reflecting a stationary pattern of reproduction. Modern societies, on the other hand, are characterised by a conception of time as a linear flow, stretching from the past and present into an open and uncertain future. The hypothesis that I want to make here is that the rise of modern linear time is closely related to the material disembedding of markets and in particular to the inclusion of labour power in the market nexus and the resulting transformation of money into capital (Deutschmann 1985). As shown above, the extension of the property claim of money to the creative potential of labour implies that the claim is no longer being redeemed in a definitive way, but that in continues on in a never-ending process. From here, the centrality of the future in capitalism, and the centrality of 'fictions' to fill in the future (Beckert 2011, 2016), again is becoming apparent.

To conclude, I argue that, while Polanyi has invested much effort into an ethnographic reconstruction of the social embeddedness of pre-modern economies, he did not enter into a similarly rigorous empirical analysis of the capitalist disembedding process itself. Instead, he accepted – as I think, prematurely – the classical and neoclassical market model as an adequate description of a reality that he qualified as 'utopian', 'absurd' and doomed to downfall at the same time. From the viewpoint of today, it is evident that Polanyi's predictions about the demise of global capitalism were erroneous. Moreover, Polanyi's understanding of disembedded markets as an 'asocial' system raises questions. Polanyi views capitalism as a system driven by the egoistic motives of hunger, on the one hand, and of profit, on the other. While economic action in pre-capitalist societies had always been an integral part of more encompassing social roles and obligations, markets in capitalism became isolated from the rest of society in an 'artificial' way. Society in its turn became subordinated to apparently 'objective' economic laws with their destructive impact on social relations as well as on the natural environment (Polanyi 1947: 109–110).

From a sociological viewpoint, Polanyi's characterisation of disembedded markets is hardly satisfying. Markets, even in their most elementary form, cannot be defined simply as a nexus of rational egoisms. Here, Polanyi mixes up the heuristic fictions of neoclassical theory with an empirically oriented analysis, which neoclassical economics could never claim to be. The disembedded markets of global capitalism are based on the institution of private property, they are governed by the social norm of exchange, and they depend on money as a medium for the interpersonal recognition and transfer of private property rights; hence, they fulfil all the criteria of a social system. Mutual recognition of private property rights is a *social* arrangement that should be distinguished clearly from simple selfishness (which would be force, fraud or murder). Therefore, the interpretation of capitalist markets as a quasi-technical system being regulated by the drives of hunger and profit is inadequate, even as a 'critical' description of capitalism, which Polanyi (and, with him, many critical theorists and economic sociologists) is suggesting. Markets, even in their most abstract form, are clearly a *social* system characterised by a high degree of functional specification on the one hand and by their universal reach on the other. The historical transition from embedded to self-regulated markets thus did not have the effect of locating markets 'outside' society, as Polanyi contends. Rather, it resulted in the creation of a new, universal form of society, which transcended the political and religious particularisms of traditional societies. At this point Marx, who interpreted the commodity nexus as the core of global capitalist society, was much clearer than Polanyi.

Indeed, Polanyi's interpretation of the Great Transformation focuses exclusively on the disruptive impact of the evolution of markets on traditional social institutions. Starting from strong 'anthropological' assumptions, he ruled out the possibility of markets constituting a historically new, universal form of sociality, that is, the possibility of no longer forming only a *sub-system* of society but of being the most encompassing social system therein. It is this hypothesis that I will focus on in the following chapters.

## Notes

1 For Streeck, the present-day counter-movements in Europe against market fundamentalism look like they are 'coming out of a Polanyian storybook' (Streeck 2013: 239, my translation).

2 As Jürgen Osterhammel states, the institution of the free work contract had become normalised and widespread in large parts of the world around 1900 However, 'Around 1800, this clearly had not yet been the case' (Osterhammel 2009: 993, my translation).

# 3 Markets as a social system

## The liberal narrative

Can self-regulated markets be called a 'social system'? Not only did Polanyi deny this, but so have many critical theorists. Joseph Vogl, for example, views capitalist markets as being dominated by 'blind, egoistic drives' (Vogl 2010: 34, my translation). Though starting from very different theoretical premises, Jürgen Habermas reaches similar conclusions in his theory of the 'colonisation' of the social lifeworld by markets (Habermas 1981: 229–230, 489–490). Central to Habermas' approach is his distinction between social systems based on communicative action – the 'lifeworld' in his terminology – and systems based on media, such as money or power. While in the lifeworld actions are coordinated via communication and consensus, coordination in media-based systems works via the functional integration of the *outcomes* of actions. The actors observe each other in an ego-centric, 'instrumental' perspective; they treat each other *as if* they were not human subjects but mere means for everybody to reach their personal objectives. As Habermas tries to show in his encompassing panorama of social evolution, the rise of modern societies did not follow the logic of a communicative rationalisation of social institutions and values alone. It also had the ambivalent effect of giving rise to media-controlled social sub-systems, amongst them markets. Communicative rationalisation resulted in an ever-increasing amount of deliberation and, hence, in an overburdening of society by unsettled complexity. To avoid the danger of social disintegration, society had no choice but to reorganise certain social processes on the basis of abstract media and to make use of their potential to manage complexity; as a consequence, not only markets but also public and private bureaucracies wound up expanding. For Habermas, the recourse of society to media and the built-in 'technicism' (Habermas 1981: 273, transl. C.D.) of media-controlled social interaction is unproblematic, as long as the reach of media is confined to the functional requirements of 'material reproduction'. However, as soon as media start invading the 'proper' domains of the social lifeworld, such as socialisation, culture, or political discourse, Habermas sees the danger of 'colonisation' subordinating the lifeworld to abstract imperatives of economic growth and political power.

With Polanyi, Vogl and Habermas, I have mentioned a few amongst many other authors interpreting markets as a non-social, instrumental or 'technical' system – an interpretation that is widespread amongst critical observers of capitalism. In espousing this view, critical theorists are showing themselves to be arguing for something quite close to neoclassical theory, and revealing a puzzling inclination to mix up the neoclassical market model with an empirical description of markets. Apparently, their view is backed by an authority no lesser than Adam Smith and his often-cited statement about the butcher, the brewer and the baker: 'It is not from the benevolence of the butcher, the brewer and the baker, that we expect our dinner, but from their regard to their own interest. We address ourselves not to their humanity but to their self-love, and never talk to them of our own necessities but of their advantages' (Smith 1999 [1776]: 119). To attribute to Smith the interpretation of market exchange as a purely utilitarian or instrumental type of action, however, would be to make a gross oversimplification. This becomes evident even from the sentences immediately preceding the above cited passage:

> But man has almost constant occasion for the help of his brethren, and it is in vain for him to expect it from their benevolence only. He will be more likely to prevail if he can interest their self-love in his favor, and show them that it is for their own advantage to do for him what he requires of them. Whoever offers to another a bargain of any kind proposes to do this. Give me that which I want, and you shall have this which you want is the meaning of every such offer; and it is in this manner that we obtain from one another the far greater part of those good offices which we stand in need of.
>
> (Smith 1999 [1776]: 118)

As recent interpreters (e.g. Herzog 2013) have argued, Smith's economic theory and his moral philosophy should be considered as a unity. In his earlier grand work, *The Theory of Moral Sentiments*, Smith had already developed his view of human actors being capable of identifying with each other and defining their own interest in the perspective of their social counterparts. Emphasising human sympathy and reciprocity, he anticipated many of the insights which George Herbert Mead developed in his theory of symbolically based interaction more than one hundred and fifty years later (Smith 1991 [1759]). People are able to identify with each other and to mirror their own behaviour from the viewpoint of external spectators. They can learn from their social experiences and correct their self-conceptions accordingly. Self-interested action in Smith's sense, including profit-seeking behaviour, is always *socially reflected* self-interest, which is governed by the quest of actors for mutual recognition (Barbalet 2008, Lenger 2018: 49–50). Hence, it can be interpreted – here Smith follows the position of Adam Ferguson – as a mechanism to constitute society in a bottom-up, spontaneous way starting from face-to-face interaction and exchange. Market exchange even in its most elementary form is neither a merely economic phenomenon nor an act of simple egoism. It is a moral act based on the institution of private property and money as a medium of interpersonal recognition and transfer of property rights. The basic rule reads that nobody is entitled to take possession of the property of others, except if accepting a reciprocal claim of others on his property. While representing a claim against everybody, money is accepted by everybody as a claim against themselves. Markets constitute themselves as a social system due to the civil norm of the personal accountability for profits and debts.[1]

Free markets enable citizens to regulate their affairs in an autonomous and rational way. Individual freedom can coincide with collective welfare without the intervention of an external authority. Though the state is required as a guarantor of the rules of competition and private property rights, it is not the state but the market contract that is basic for civil society. At this point, the Scottish version of liberalism deviates from the republican one (Montesquieu, Immanuel Kant), focusing on the role of the state to constitute civil rights and the separation of powers. For the Scottish liberals, freedom ultimately does not rely on the state but on the pre-political basis of free contract. Hence, the message is a *universal* one, addressing itself to all mankind irrespective of religion, culture or nationality. Market liberalism developed its own version of the idea of individual freedom that was central to the enlightened philosophy of the time. It became a social message that spread far beyond intellectual and philosophical circles and found vast resonance amongst contemporaries:

> Indeed, the arguments of *The Wealth of Nations* seemed to lend a certain sanctity to the self-interested pursuit of gain, by showing that such activity was productive of benefit to society at large; by demonstrating that the enterprise of individuals was capable, when left free of regulation, of carrying the standard of material well-being to heights hitherto impossible and scarcely calculable. … To some contemporaries Smith's message was both powerful and attractive, while to ourselves, armed with the benefit of hindsight, he appears as the herald if not the prophet of a new order.
>
> (Skinner 1999: 8–9)[2]

The usual objection against the liberal market narrative is that the justice underlying markets is only a minimal and abstract kind of justice. Indeed, what is required is not more than the formal obedience to market rules. The exchange partners have to refrain from force and fraud, and to pay the prices agreed upon; beyond that, no deeper interest into the well-being of the other is required. Again it was Smith who emphasised that in a commercial society there is no room for the old, Aristotelian concept of *iustitia distributiva*, that is, the idea of 'just' prices in the sense of a 'substantial' understanding of justice taking account of the social status and the material needs of the exchange partners (Wilson 1997; Nutzinger and Hecker 2008). Classic political economy divorced itself from the moral underpinnings of scholastic economic theory. What is relevant are only the signals of prices and money as the most 'impartial observer', with actual prices oscillating around 'natural' prices, the latter in turn being governed by labour as 'the real price of everything' (Smith 1999 [1776]: 133). The self-regulation of markets indeed opens a lot of room for the pursuit of individual gain. Depending on the local power relationships in the market, this may result in relationships of exploitation and excessive inequality. A key problem in this context was how to include the poor in the market – a problem that could be solved only by the dubious invention of a commodity called 'labour power'. I will come back to this point below (Chapter 8).

The usual answer given by liberals to such objections is threefold. First, the actors should be given as much room to settle their concerns by direct negotiations instead of by referring to dubious political standards of social justice. Second, the lack of genuinely altruistic motivations in market transactions cannot justify fundamental criticisms of the market, given the factual presence of latent egoistic motives in most other types of social action, even in those appearing to be purely altruistic on the surface. Third, even in the case of gross inequalities arising, there is the countervailing mechanism of the 'invisible hand': free competition will curb excessive profits as well as excessive losses by shifting the supply–demand ratio either into the positive or the negative direction. In the liberal scenario, the main hope for social justice rests on the idea of self-interested individual market action having unintended beneficial effects at the collective level.[3]

The justice which the invisible hand may provide is obviously a minimal and weak one.[4] However, one should not forget the other side of the market narrative, which is its *universality*. Just *because* of their relative indifference towards local solidarities and standards of justice, markets are most likely to transcend national and cultural boundaries. The moral minimalism of markets thus can be interpreted as the price to be paid for their universality; they are two sides of the same coin.[5] As was recognised even much earlier than the eighteenth century,[6] markets did not originate within socio-culturally integrated communities, but between strangers; they tended to cross-cut the boundaries between communities, states and cultures, creating transnational relationships of economic interdependence. The 'natural' order of markets, which liberal economists conceptualised in line with Smith, is a universal one that is capable of co-ordinating billions of decisions of mutually unknown actors. The discussion about the 'civilising' impact of markets on society, which was a key theme of the liberal defences of capitalism in the eighteenth century (Hirschman 1977) departed right from this point. Due to the capacity of markets to calm down violent political and religious passions to profane 'interests', foreign trade would create mutual dependencies even between rival political powers, and hence would pacify international relations ('*doux commerce*', as Montesquieu called it). The message of the free contract, constituting the basis for a peaceful and prosperous society, extended principally to all mankind (Asbach 2014: 20), and this is what made it so powerful. Even Marx followed Smith this far, as he acknowledged the potential of capitalism to generate a world society, though he focused on the antagonising sides of capitalism instead of its integrative ones.

## Notes

1 Money does not 'replace' language, as Habermas argues, but functions to represent the claims and performances of all actors involved directly or indirectly in market transactions in a mutually acknowledged way – a point that had been emphasised by the institutionalist school of economics (and by John Commons in particular).

2 Even two hundred years later, Hayek (1960) would come up to revive the same message and make it the core of so-called 'neoliberalism'.

3 As is well known, this idea had been brought forward in the eighteenth century even before Smith by authors such as Bernard Mandeville with his popular 'Fable of the

Bees' (1705) and the Neapolitan economist Ferdinando Galiani with his book *Della Moneta* (1751) (Galiani 1751, 1999).

4 As mentioned above, the scientific validity of the invisible hand theorem never could be demonstrated convincingly. A key problem lies in the circular logic of the theorem: free markets produce the welfare optimum, which in turn is nothing but the result of the free working of market forces. To remove obvious deficiencies of empirical markets, the liberal doctrine calls for liberalisation moves; however, empirical markets will always remain 'imperfect' in some sense and can *never* be free enough to avoid all deficiencies. Whether the invisible hand hypothesis should be preferred to the countervailing hypothesis of Matthew's law is an issue that cannot be answered on *a priori* grounds but only empirically; and there appears to be no lack of empirical instances where Matthew's law seems to be the more promising assumption (Matthew 25:29: 'For every one who has will more be given, and he will have abundance; but from him who has not, even what he has will be taken away' [NRV]).

5 A similar point had been made by Georg Simmel in his work on social differentiation. As he emphasised, the development of social relations over large distances coincides with processes of individualisation, which tend to undermine the moral cohesion of local circles (Simmel 1989a [1890]: 173–174).

6 David Graeber (2011: 251–252) points to similarities in the interpretation of markets between Adam Smith and Islamic philosophers in the medieval period such as Al-Ghazali (1058–1111) and Al-Tusi (1201–1274) as an expression of general human reason.

# 4 Dimensions of disembedding

So far, I have reminded the reader of the positions of classical market liberalism, views that go back mostly to authors of the eighteenth century and that culminate in the idea that markets are the basis of civil society. A common critique of this idea is that it only reflects the moderate level of capitalist development of its time. Its implicit sociological premises were a strong national state and the limited internationalisation of trade that was controlled largely by colonial rule. After the revolutions in seventeenth-century England, a stable political class compromise had been achieved, with a still strong aristocracy and rural gentry, on the one hand, and a rising bourgeois middle class, on the other; there was still no significant industrial proletariat. What Smith had in mind when he spoke of 'markets' were the moderately liberalised national markets of his time, which had hardly been touched by the industrial revolution setting in only in the last two decades of the eighteenth century (Acemoglu and Robinson 2012: 191–192). Within such a traditional society, the market system itself apparently could not become the source of large social inequalities beyond the inherited inequalities of status and wealth. The liberal model does not take into account the social consequences of the disembedding of markets that started only after Smith's death. The eighteenth-century liberals could be so optimistic about the future of their own ideas only because their historical background was a nationally based semi-aristocratic society that was still far away from thorough liberalisation.

With the historically unheard of expansion of markets developing in all dimensions of social life from the early nineteenth century onwards, the liberal market narrative became overwhelmingly successful – a success, whose dimensions even the liberals themselves could hardly have anticipated. Capitalism indeed has been promoted by a 'spirit' much greater than Weber's often cited 'Protestant ethic': the narrative of the market as a key place for individual freedom.[1] The liberal creed became a part of the constitutional value system of the United States; in Europe, it became the legitimating background for a series of social reforms, including the introduction of the gold standard, the expansion of free trade, the liberation of peasants, the abolition of guild controls and state-granted monopolies, and the changing of poor laws. In Britain as well as on the continent, a broad movement to reorganise the economy and the political system according to the model of the self-regulating market set in. In the words of William Grampp: 'All this can lead one to believe that Britain must have been under the rule of the free markets and its apologists, as if the idea of laisser-faire had taken hold of the country about 1776, when the *Wealth of Nations* was published, and informed it with a grand design that was executed in the next century' (Grampp 1965: 85). The power of the market narrative did not exhaust itself in the Great Transformation of the nineteenth century. It was revived again in the so-called 'neo-liberal' ideologies of the second half of the twentieth century, a revival which triggered new waves of deregulation after the end of the Bretton Woods system in 1973, and which helped to bring about the downfall of the socialist system. Thus, Karl Polanyi certainly was on the right track when he characterised the liberal credo as a 'militant creed'.

What happened with the liberal creed, once it dissociated itself from the context of eighteenth-century society and entered into practice, becoming a message for social transformation? In the course of its practical implementation, the narrative did not only generate beneficial, but also unintended, contradictory and socially antagonising outcomes, as is to be expected from any great political idea becoming a force of real change. The Great Transformation gave rise to a new type of society entirely different from eighteenth-century civil society – global capitalism, whose antagonisms became the focus not only of Marx's critique, but also those of a large variety of anti-liberal and anti-capitalist counter-movements (Mishra 2017). In this chapter, I will deepen the historical analysis of the disembedding process, focusing on its different dimensions and in-built contradictions. The result – to put it in advance – will not be a revocation of the liberal argument about the social character of markets. Rather, as I am going to argue, the disembedding of markets led to an unprecedented expansion of the opportunity context of markets and money as their medium. With markets no longer being framed by an overarching political authority, the implicit sociological premises of liberal theory became obsolete; an entirely new global form of society arose. In some sense, Alexander Rüstow (2001) indeed was right when he warned of the danger that markets may exceed their proper social domain and that liberalism may become a 'religion' in a dubious sense.

Here, I am not engaging in the debate on the nature of money that has become so influential in recent times (Zelizer 1997, Ingham 2004, Ganssmann 2011, Paul 2012, Dodd 2014, Engster 2014, Konings 2015). Nor am I entering into the discussion about the possible historical origins of money in the sphere of the sacred, or about the religious connotations of the concept of debt (Laum 1924, Goodchild 2007, Graeber 2011, Dodd 2014, Türcke 2015). In a modern context, which I am confining myself to here, money as such can be understood first as nothing but a medium for the interpersonal recognition and transfer of private property rights. It is a claim against the property of others that everybody accepts as a claim against oneself. The point I want to make is not about money per se, but its real opportunity context. What money 'is' depends on what it 'does' and on what it 'can do', that is, on the institutionalised realm of private property rights (Koddenbrock 2017). Money that is valid only at local markets is different from world money; money that can only buy products is different from money that can also buy the conditions of production, or that can even buy money itself. To understand the nature of contemporary money, therefore, it is vital to consider the historical expansion of markets from the early nineteenth century, which was promoted by the promises of an ever-present liberal narrative. The consequences were indeed spectacular, as they did not only include the territorial opportunity context of money, as the 'globalisation' debate suggests, but also its social, material and temporal ones. In the course of these transformations, money became a vehicle of vast, historically unheard of potentials. In its capital form highlighted by Marx, it became a private claim no longer only on existing but also on *possible* wealth. The range of possible objects to be bought with money became undefinable, a new situation which transformed money into an incarnation of wealth 'as such'; Marx spoke of the 'third' form of money (Marx 1988 [1867]: 143–144). The 'iconic' qualities of money, which Martijn Konings (2015) has focused on, were a reflection of the modern universalisation of markets.[2] The counterpart of this rise in the potential of money, however, was the parallel rise of debt and alienation, which in turn gave rise to new and deep social antagonisms. The homogeneous commercial society of Adam Smith's time gave way to a capitalist class society, making it largely impossible for capitalists and workers to identify with each other and to switch between their roles.

With disembedding, the place of markets and money in society changed profoundly. As Marx and Simmel had emphasised, the very presence of money in market exchange indicates that exchange is more than a bilateral affair, but a transaction, where 'society', as a third partner, is always involved (whether it wants to or not). It makes, however, a crucial difference whether society comes in as a political agency controlling the use of money and restraining it to particular social sub-systems, or whether the use of money becomes generalised to a degree that makes it coincide with society itself. In modern, global capitalism, as Marx viewed it, markets no longer form an economic sub-system *within* a politically constituted society, but form an all-encompassing social system. In such a society, the dominance of markets and money as their medium is due not primarily to their functions for material reproduction (as orthodox Marxists continue to contend even today) but to their *universality*, that is, their global reach and their omnipresence in social life. The dominance of markets over society becomes effective, as I will argue, not only via external constraints, but via their capacity to govern subjectivity from within too, that is, to generate meaning, visions and utopias.[3] This will lead me to discuss the following question in the remainder of this book: can markets under such conditions take the role of defining the collective unity of society in much the same way as religion held sway over pre-modern societies and even over eighteenth-century civil society?

I will start with a closer explication of the concept of disembedding, taking up the distinctions met in Chapter 2. In a formal sense, the disembedding of markets can be defined as their expansion in the territorial, social, material and temporal dimensions. This means a spectacular enlargement of the options embodied in money: the spatial reach of money-based transactions increases; the variety of possible exchange partners increases – as is that of possible objects to purchase; and the temporal horizon of transactions is continuously broadened. In the following sections, I will develop a stylised historical description of the disembedding process, including its in-built contradictions.[4] Again, my intention is to elaborate and actualise Polanyi's double-movement theorem and to correct its analytical asymmetry.

## Territorial disembedding

With territorial (or spatial) disembedding, markets get integrated across national, regional and local borders. As a consequence of market liberalisation, transnational commodity markets, as well as capital and labour markets, grow at the cost of national and local markets. With the geographical reach of markets, the quantity and quality of commodities available to the individual customer starts to increase. On the side of the producers, transnational competition, the division of labour and economies of scale, and foreign direct investment (FDI) begin to develop. At the same time, transnational trade does not only extend to finished goods and services, but increasingly to intermediate ones too, resulting in the internationalisation of value-creation chains (VCCs).[5] As a consequence, the local and national self-sufficiency of markets and production circuits declines; likewise, local and national markets are exposed to global fluctuations to a higher degree. This has adverse effects on national states as agencies of economic and monetary governance, and may even threaten their political sovereignty. National taxation systems and market regulations (including work, production, and social and environmental standards) are subject to the pressure of international competition, as national laws can be easily circumvented by transnationally mobile, profit-seeking investors. Labour markets, too, are influenced by transnational labour migration, affecting employment and wage levels. The parallel processes on the monetary side are the rise of transnational financial and capital markets and the increasing preponderance of transnational forms of money (gold in the nineteenth century and international reserve currencies today) over national currencies. As cross-border flows of capital and credit increase, cyclical and speculative movements get amplified on a global scale.

As a broad historical overview reveals, territorial disembedding did not develop in a straightforward way. A first phase consisting of the marked internationalisation of markets, starting in the early nineteenth century and lasting until the First World War, led to a historically unprecedented upswing in world trade (Osterhammel 2009: 1033). A second phase, lasting until the end of the Second World War, was characterised by a revival of national economic protectionism and political and military antagonisms, which had adverse effects on international trade. A third phase, lasting from 1945 to 1973, saw the emergence of a politically 'embedded' transnational currency and trade system based on the agreement of Bretton Woods (Helleiner 1995), which gave rise to a revival of international trade within the Western bloc, and allowed a moderate level of trade between the Western and the Soviet bloc. Finally, full-fledged liberalism resurged in the late twentieth century in two steps, the first one being after the end of Bretton Woods in 1973 and the second one being after the fall of the Soviet bloc in 1991. This resurgence led to further spectacular increases in world trade and global economic integration (Halperin 2016). A simple indicator of this development is the ratio of merchandise exports to GDP (gross domestic product) at the world level, which rose from 4.6 percent (1870) to a preliminary maximum of 7.9 percent in 1913. After a marked decline due to the impact of two world wars and the Great Depression of the 1930s, the ratio rose again from a 5.5 percent in

1950 to 17.2 percent in 1998 (Maddison 2001: 127). In the first decade of the twenty-first century, the share of world trade in GDP continued to soar up to an all-time high of 31 percent in 2008, before dropping sharply due to the financial crisis in 2008–2009 (WTO 2015).

Ideally, territorial disembedding would culminate in a single global system of markets and production, with nationally or locally bounded economic circuits no longer playing a significant role. There have been extended debates about the empirical chances of such a development. World system theorists (Wallerstein 1979; Arrighi and Silver 1999) insist that market globalisation meets its limits in a *politically* constituted hierarchy of 'core', 'semi-periphery' and 'periphery' countries, with the core countries dominating the bulk of world trade and leaving the semi-peripheral and peripheral countries in a dependent and marginalised position. In light of the most recent development, critics of world system theory have called this hierarchy model into question. As a consequence of the resurgence of globalisation after the 1970s they see a 'single global production system' (Robinson 2004: 33) coming into existence, which includes emerging and developing economies. While trade even between emerging and developing nations has increased, the transnational integration of the economy has become more dense than it had been in the first wave of globalisation before the First World War. The globalisation of financial markets after 1973, for example, was intensified by the digitalisation of operations and by the mushrooming of new financial instruments, such as swaps, options and futures. Further characteristic developments were a marked growth in FDI, interlocking networks of control, and transnationally integrated VCCs. At the turn of the millennium, transnational corporations accounted for around one third of world output and two thirds of world trade (Robinson 2004: 55). In connection with the integration of firms across borders, some authors see a 'transnational class and even a 'transnational state' emerging, which is reflected in the increasing influence of transnational institutions, organisations and networks, like the World Trade Organization, the United Nations and the European Union (Sklair 2001; Robinson 2004; Caroll 2010). Rising cross-national labour migration has led to the formation of 'global cities' as centres of a new world-wide division of labour (Sassen 2007). An analysis that is largely complementary to such accounts has been offered by Manuel Castells and his theory of a capitalist 'network society', which focuses on the spread of digitally based social networks across national and cultural borders, and into almost all sub-systems of society (Castells 2000). The global 'information economy', which Castells sees as being on the rise (following partly older approaches of modernisation and post-industrialism) is based on the superior power of IT technologies to coordinate not only markets, but a large variety of social functions as well. This does not mean the end of capitalism, or of class conflict, but conflicts are arising increasingly from the socially exclusive and antagonising effects of network structures. Authors of the institutionalist school of world society theory point to institutional 'isomorphism' as a factor behind global integration (Meyer 2009) – that is, the spread of uniform models of institutional governance around the world.

Summing up these interpretations, present-day capitalism seems to have made considerable progress on the way towards a world of transnationally integrated markets and one global finance and production system.[6] Even more so, the global integration of the economy has had a transformative impact on all of society, including the formation of a global state, of global cities, and of a world-wide culture of social media and consumerism. According to such accounts, these developments could pave the way for a global civil society and for the world-wide victory of democracy as a political system. Francis Fukuyama anticipated such a scenario already in the early 1990s under the impression of the fall of the socialist system (Fukuyama 1992). Though the disembedding of markets did not guarantee the success of democracy and human rights, Fukuyama expected it to lay the groundwork for it.

The hypothesis of a long-term historical trend of capitalism towards global integration nevertheless continues to be controversial. For Paul Hirst and Grahame Thompson, globalisation is largely a myth (Hirst and Thompson 1999). As they have emphasised, the present-day international openness of the economy is not unprecedented; in some respects, globalisation is returning only to the level already reached before the First World War. The significant decline of in the growth rates of world trade after 2009, too, can be read as an indication that there is no iron law of ever-increasing transnational integration of markets. Contrary to theories of a transnational class, the globalisation of markets and production systems so far has not led to a corresponding internationalisation of biographies and careers of CEOs and corporate managers. Rather, most global companies still have a national focus that reflects itself in the nationally based compositions and careers of their management and their CEOs (Hartmann 2016). Moreover, the mounting transnational integration of markets and corporations should not be equated with a simple retreat of the national state, as Susan Strange (1996) has argued, but requires the development of new forms of national and transnational regulation and institution-building (Djelic and Quack 2003; for a recent overview, see Malets 2017). Transnational markets depend on common technical and accounting standards, and on intact governance structures and legal institutions at the national and local levels; otherwise, global investors could not meet a calculable local environment and have a chance of enforcing their legal claims. Paradoxically, the global territorial disembedding of markets depends on the countervailing moves of their local re-embedding, with the national state now partly becoming an executor of a new type of international law. Some authors have suggested the concept of 'glocalization' (Robertson 1995; Roudomelof 2016) to circumscribe these contradictory developments.

This means, however, increasing tensions between the role of the national state as an agency of transnational economic integration and its commitment towards its local electorate. Vital policy decisions in many areas can no longer be met at the national level alone; national legislative standards, such as in the fields of work, social policy and environment, are coming under pressure. The scope of decisions still being accessible to national politics is getting narrower and narrower, with the consequence of increasing legitimacy problems for national democracy. This may indeed permit obstacles against economic globalisation to go on. Dani Rodrik has raised this issue with his so-called 'globalization-trilemma' model: 'We cannot simultaneously pursue democracy, national determination, and economic globalization' (Rodrik 2011: xviii). Ongoing economic globalisation will not necessarily undermine the national state as an agency of market regulation; what will suffer, however, is the *democratic* governance of markets at the national level. There are only two possible ways out of the dilemma, as Rodrik argues: either democracy will have to be transplanted to the transnational level, which he deems to be unrealistic, or the transnational expansion of markets would have to be contained, which in his view is the most desirable solution. In a similar vein, Wolfgang Streeck (2013) has emphasised the fundamental threats that national democracy is exposed to by the globalisation of markets.

Castells' influential network approach has not remained uncontested either; for some critics, it seems to rely on a reified understanding of the social impact of network structures and IT technologies, and on an underestimation of the embeddedness of networks in conventional group, power and class structures and their inherent antagonisms (van Dijk 1999; Stalder 2006). With regard to John Meyer, Jens Beckert (2010) has shown that the same factors underlying institutional isomorphism can also be interpreted as a source of conflict and divergence. A key factor neglected by globalisation-optimistic approaches are regionally and nationally based cultural traditions and collective identities. As Samuel Huntington (1996) and Benjamin Barber (1996) have argued, economic globalisation cannot neutralise the countervailing power of cultural and religious traditions. According to the former:

> Differences among civilizations are not only real; they are basic. Civilizations are differentiated from each other by history, language, culture, tradition and, most importantly, religion. The people in different civilizations have different views on the relations between God and man, the individual and the group, the citizen and the state, parents and children, husband and wife, as well as different views of the relative importance of rights and responsibilities, liberty and authority, equality and hierarchy. These differences are the product of centuries. They will not soon disappear.
>
> (Huntington 2000: 28)

The globalisation of markets and production chains certainly will not only produce winners. The losers should not be neglected, and both, winners and losers, are likely to be positioned unevenly in the territorial as well as in the social dimension. In the advanced economies, many of the less-skilled workers will be hit by increasing transnational competition on the labour markets, be it in the form of production outsourcing to low-wage countries or on the form of mounting labour immigration. For them, the national welfare state remains the only entity in which they can place their hopes to defend their living standards. The losers may mobilise nationalistic or xenophobic currents in order to fight labour immigration and to prevent social downgrading. Anti-liberal policies aiming to protect national or regional markets may receive increasing popular support, as the globalisation pessimists are predicting in line with Polanyi. I will come back to this issue below (Chapter 8). For the time being, however, it appears safe to conclude that the territorial disembedding of markets will reach social and cultural limits, and that it is likely to mobilise political counter-movements. Though transnational economic integration has made undeniable progress since the late twentieth century, the hypothesis of a single global production system still has a long way to go before it can materialise.

## Social disembedding

The expansion of markets in the social dimension means the progressive inclusion of the population into the market nexus and the parallel elimination of rural and family-based subsistence economies. A 'social division of labor' (Perelman 2000) emerges, replacing tradition-based forms of work organisation and requiring people to make a living via market-based transactions instead of supplying themselves locally. In contrast to the extensive dynamic of territorial disembedding, this means an *intensification* of market relationships, resulting in an erosion of household-based forms of solidarity, of kinship and of neighbourhood ties and their replacement by buyer–seller relationships. Historically, the social disembedding of markets was initiated by what Marx had called 'primitive accumulation' ('*ursprüngliche Akkumulation*'), that is, the violent separation of peasants from their natural subsistence bases, forcing populations into the regime of a labour market. Primitive accumulation started in fifteenth-century Britain; however, as Michael Perelman has emphasised, this process is not confined to a distant past. It continued up to the present day with the proletarianisation of the small peasantry of many countries in Asia, Africa and Latin America (see also Harvey 2003). The 'liberation' of peasants in nineteenth-century Europe (Austria, Prussia, Russia) and of slaves in the United States coincided in its effects with primitive accumulation; though releasing peasants and slaves from personal dependence, it 'released' them and subjected them to the labour market (Osterhammel 2009: 992–993). Primitive accumulation is not the only arena where the social disembedding of markets developed. During the nineteenth century, the process was intensified by the erosion of family work in agriculture and the traditional craft industries, with the result of even more workers being mobilised for the emerging industrial labour market, which subsequently became institutionalised on a large scale.

In the twentieth century, the social disembedding process continued with the commercialisation of household work and child care, in combination with the further inclusion of women into the labour force.[7] Today, dual career couples, outsourcing homework to externally hired nannies and service personnel, many of them being migrants, have become a widespread phenomenon no longer only in the wealthy milieus of advanced capitalist countries (Hochschild and Ehrenreich 2002). The spread of digital platforms, such as Facebook and Uber, have opened ways to commercialise private relationships and networks on a large scale. A further variant of social disembedding, which became relevant in the late twentieth century, was the permeation of the public sector by market forces. Formerly public industries and services, such as energy, railways, and telecommunication, were privatised; large parts of the public sector, including health care and education, were reorganised according to market principles and became subject to the logic of profit (Schimank and Volkmann 2008, 2017). Even the private sector itself was restructured accordingly; private corporations outsourced parts of their operations, decentralised their structures, and simulated market mechanisms internally (e.g. by introducing internal 'profit centres' or 'benchmarking' practices) to enhance their competitiveness. As a consequence, the difference between organisations as formalised and hierarchically structured systems of action, on the one hand, and networks and markets, on the other, became porous, though it did not vanish completely (Davis 2009). As Michael Sandel (2012) has shown, the transformation of hitherto non-market-based social relationships into commercial contracts is proceeding in a variety of ways in contemporary society, ranging from the possibility of buying citizenship or academic degrees, to buying privileged health-care services, line-standing services, and pollution rights. The development of artificial reproduction technologies may be even paving the way for markets to invade the reproduction sphere by enabling parents (of whatever sex) to 'buy' their children: 'Today, the logic of buying and selling no longer applies to material goods alone, but increasingly governs the whole of life' (Sandel 2012: 6). With markets, money and its logic are permeating daily life,[8] undermining everything that has been left from former local solidarities and subsistence economies.

Ideally, such a development would terminate in an 'individualised' society, with everybody taking the position of an autonomous private proprietor while nevertheless being perfectly 'socialised' via the nexus of markets and money. It was Georg Simmel who first – almost one hundred years before Ulrich Beck and Anthony Giddens came up with their well-known theories of individualisation – developed a thorough analysis of such a constellation. Simmel's analysis concentrates on the generic impact of the spread of money and markets on the rise of modern individuality (Simmel 1989b [1900]; see also Deutschmann 1996, 2001). Money does not promote the autonomy of the individual by segregating them from society. The modern individual is not the lone settler in the woods; to the contrary, their social interconnectedness is becoming more complex and universal than ever, with the modern city as their characteristic arena. 'Autonomy' does not mean independence, but freedom of *personal* dependencies provided by the anonymity of money and money-based networks. Not by chance was it the 'strangers', that is, ethnic minorities like the Jews in Europe, the Armenians in Turkey, and the Parsis in India, who established themselves as pioneers of commerce and of the monetary economy. As the monetary economy spreads, however, *everybody* becomes a 'stranger'.[9] Money thus has a thoroughly undermining effect on all traditional, feudal, kinship, and local solidarities. As everybody now 'carries his claims on the performances of others along with him in a condensed, potential form' (Simmel 1989b [1900]: 463, my translation), they can free themselves from personal dependencies and particularistic social contexts, replacing them by relationships characterised by emotional indifference and cool opportunism.

The ideal of individual autonomy corresponds to that of cosmopolitanism. As it embodies an infinite variety of territorial, social, material and temporal options, money lays the groundwork for individual autonomy *on a global level*. Indeed, it was Simmel who pointed to the centrality of money for modern cosmopolitan and consumerist lifestyles. As an owner of money – given only I have enough of it (which, though, is almost never the case) – I do not only have the free choice about *where* and from *whom* to buy, but also *what* to buy, and at *what time*. In other words, money enables actors to treat all givens of their life as variables and to continuously invent their individuality anew.[10] Cosmopolitan individual autonomy, however, is bound to the implicit condition of money becoming overwhelmingly dominant over society and individual life. Money takes on the paradoxical character of an 'absolute means' (Simmel 1989b [1900]: 298, my translation) – a means, which due to its absoluteness, turns out to be more than just a *means*. Whether voluntary or not, it becomes and end in itself for the individual actor, as it represents the key to attaining most of the relevant aims of their life. Beyond what actors actually do with their money, the truly important thing is what they *could do*. Money, in other words, is much more than a mere vehicle of material interest, or a profane medium of exchange, as the common opinion goes. Rather, it embodies an option of a higher order, a utopia of perhaps the strongest possible kind: personal freedom *within* a global society. Freedom is being guaranteed not only on the level of the law (this being the focus of philosophical theories of justice), but also as a matter of factual purchasing power beyond the nationally bounded reach of the law. The centrality of this utopia for modern society could provide an initial answer to the question left open by Karl Polanyi: how can the 'liberal credo' be so successful despite its incompatibility with apparently 'anthropological' facts? It is Simmel's point that the practical success of the modern idea of individual freedom – which Polanyi himself subscribes to – would have been unthinkable without the key role of money in a market society and the model character of money-based lifestyles for all of society. Money and individual freedom are complementary and not at odds with each other, as Polanyi contended.

Nevertheless, Simmel was aware of the limitations of money-based individual freedom. As he observed, even the rich often feel overtaxed by the promises of wealth and fall into diverse forms of money greed, either excessive spending or stinginess, with the ultimate level of money pathology being 'smugness' ('*Blasiertheit*') (Simmel 1989b [1900]: 322–323). The poor, on the other hand, do not experience any freedom of choice, as their expenses are predetermined by their pure subsistence needs. Poverty, thus, is much more than just material deprivation, as it deprives the individual from the very freedom of choice itself (Simmel 1989a [1890]: 277). Beyond Simmel, it needs to be emphasised that the poor see themselves confronted with the negative side of the money utopia: debt. What Simmel neglects is the double character of money as a claim of myself against others *and of others against myself*. With the capitalist expansion of claims and promises, the debts expanded accordingly. The extension of the claims of money to the potential of labour via the social construction of labour as a commodity meant a further dramatic widening of the social gap between promises and debts. The counterpart of the capitalist freedom utopia was the permanent attribution of the debt side to the working class, giving the lie to liberal ideologies of markets as a sphere of peaceful and harmonious exchange. Capitalism is no longer a harmless 'commercial society' where everybody can switch easily between the roles of debtor and creditor. The social disembedding of markets has meant the transformation of civil market society into a class society, with the claims of the one class becoming the debts of the other. The problem with money is that one must have it, and in capitalism the haves and have-nots certainly are not distributed across society in a random way. Marx was much clearer than Simmel in highlighting these reverse sides of the capital form of money.

The social obligation which the market nexus implies confines itself to the formal fulfilment of contracts. Hence, it is an utmost thin one, as it abstracts from all the real differences of the exchange partners. In comparison with other types of social relationships, the market nexus appears unique with regard to its universality, as well as with regard to its abstract character. It represents one extreme in a continuum of social structures, each of them being characterised by more binding forms of solidarity – such as the state, organisations, civic communities, and the nuclear family – while at the same time confining themselves to particular social contexts. As reciprocity becomes more binding and encompassing, it becomes more exclusive and personal. The opposite extreme of the continuum is marked by love as an utmost exclusive social relationship that is characterised by a maximum amount of mutual commitment. The price to be paid for the universality of markets is their moral minimalism; conversely, the exclusivity of love may be interpreted as the price for its communicative intensity.

Despite all the advances that market logic has made, modern capitalism is still far away from being a 'pure' market society. There continues to exist a rich variety of social relationships between the extremes of markets and love, which Marshall Sahlins has categorised by his well-known conceptual dichotomy of balanced and generalised reciprocity (Sahlins 1972; see also Graeber 2011).[11] Even the wealthy cannot live in a world governed by the money nexus *alone*; all the more does this apply to those less endowed with financial (and social and cultural) capital. Bear in mind that the labour market inclusion of the working-age population even today is far from being complete; most social work is still being done in households and in other non-market contexts.[12] It is a commonplace of economic sociology that embeddedness – in the sense of generalised reciprocity – is not restricted to primitive societies, but continues to be present in modern ones too, and that it is a vital precondition for markets to work in practice.

Viewed from this side, Polanyi indeed was right in his verdict that socially disembedded markets comprised a 'stark utopia'. The reverse side of embeddedness, however, is its built-in particularism. While markets are transnational, and capitalist firms are operating globally, the reach of states, communities, organisations and families is mostly bound to the national or even local level. This makes them vulnerable to the forces of global competition, as those depending exclusively on local solidarities are in an inferior position vis-à-vis globally mobile capital investors. Though they depend on the accountability of the local environment too, the investors can always opt to exit. The hollowing out of non-market solidarities by market forces may mobilise social resistance, and even militant counter-movements, which aim to restore the exclusive character of local or national collective identities. The upshot is that the functional coexistence of markets with non-market solidarities, due to the former's parasitic traits, is anything but a stable and harmonious one. Rather, it is susceptible to self-destructive counter-movements and vicious circles, which finally may endanger the market nexus itself.

## Material disembedding

The material disembedding of markets refers to their extension from raw and finished products and services to the factors of production – labour, land, technology – and finally to the medium of markets itself: money. Gradually, the entire circle of human reproduction, including production, distribution and consumption, is subject to the market nexus. From a historical viewpoint, this definition needs several qualifications. As Braudel (1992) has emphasised, it would be erroneous to assume that before the end of the eighteenth century there were no markets for land and paid labour; slave markets, of course, did pre-exist the eighteenth century too and looked back on a long tradition. Indeed, land in Europe was barred to a large degree by the institution of entails, which prevented the sale of landed estates in order to secure the property basis of noble families from one generation to the next (as mentioned already by Adam Smith (1999 [1776]: 486). Nevertheless, monasteries enlarged their possessions by taking over communal and agricultural lands. There were also moves made by bankers (such as the Fuggers), merchants and rich noblemen to invest their idle money into land, industry and transport. It was not money that was lacking, but 'what *was* lacking, for a number of reasons, was the opportunity to invest it into a really profitable enterprise' (Braudel 1992: 248). The agricultural investor had to accept feudal dues and peasant quit-rents, and he could do little to change the traditional work culture of the peasantry; parallel experiences were had by industrial investors (e.g. in mining). Except in cases where the investment was guided by motives of representation, the investors gained little joy from their projects; due to a lack of profitability, capital soon moved out again. Industrial technology was hardly developed before the eighteenth century; it remained in a poor state. Thus, there hardly existed any markets in this sector too. Paid labour was usual to some degree only in agriculture, mining, transport and construction. As Braudel concludes, it is no surprise that 'the capitalism of the past is essentially found in the commercial sector, that its greatest efforts and investments went into the sphere of circulation' (Braudel 1992: 247). This also had a retarding effect on the development of the financial sector, which nevertheless did exist too in many forms before the nineteenth century. However, even the market for public bonds developed on a transnational scale no earlier than in the nineteenth century, and this was largely due to the efforts of the Rothschild dynasty (Ferguson 1998).

What was really new in the Great Transformation was less about the factors of production going to market *as such* and more about land, industrial technology, free labour, and money entering the market *separately*. The workers were no longer artisans, bringing their tools with them, but 'pure' workers equipped with nothing but their personal capacities. The buyer of land was released from the traditional obligations towards the peasantry inhabiting it and from feudal dues. The land was 'freed' from the peasants, as Weber had remarked sarcastically (Weber 1981: 206, my translation). With the 'liberation' of peasants, the problem arose of how to include those who literally owned nothing into the market. The solution was found in the social construction of labour power as a commodity. It was only due to this particular social design of property rights, and not to any intrinsic qualities, that land and other means of production took on the character of capital and that work took on the character of labour.

The invention of the free work contract was a key step in the social disembedding process of markets. What was even more important, however, was its impact on material disembedding, as it came down also to a spectacular enlargement of the *possible objects* to be marketed. This appears paradoxical, since the liberalisation of work at first glance did not mean an expansion but a contraction of the market sphere, as it implied the abolition of formerly flourishing slave markets.[13] My point here is that the apparent contraction of markets due to the prohibition of slavery actually had the contrary effect, namely, a historically unprecedented *expansion* of markets, since the free work contract resulted in the extension of the property claim of money from finished goods to the creative and innovative *potential* of labour. Money now no longer could buy only what actually *had been produced*, but also what *could be produced* via the organised employment of free labour. As a consequence, the difference between the 'real' and the 'imaginary' sides of the economy became fluent and entered into the dispositions of the market actors. As it is impossible to determine the creative potential of labour exhaustingly, the property claim on this potential can never be finally redeemed. In its capital form, therefore, money is bound to grow and to get invested into an uncertain future of never-ending innovations. Instead of merely mediating the exchange of use values (C-M-C in Marx's terms), money now took on the character of a self-referential entity (M-C-M): it was to be accumulated not with the purpose of 'single profit, but of the restless determination to gain' (Marx 1988 [1867]: 168, my translation).

The term 'creativity', which I am taking up from John Dewey (1958 [1925]), Hans Joas (1992) and Jens Beckert (2002), circumscribes the capacity of humans to create something new beyond the mere observation of rules and routines (see also Deutschmann 2011a). Only free individuals possessing sovereignty over their own abilities, not slaves, can be creative. Creativity is different from 'rational' or even 'intentional' action, as it does not follow a logic of utility maximisation but one of 'enquiry', as Dewey (1938) had called it. Creative actions do not merely exploit the chances of a given situation. Rather, they result in a *transformation* of the situation, not only in the sense of the actor unilaterally transforming the environment (such as in the case of planning), but also in the reverse sense of the actor learning from the environment: the actor, in other words, is letting himself be transformed in an indirect way. No one can 'intend' to make an invention or predict its course; it comes or does not come in a process of experimentation, though hard work may prepare the ground for it. Not only are creative individuals able to find hitherto unknown solutions for given problems, they may even discover new problems or identify problems for given solutions (Popitz 1997; Stark 2009). Creativity does not mean complete disruption, as it emerges on the basis of given knowledge, routines and acquired skills, though it makes use of them in a new and unforeseeable way which is impossible to reproduce in any algorithm. Though it develops on the basis of given technologies and knowledge, creative action has destructive consequences, as it renders established technologies obsolete and leaves behind industrial ruins (e.g. the petrol engine was developed according to the model of the steam engine while replacing the latter to a large degree).

The creativity of labour – of entrepreneurs, inventors, engineers, as well as that of blue- and white-collar workers – is a key resource for the growth of capital; firms compete to mobilise this resource. Clearly, this is not the only way to reap profits. *Single* actors or firms can also generate profits by simpler means, such as by cutting wages or costs, exploiting market imperfections, or erecting political monopolies. However, the business strategy of exploitation appears rational only in the short term, as it can be copied most easily: it tends to end up in zero-sum games, with some market players winning and others losing. As an *aggregate*, capital can only grow on the basis of innovation, promoting new combinations such as new products, technologies, logistics, markets and resources, as Joseph Schumpeter had emphasised (Schumpeter 1934 [1911]; following him are Lazonick 1991 and Baumol 2002). As the success of innovations cannot be calculated in advance, it is not simply rational calculation but creativity that is basic for capitalist growth.[14] Due to the uniqueness of their products, innovative firms may gain an edge over their competitors. They are able to reap profits as a premium on their temporary monopoly, and are thus able to grow faster than their competitors, who, since they do not sleep, may eventually catch up. The original innovators are therefore put under pressure to once again come up with new inventions. In this way, a self-reinforcing growth process may be generated, making the economy grow as *an aggregate*, not only on the level of the firm. In such a constellation, growth does not reduce itself to a zero-sum game, but comes from additional value creation, enabling all market participants to benefit. Accordingly, the aggregate volume of money and credit must increase too, as Schumpeter had argued (Schumpeter 1934 [1911]).

For Schumpeter, the key instance to promote innovations is the capitalist entrepreneur. The industrial revolutions of capitalism, nevertheless, did not simply go back to the ideas of any single entrepreneur or inventor. They would have been unthinkable without the small, incremental inventions of millions of engineers, technicians, and white- and blue-collar employees making great inventions work in practice. It is not only the entrepreneur, but also the personal commitment of their employees and partners that is vital for the market success of innovations. The vast majority of innovations, 'then and now were incremental improvements to existing processes and products and, as Adam Smith observed, were often made by workers who used machines in different types of workplace' (Freeman and Louca 2001: 157). Despite its individual origin, the innovative process needs to be communicated, coordinated and organised in order to materialise itself in marketable products or technologies (Dopfer 2006). Beyond Schumpeter's heroic picture of the entrepreneurial individual, it is vital to understand how capitalist firms were able to manage innovation as a collective process involving not only their employees, but also their external partners, financiers and customers (Lazonick 1991; McCraw 1997).

As a first step, a closer understanding of the work contract is required. Still in Adam Smith's time, the work contract hardly differed from the conventional sales contract. Workers were mostly artisans, who saw themselves as small producers and who gathered under the roof of the shop and sold their products to the employer. In Britain, this understanding of the work contract continued to prevail for a long time (this had been Richard Biernacki's point, as mentioned above in Chapter 2). It was Karl Marx who discovered the peculiar character of the work contract as an agreement giving the employer not only the right to dispose over the *product* of the worker, but to dispose over the work *in actu* (within certain temporal and material limitations). What the worker sold to the employer was the right to dispose over their *labour power*, not only the results of their work. As Biernacki (1995) has shown, this interpretation coincided with the contemporary practice in Prussia, which was both less and more modern than the practice in England at the same time. It was less modern because industrial management in Prussia followed the authoritarian and paternalistic traditions of the state bureaucracy; hence, managers were much less hesitant to intervene directly in the work process than the employers in liberal England. It was more modern because it provided more room for managers to make use of their prerogative in an innovative and productive way and to develop the potential of industrial organisation. Today, the interpretation of the work contract as an entitlement for the employer to dispose over the *capacities* of the employee is generally considered to be well established (Simon 1976 [1945]). Closely associated with this interpretation is the notion of the incompleteness of the work contract, leaving both, the employer as well as the employee, a zone of informal discretion which can be occupied by both sides in different antagonistic and cooperative ways (Marsden 1999).

There can be no doubt that not only managers but key groups of workers too were ready to cooperate; otherwise, the success of the industrial revolutions would have been unthinkable. How could this be possible, given the class character of industrial relations and the social antagonisms between capital and labour? Human creativity – to emphasise the point again – is a capacity that cannot develop under conditions of force and alienation, but presupposes personal freedom. The key to solving the puzzle lies in what I will describe below (in Chapter 9) as the 'double-bind' character of capitalist class relations. While being collectively closed, the demarcations between capital and labour are individually open at the same time, as the individual affiliation to capitalist classes (differently from pre-modern status groups) is defined not by social origin but by the mere fact of ownership. Though the social gap between the classes may appear unsurmountable to the poor, the formal openness of class membership could give rise at least to *aspirations* of social advance. Despite the poor conditions of the European working classes in the early nineteenth century (and still today in many emerging and developing countries), these aspirations turned out to be more than just illusions. In the United States, around 20 percent of the members of the economic elite in the nineteenth century had a petty bourgeois, clerk, or white-collar family background (Bendix and Howton 1978: 228). Between 1820 and 1845, 'only 19 percent of patentees in the United States had parents who were professionals or were from recognizable major landowning families. During the same period, 40 percent of those who took out patents had only primary schooling or less, just like Edison. Moreover, they often exploited their patent by starting a firm, again like Edison' (Acemoglu and Robinson 2012: 33). In nineteenth-century Germany, too, there was no lack of similar success stories of entrepreneurs coming from a small bourgeois background (e.g. Friedrich Krupp, August Thyssen, the Siemens brothers, Gottlieb Daimler), and they continue to occur even today. Due to a variety of factors, such as social reforms, the expansion of technical and general education, and the institutionalisation of industrial relations and internal labour markets, the chances for qualified blue- and white-collar employees to advance have also increased (e.g. Kocka 1969; Gall 2000; Deutschmann 2002; Lesczenski 2008).

Even as early as during the Industrial Revolution, factory owners began to recognise the importance of incentives for worker cooperation: 'The equipment and materials used by the workers belonged to the capitalist and were costly. Factory owners needed to instill in workers a culture of loyalty and sobriety, and a willingness to take instructions from and cooperate with other workers' (Mokyr and Voth 2010: 32). After the turn of the twentieth century, traditional paternalistic patterns of labour relations gave way to modern approaches to management, which were pioneered, for example, by Werner von Siemens and Ernst Abbé in Germany (Kocka 1969) and Elton Mayo in the United States (Roethlisberger and Dickson 1939). Gradually, the employers had to learn that the traditional despotic factory regime was neither helpful in raising productivity, nor useful in fighting the high fluctuation amongst workers. Complex performances of workers, such as cooperation in innovative projects, or even simply safeguarding the smooth flow of shop-floor operations, cannot be achieved only by command. Higher productivity and innovation require workers to cooperate voluntarily with each other and with superiors, and to feel committed to their tasks. To generate workers' commitment, however, capital had to pay a price not only in terms of contract, that is, higher wages or financial incentives, but also in terms of social status (Streeck 1990). To do this required the introduction of the pattern of generalized reciprocity (according to Marshall Sahlins' above-mentioned concept) into the sphere of industrial relations, with workers committing themselves to the firm in exchange for receiving status. Status materialised itself in employment guarantees and institutionalised internal qualification and career systems. Initially, these systems were confined to a small elite of white-collar employees. In the course of time, they were extended to other groups of the workforce too, though the degree of inclusion of the workforce varied considerably between nations and industrial sectors. This phenomenon paralleled the emergence of industrial relations, that is, of nationally different forms of collective bargaining, labour laws, sectoral and enterprise-level institutions of co-determination, qualification and social policy.

The extension of markets from finished products to the creative capacities of labour certainly was one of the biggest historical achievements of capitalism, as well as a key aspect of the disembedding of markets. Money became a property title no longer only on the *products* of labour, but also on its *potentials*; and it thereby transformed itself into capital. However, as I have tried to show, material disembedding is anything but a smooth and continuous process; it is a contradictory and conflict-ridden transformation, which depends on simultaneous moves to re-embed markets into non-market institutions. There can be little doubt that the big industrial innovations of capitalism would have been impossible without the institution of a privileged, 'primary' segment of the labour market, giving engineers, technicians and core workers a social status beyond a 'normal' contractual relationship of hire and fire. The extension of markets into the cooperative and creative potential of labour paradoxically was contingent upon a prior 'decommodification' of the labour market status of certain groups of employees in various forms, giving them a socially acknowledged position beyond the cash nexus, and opening prospects for social advancement.

Not all sectors of the labour market – just to make it clear – were involved in these changes to the same degree. Depending on sectoral conditions, and on diverging national institutional traditions, large segments of semi-skilled and unskilled work, which were characterised by poor work and pay conditions, have remained. In the most recent past, these 'secondary' segments of the labour market seem to have increased. At the same time, the mounting influence of financial investors on corporate governance has led to a dismantling of organisational hierarchies and to a reorganisation of firms according to market models, resulting in the spread of short-term employment contracts even in formerly privileged segments, as mentioned above (Davis 2009; Deutschmann 2016a; Roberts and Kwon 2017; Schimank and Volkmann 2017). Could the trend towards hire and fire endanger the capacity of firms to innovate? There seems to be little concern in management consultancy about that. Perhaps, this nonchalance has to do with the spread of new management concepts about innovation and creativity, which aim to release something like 'pure' creativity. As I have emphasised above, real innovation is never pure, but is always historically and socially contingent. Creativity develops within a framework of given institutions, routines, expertise and knowledge without transforming them completely. The idea of 'pure' creativity, by contrast, would come close to the old theological concept of *creatio ex nihilo*, creation out of nothing, which was considered to be the privilege of God. The most recent move made by management consultants to approach the idea of pure creativity can be categorised under the heading of 'disruptive innovation' (Christensen 1997). Here, the break with given technological routines and management knowledge *as such* is being declared as the cornerstone of a new gospel for management. Managers are being advised to invest not in established markets, but in insignificant or emerging ones that offer low margins.[15] Mature firms are advised to become juvenile and to focus their strategies on their capabilities and their blind spots at the same time. Under such premises, a high turnover of personnel even in firms' research and development departments would be a virtue instead of a problem. The reactions of practitioners to this phenomenon continues to be mixed. It remains controversial whether disruptive innovation comes down to more than mere rhetoric, which – if being put seriously into practice – would simply institute arbitrariness and vastly overtax real actors (e.g. Lepore 2014). In the end, the innovative process itself would be paralysed and bring about disorganising consequences for the economy and society as a whole. As we have seen in the case of social disembedding too, the capitalist dream of absolute wealth vanishes and becomes self-destructive just by radicalising itself.

Material disembedding does not exhaust itself in the mobilisation of the potential of free labour by capital; we have to consider the other 'fictitious' commodities listed by Polanyi as well, namely, money and land. As in the case of labour, it can be shown that the successful inclusion of money and land into the market nexus depended on parallel moves of decommodification.

To begin with, I will look at money: today, there is a widespread consensus amongst historians that pre-modern money originated outside of the sphere of markets. What later became money were originally sacrificial offerings to the gods, or goods serving as accounting standards for redistributive payments (taxes and transfers) arranged by the state (Laum 1924; Ingham 2004; Graeber 2011; Türcke 2015; Paul 2017). The state created money by fiat, issued it the form of transfer payments, and accepted it in the form of taxes. As the state combined the role of the debtor and the creditor in itself, the money circuit was a static one. As Ingham has argued, all money is rooted historically in institutionalised 'money of account' in this sense. Originating as a public good, money gradually spread into the market sphere, taking on the function of a medium of exchange in private contracts while being issued and certified by the public authorities.

Beyond its pre-modern history, however, money also has genuinely modern origins as privately created credit money which developed in the transactions between merchants and bankers in Southern and Western Europe (Italy, England, the Netherlands) starting from the fifteenth and sixteenth centuries. Credit money emerged from individual bills of exchange, which were increasingly depersonalised and transferred to private and public banks (Ingham 2004: 107–108). This development meant the beginning of the commodification of money, as money now took on the character of an asset to be traded in special markets. Private credit money is dynamic by its very nature, since it depends on the continuous creation of new debts; it would only '*disappear* if everyone paid their debts' (Ingham 2004: 221, n. 6). Given the stationary economic logic of stratified societies, as they were prevailing in Europe still in the eighteenth century, however, the creation of credit money had narrow constraints. If the income of debtors remained more or less constant – which was the normal case under pre-capitalist conditions except for a small sector of merchant capital – the obligation to repay credit with interest often had economically ruinous and socially disruptive consequences. Likewise disruptive was the impact of inflationary turbulence caused by the importation of precious metal or by the issuance of fake coins, which states often resorted to in order to cover their deficits. Though the economy could 'take off' in terms of nominal monetary expansion, as it did in several financial bubbles in the seventeenth and eighteenth centuries (Kindleberger and Aliber 2005: 256–257), the subsequent real crash to be expected sooner or later became all the more devastating. Preventing such crises was a key motive lying behind states' attachment of currencies to metal and the religious prohibition of interest.

The Great Transformation of the nineteenth century, however, enabled the economy to take off in *real* terms, not only in nominal terms. As I have tried to show, a key step here was the capitalist inclusion of free labour into the market nexus and the mobilisation of the creative capacities of labour, which laid the groundwork for the Industrial Revolution and a historically unprecedented upswing in economic growth. With growth instead of stationary reproduction now becoming the normal condition of the economy, the commodification of money and the expansion of credit and financial markets could proceed too, and this became vital to securing the accumulation of industrial capital. As Samuel Knafo (2013) showed in his above-cited analysis (Chapter 2), the introduction of the gold standard in Britain in 1821, and subsequently in most other European economies, played a key role in this process. Nevertheless, it did not lead to the complete liberalisation of financial markets. Though the gold standard left considerable room for discretionary monetary policies, state governments aimed to set tighter rules and to strengthen national control over an enlarging finance and banking system. The capitalist mobilisation of the real economy did not mean that credit now could be generated at will. The limits of a 'neutral' expansion, however, never could be known in advance, as they depended on the *a priori* incalculable response of markets to entrepreneurial innovations. As a result of this dilemma, the classic 'business cycle' emerged, with alternating phases of excessive expansion and contraction.

While there were some attempts to reintroduce the gold standard after the First World War, it was removed again as a consequence of the world economic crisis in the early 1930s. Again, this did not mean the complete liberalisation of finance. Knafo interprets the gold standard as a forerunner of later Keynesian 'functional' finance, not as its counterpoint. As he showed, monetary policies move in a triangle of three objectives which are impossible to implement at the same time: *fixed exchange rates* (aiming to stabilise trade and investment), *free capital movement*, and *domestic autonomy for policy-makers* (Knafo 2013: 8). Whatever priority is taken, it always requires political intervention, and, hence, some level of embeddedness. The complete self-regulation of financial markets, which Polanyi had in mind, would require an elimination of national central banks. Not only the creation of private credit, but the generation of any kind of money would become a private business. This is what Hayek suggested in his concept of denationalised money (Hayek 1990). In the last instance, the full extension of the market nexus to money would mean that money would become purely self-referential and that capital would be transformed into an agency of unrestricted speculation.[16] However, as long as money remains indispensable as a profane medium of exchange to safeguard property rights over the real economy, it cannot be disposed of purely at will by private actors. It remains a public good requiring state authority to secure its acceptance and to guarantee its value (Paul 2010). The recent financial crisis has given abundant evidence about the risks of decoupling money from state and central bank control and from the non-financial sphere. These risks, which were greatly enhanced by the globalisation of capital markets after the fall of the Bretton-Woods system in 1973, have been discussed extensively in the financialisation literature since the late 1980s (Strange 1986; Phillips 2006; Reinhart and Rogoff 2009; Lounsbury and Hirsch 2010; Heires and Nölke 2014). In the crisis of 2007–2008, like in that of the 1930s, rescue finally came from national state and central bank rescue programmes, not from denationalised money. Today, the insight has grown again that political regulations on the national and international levels – such as minimum capital requirements, firewalls between credit and investment banking, and prohibitions against dubious financial products (Admati and Hellwig 2014) – are vital to the avoidance of catastrophic market collapses.[17]

The case of land again demonstrates the impossibility of fictitious commodity markets becoming completely disembedded entities. For Smith, Ricardo and Marx, land rent did not constitute a premium for net value creation, but was a deduction from the latter. Land rent is based on the monopoly of the landowner over the 'fictitious commodity' of land, enabling him to extract revenues from the rest of society.[18] A key concern in the early-nineteenth-century discussions (e.g. by David Ricardo and Thomas Malthus) had been that rising prices for land and agricultural products, which was due to population growth and industrial development, was leading to an increase in the exploitation of industrial capitalists and workers alike by the landowners, thus gradually curbing economic progress. While productivity growth in agriculture invalidated these concerns to some degree, new problems arose. In particular, there was the devastation of the natural environment that resulted from the application of industrial technologies to agriculture and the soaring of real estate prices in the urban agglomerations, which was due to population growth and migration. The only way to cope with these problems was to have political interventions, such as environmental regulations and locally managed systems of resource control (Ostrom 1990). In most metropolitan areas, public real estate ownership has become the only way to keep housing affordable for the less wealthy. An alternative device to neutralise the negative distributional consequences of private land ownership is a land-value tax, which would syphon off speculative land value increases. Such a tax scheme, which had been advocated by Adam Smith, David Ricardo, and the popular American land reformer Henry George (1879), is currently being implemented in many countries, including Denmark, Estonia, Lithuania, Russia, Hong Kong (China), Singapore and Taiwan.

## Temporal disembedding

The disembedding of time in some sense can be interpreted as the upshot of the hitherto-discussed processes of territorial, social and material disembedding. As noted above (Chapter 2), sociologists have learnt to conceptualise time as a social emergent (Bergmann 1992). According to this view, there is no such thing as abstract physical time, pre-existing history and all historical forms of society. Rather, as Alfred Schütz (1971) has shown, time is inherent in human *action* as distinguished from mere instinct-based *reaction*. Action by definition arises from an intentional anticipation of the future, which presupposes language-based communication. The social division of labour gives rise to interpersonal standards of time, making the coordination of diverse and detached operations possible. With the rising complexity of society, social time standards tend to become increasingly abstract. Simple societies can manage with experience-based standards of time (such as daylight, the rhythms of agricultural work, or the seasons); here, we can speak of 'embedded' time in the sense of time merely reflecting traditional collective and nature-based rhythms of life. By contrast, complex societies require abstract levels of time commensuration and reflexive forms of time discipline, which take account of a vast plurality of individual biographies and collective histories, with 'world-time' (Luhmann 1975) being the final stage in this plurality.

With the territorial, social and material disembedding of markets, the complexity of society rose spectacularly in all three dimensions. Capitalised money became a key medium in the controlling of a vast range not only of spatial, social, and material action options, but of temporal ones as well. With the spread of the capital form of money, the temporal dimension of economic reproduction gained new relevance. Again, Marx's formula M-C-M brings this to the fore: capital is bound to get invested and to deliver a surplus value, which becomes the starting point for a new investment cycle, and so on. The circular and stationary time pattern of traditional reproduction gives way to a process of continuous 'growth' fed by the accumulation of capital. Marx's analysis, however, confines itself to the systemic level while largely neglecting the situation of the individual actors, who as entrepreneurs, investors and workers are confronted with uncertainty. Forecasts, planning and visions, therefore, are vital preconditions of economic action (Dosi 1982; Garud and Karnoe 2001; Freeman and Louca 2001; Sturken et al. 2004; Esposito 2007; Beckert 2016). Though being aware of the fictitious character of their anticipations, entrepreneurs may speculate on the social resonance of their scenarios and their possible self-fulfilling prophecy effects. Economic 'prophets', depicting future worlds and giving forecasts, play a key role not only in financial markets, where self-referential expectations are a common phenomenon (Kraemer 2016), but also in the fields of new technologies and consumer fashions. In their initial phases, economic inventions are often surrounded by intense concerns and scenarios about their possible impact on future life.[19] In the positive case, these scenarios describe a better and fascinating world to come, such as the Fordist visions of a 'mobile' society in the early twentieth century associated with the invention of mass motorisation. More actual examples are the utopia of a 'global community' where people are linked with each other around the globe via the internet and the dream of eternal youth and health connected with modern biotechnologies. A further contemporary case is the idea of a 'green' or 'sustainable' economy organised around inventions like wind power and/or electrical cars. Partly, such visions come from writers, intellectuals, politicians, and journalists engaging in the public debate, and partly they are generated intentionally by the inventors and investors themselves. Firms and entrepreneurs operating in innovative fields strive to communicate visions about future worlds, whose realisation would depend on the implementation of their projects. If potential customers, investors and the public would identify with their vision and help get the project off the ground, further actors might join in and make the project a success.

Thus, inventions, collective visions and growth tend to stimulate each other in a feedback circle, which may spin in either a positive or a negative direction. In the positive case, the vision will generate an optimistic mood, which will help organise a critical mass of entrepreneurs, experts, customers and political supporters who are able to realise the potential of the invention. Ideas that may appear utterly phantasmal at the outset – consider only the idea of the airplane in the early twentieth century – may become a realistic project due to the self-fulfilling prophecy dynamics of the underlying vision. In this sense, innovative utopias, like religious beliefs, may literally 'move mountains'. However, the visions connected with new technologies are not always positive. Inventions can also give rise to intense collective fears and anxieties. Consider the fears of nuclear disaster associated with atomic energy, or the fears of an erosion of freedom and privacy evoked by information technologies. New technologies, therefore, may become self-destroying instead of self-fulfilling prophecies. It is difficult to assess in advance whether the feedback process will develop in a negative or a positive direction; history shows that reliable forecasts of the career of innovations are mostly impossible.

Visions of innovation are relevant not only in a narrowly economic sense. Given the key role of capitalised money in managing social complexity, such visions have a dynamising impact on society as a whole, an impact which is not confined to national borders but has a global reach. Fictions and visions influence the rise or decline of firms, of economic sectors and of entire national economies. They affect the ups and downs of labour markets, income chances, consumption, and lifestyle fads; they have an impact even on the success or failure of individual work biographies. Beyond individual action orientations, the capitalist system 'institutionalizes systemic pressures that enforce a temporal orientation toward future economic opportunities' (Beckert 2016: 3–4). Even beyond the economic sphere, society follows a conception of time as of a linear flow stretching from the past into an open and uncertain future to be filled with ever-new imaginations. While the social esteem of traditions and experience is declining, learning, adaptation and flexibility are becoming top virtues. Moreover, social time horizons are being opened not only in the extensive, but also in the intensive dimension, as Hartmut Rosa (2005) has shown. As the accumulation of capital does not depend only on future opportunities, but also on the speed, efficiency and continuity of current operations, a permanent pressure to accelerate economic processes evolves. Again, the technical acceleration of production and market operations has an impact on society as a whole, as it results in an acceleration of social life and in increasing the pressure that times place on individual actors (Deutschmann 1985; Rosa 2005: 124–125).

A key element of the systemic mechanisms underlying the temporal disembedding of markets is *credit*. Credit opens the horizon of what money can buy in the dimension of time. This is the key for understanding the logic of modern consumption as well as that of investment. Not only consumption growth but capital accumulation as well is possible only under the condition of a permanent expansion of the quantity of circulating money. From this viewpoint, the creation of credit by the banking system (Ingham 2004) has a key function to secure the continuity of the accumulation process, as it links the macro-process of economic growth with the micro-process of investment and consumption decision-making. Credit does not simply generate growth as such, as some authors (e.g. Esposito 2010; Kuhn 2015) seem to believe. Rather, as I have argued above, growth comes from relating the contingencies of credit and those of the capitalist exploitation of the creativity of labour which each other.[20] What we are facing here is a dilemma of interdependent contingencies: on the one hand, without a successful mobilisation of the creative potential of labour in the real economy, an expansion of credit would end up in inflation. On the other hand, real growth would be impossible *without* credit. Aggregate capital can be profitable and grow only if the supply of newly produced goods meets a demand *higher* than the aggregate demand created by the entrepreneurs themselves due to their prior cost payments. This requires an *additional* inflow of demand, which cannot come from the mere expenditure of incomes or savings, but only from additional investment or consumption expenditures financed by newly created credit (Binswanger 1996). This in turn presupposes entrepreneurs engaging in new, credit-financed projects and guaranteeing the repayment of the credit. Again here, the centrality of fictional expectations and economic myths to resolving the dilemma of interdependent contingencies is apparent. The only common ground where givers and takers of credit can meet is a positive vision about the future.

As an emergent result of credit-financed economic innovation, change seems to intensify in all dimensions of social life. It would be a shortcut, however, to assume that change could be intensified infinitely. In a world where *everything* would change at once, with no continuity and cyclical time sequences remaining, the experience of change as such would vanish, as Reinhart Koselleck has emphasised (Kosellek 2003: 19–20). The perception of change is bound to the implicit condition of continuity. Though the collective experience of time in capitalism is deeply influenced by the ideas of progress and innovation, and the underlying logic of capital accumulation, it would be premature to conclude that repetitive and cyclical forms of time experience no longer matter. Rather, such repetitive patterns continue to exist on the collective level as well as on the individual level. They cannot be neutralised completely by the capitalist economisation of time; examples of cyclical time are the rhythm of seasons and the seasonal holidays, the time prescriptions of legal and political procedures (e.g. elections), the pattern of working time and leisure, and the institutionalised phases of the individual life course (e.g. birth, marriage, death). These repetitive patterns are important, as they represent an element of continuity in social life. Again it becomes evident here that temporal disembedding, like the other forms of disembedding, is a contradictory process, being contingent upon parallel contrary moves of re-embedding.

## Notes

1 The spiritual and cultural dimensions of capitalism are an increasingly important topic of discussions in economic sociology (see Sachweh and Münnich 2017).
2 'Traditional societies typically had a range of monetary media whose commensurating capacities were limited to a particular region or sphere of life. Their ability to translate and transfer social obligations remained circumscribed and conditional. This changes in capitalist society, where the commensurating capacity of one sign increases dramatically' (Konings 2015, 60).
3 For an earlier version of this argument, see Deutschmann 2015 and Beckert 2016.
4 German authors, such as Burkhard Lutz and Klaus Dörre, have introduced the concept of *Landnahme* (the taking of lands), which they borrowed from Rosa Luxemburg, to circumscribe the disembedding process (Lutz 1984; Dörre 2009). While this conceptualisation focuses on the territorial dimension (though actually being employed in a much broader sense), the approach which I am suggesting here allows a more comprehensive view by differentiating systematically between the four dimensions of disembedding.
5 In 2011, no less than 49 percent of world trade in goods and services took place within global VCCs (WTO 2015: 18).
6 For globalisation optimists, such as Martin Wolf (1999), this confirms the unbroken actuality of the liberal market narrative about the beneficial effects of the ever-increasing transnational integration of markets.
7 A rough statistical proxy for market inclusion is the market participation rate of the working-age population, which today amounts to an average of 60 percent in the OECD countries (OECD 2016).
8 As Lendol Calder has argued in his analysis of the 'monetarization' of American society in the nineteenth century, the Americans were 'the first people in history to deal with the spread of a monetary economy into every part of daily life' (Calder 1999: 75).
9 Originally, the 'strangers' were foreigners not subject to the religious restrictions of usury instituted in Judaism as well as in Christianity and Islam. The social disembedding of markets went parallel with a gradual relaxation of these restrictions in the Protestant countries after the sixteenth century and in Catholicism and Judaism after the nineteenth century, which Benjamin Nelson (1969) has circumscribed with the formula 'from tribal brotherhood to universal otherhood'.
10 Present-day literature on the 'financialization of everyday life' and on the 'investing subject' hedging himself or herself against all life risks through financial literacy and self-discipline (van der Zwan 2014: 113) indeed points to actual developments coming close to such a scenario.
11 Balanced reciprocity is characterised by functionally specified and one-to-one give and take, with markets being a paradigmatic case. Generalised reciprocity, on the other hand, is based on permanent mutual commitment; neither is it functionally specified, nor does it depend on favours to be reciprocated immediately and on a one-to-one basis (Sahlins 1972: 193–194).

12 In the weighted average of twelve Western European countries, the ratio of employment to total population did not show a marked trend between 1870 and 1999, varying between 44.4 percent (1870) and 43.5 percent (1998). Though the labour market participation rate of the working-age population rose during the same period, this effect was compensated for by the shortening of the working age itself relative to extended education periods and by longer post-retirement life. In the United States, however, the ratio of employment to total population rose from 36.6 percent in 1870 to 49.1 percent in 1998 (Maddison 2001: 355).

13 As I emphasised above, the disembedding of markets resulted from the spread of the liberal narrative and had to conform to its normative principles. Hence, it was incompatible with the institutions of serfdom and slavery, which, therefore, were abolished gradually during the nineteenth century (Osterhammel 2009: 992–993).

14 This is not to deny Weber's point about the 'rational' character of capitalist accounting in general. However, Weber's concept of 'means-end rationality' (*Zweckrationalität*) is applicable only to advanced phases of the innovative process, wherein a stable definition of a technological paradigm has already being achieved, and not to the innovative process as a whole. Moreover, increasing the rationalisation of production tends to be associated not with rising but with declining profitability (Deutschmann 2016a; see also below Chapter 9).

15 'First, disruptive products are simpler and cheaper, they generally promise lower margins, not greater profits. Second, disruptive technologies are first commercialized in emerging or insignificant markets. And third, leading firms' most profitable consumers generally don't want, and initially won't use products based on disruptive technologies. By and large, a disruptive technology is initially embraced by the least profitable consumers in the market' (Christensen 1997: xx).

16 Present-day experiences with private currencies like Bitcoin may serve as an illustration of this.

17 In practice, nevertheless, little happened after the financial crisis beyond immediate political rescue interventions and 'quantitative easing' policies of asset purchases and negative interest rates. As the inflation of assets today seems to be guaranteed politically, financial market players continue to play their games as usual (Mayntz 2012).

18 'The rent of land, therefore, considered as the price paid for the use of land, is naturally a monopoly price. It is not at all proportioned to what the landlord may have laid out upon the improvement of the land, or to what he can afford to take; but to what the farmer can afford to give' (Smith 1999 [1776]: 249).

19 Jules Verne became a father of science fiction by inventing an entirely new genre of literature connected with technical utopias, and his work became overwhelmingly successful from the nineteenth century onwards.

20 As I will argue later (Chapter 7), my position differs from the orthodox Marxian position on this point. Though I would agree with Marx with regard to the centrality of labour for value creation, I disagree with his treatment of labour as a quasi-'objective' and measurable 'substance', which he took up from Ricardo. The centrality of labour results just from its creativity, and, hence, its contingency.

# 5 Religion as a self-representation of society

In this chapter, I will switch gears, as it were, in order to focus on the disembedding of markets as seen from the perspective of social theory, asking: what is the place of disembedded markets in society as a whole? So far, the essence of the historical discussion of the previous chapters can be summarised in two points. First, disembedded markets are clearly a sub-system of *society*, not a quasi-technical system invading society from the outside. Second, disembedded markets are clearly a *sub-system* of society and should not be identified with society as a whole. As we have seen, the expansion of markets beyond given territorial, social, material and temporal borders, which characterises the development of modern capitalism, clearly meets its limits and cannot go on infinitely. A 'society' consisting of nothing but markets would indeed be a 'stark utopia'. Even the 'economic' system in the narrow sense does not depend solely on markets, but also on different forms of social coordination, such as organisations, hierarchies and networks. Economic actors, in their turn, cannot do without a variety of functionally different institutions, which differ in their social and territorial reach. The state, for example, takes responsibility for guaranteeing external and internal security; for setting and executing legal norms; and for caring for material and social infrastructure, including education, science, welfare, and health care. Beyond political governance, society can hardly do without families, local communities, and institutions providing an environment for the rearing of children. Churches and professional, cultural and political associations are further sub-systems performing vital social functions on a non-market basis.

What is the precise location of markets within this mix of different albeit interdependent systems? It is a commonplace of sociology that modern society is made up of a plurality of functionally different social sub-systems. The general answer to the above question provided by the two main versions of the functional differentiation approach (as expounded by Talcott Parsons 1951 and Niklas Luhmann 1984) is well known: markets constitute a key part of a functionally differentiated economic sub-system, which specialises in the requirements of material 'adaptation' (Parsons), or on the management of the problem of 'scarcity' (Luhmann). This discussion, however, gives rise to the following question: can markets and their particular codes – given their disembedded character in modern capitalism – still be understood sufficiently as only one sub-system amongst others on the same level as politics, science, art or love? Considering the vast extensive and intensive expansion of markets in contemporary capitalism, and their apparent dominance over society, this appears doubtful (Paul 2012; Schimank 2013, 2015). Likewise, the system-theoretical conceptualisation of money as a medium specialised in the functional requirements of an economic sub-system can no longer convince, given the universality and inexhaustibility of the options embodied in the capital form of money, which apparently bypasses all attempts at a 'functional' definition. Not without reason, therefore, did Georg Simmel suggesthis paradoxical formula of money as an 'absolute means' – a means incorporating all ends in itself. In the following, I will take up and discuss these concerns with the aim of developing an alternative to the functional differentiation approach.

A key problem, first, seems to lie in the precise meaning of the term 'functional differentiation' itself. It is at this point where differences between the two main schools of system theory emerge. On the one hand, there is the structural-functionalist approach going back to Parsons; on the other hand, there is Luhmann's radical system functionalism, which he circumscribed with the term 'systemic *autopoiesis*' (Luhmann 1984). At first glance, the difference between the two approaches is related to the ambiguities in the term 'function', which have been highlighted prominently by Robert Merton and Jon Elster (1985). In his critique of functional analysis, Merton (1968: 73–74) lists a set of methodological postulates which sound enquiry has to observe. According to his first postulate, the units of functional analysis should be defined properly. The statement 'x fulfils function y for z' is meaningless, unless the subject unit 'x' as well as the reference unit 'z' are defined clearly in analytical as well as in operational terms. As Merton argues, anthropological studies have often violated this criterion when introducing holistic terms like 'society' or 'the cultural system' as a reference unit of functional analysis. The diffuse holism of such studies reveals itself also, as Merton notes, in a widespread overestimation of the integrative power of religion while neglecting its conflict-generating potential. This may lead to false conclusions even in the case of primitive societies, let alone in the case of modernity, where the 'integrative' power of religion is anything but self-evident.

In Parsons' approach, the reference unit of functional differentiation is the pattern maintenance system constituting the cultural identity of society. In his emphasis on the centrality of the institutionalised value pattern even for modern societies, Parsons follows Emile Durkheim and his theory of organic solidarity. Distancing himself from the liberal idea of decentralised, bottom-up institution-building by contract, Durkheim had characterised institutions as a collective reality *sui generis* exerting a particular kind of moral force on private contracts (Durkheim 1982 [1895], 2014 [1893]; see especially Tenbruck 1981). Durkheim devoted almost his entire scientific life to a closer enquiry into the nature of the 'reality' of institutions. Drawing on anthropological studies on Australian totemism, he finally detected religion as the ultimate basis of social integration (Durkheim 1995 [1912]). For Durkheim, the integrative power of religion arises from the encompassing character of religious belief, which goes beyond particular (primordial or political) group identities and which marks the utmost general level of collective identity. Differently from particular groups, religious communities form not only one amongst other communities of a similar kind (e.g. families, tribes, nations), but are perceived as singular by their believers (see also Brubaker 2012). As Durkheim tried to show in his studies on the social division of labour, not only primitive, but even modern societies depend on a set of institutionalised collective values to maintain their cohesion.

Parsons, as the originator of structural functionalist system theory, followed Durkheim this far, putting the religion-based cultural value system into the centre of his model of modern society. Aiming at a larger synthesis of contemporary social theory, however, he tried to combine Durkheim's approach with Max Weber's idea of different social value spheres. In his well-known AGIL concept, he took the institutionalised cultural value system (L) as a reference basis to define a set of four functionally specialised social sub-systems, each of them managing a particular type of boundary relationship between the culturally constituted core system and its social and non-social environments. Within that frame, the economy took the function of 'adaptation' (A) (Parsons 1951). Nevertheless, Parsons agreed with Durkheim in his focus on the issue of social cohesion. Pre-modern societies, like modern ones, depend on an institutionalised value system which provides a basic framework in which to solve the problem of the double contingency of action, and which buffers society against existential uncertainty. In modern societies, the paramount value system emerges from a process that Parsons calls the 'generalisation' of religious values. Culmination points of that process are the American 'civil religion' of constitutional democratic, humanistic and universalistic values (Parsons 1999), or the ideology of socialism, which Parsons interprets as the secularised offspring of religious traditions.[1] Due to the centrality of the nation-state as the institutional basis of civil religion, Parsons' as well as Durkheim's approaches end up with a state-centered conception of society that does not take account of the phenomenon of globalisation in a systematic way.[2]

Different from Parsons, Luhmann did not see any need for a common reference unit for functional differentiation. He commented on the idea of a supreme social value system with subtle irony: 'Values are no longer like fixed stars, but they resemble balloons which one keeps at home in order to inflate them on occasion, in particular on festivities' (Luhmann 1998: 342, my translation). Given the vast complexity of modern society, values are by far too general to guide concrete decisions and actions, as Luhmann argues. In his understanding, functional differentiation does not depend on an overarching institutional framework. Modern society, which he understands as a world-society, does not need an encompassing value system to maintain its cohesion and to manage its encounter with the complexity of the world. Rather, the key mechanism to manage complexity is nothing but functional differentiation itself. Functionally differentiated social sub-systems, though factually being dependent on each other, are autonomous, self-referential units controlled by nothing but their special media and codes. This emphasis on functional differentiation did not prevent Luhmann from elaborating a highly sophisticated functional analysis of religion as a social system, focusing on the problem of transforming an indeterminate amount of complexity into a determinable one (Luhmann 1992, 2000). In his account, however, religion appears only as one more social sub-system amongst others that is specialised in its internal code of immanence and transcendence, but that has no clear place in the overall structure of modern society (Luhmann 2000: 317–318). Unlike Parsons, Luhmann takes account of Merton's critique of holistic concepts of society. At the same time, Luhmann's position about religion is closer to Weber's than to Parsons', though Luhmann builds his theory on system- and not on action-theoretical premises, as Weber does. Weber's well-known concept of 'secular rationalisation' culminates in the interpretation of modernity as a force of cosmological disenchantment, attributing the institution of 'last' values no longer to society but to the responsibility of the autonomous individual. With regard to his sceptical assessment of the place of religion in modern society, Luhmann's position is close to Weber's.

Do societies require a sub-system that is focused on the representation of collective identity and on the management of existential uncertainty? Concerning pre-modern stratified societies, there is little disagreement about religion fulfilling this very function – 'function' in the sense of religion having the intended or unintended *effects* of generalising collective identity and creating a universal social nexus beyond kinship affiliations. Anthropologists as well as sociologists have concentrated their studies on the role of religions in the integration of society as well as in its contribution to coping with experiences of the unknown and uncertainty (for an overview, see Riesebrodt 2007). As these studies have made clear, the emergence of a separate institutional sphere of 'religion' itself had been the product of a long and complex social evolution. Contrary to Durkheim's assumptions, there seems to have been still no marked difference between the spheres of the profane and the sacred in many primitive societies. Rather, as already Weber had noted (Weber 1972: 245–246), 'magic' or 'religious' actions formed an integral part of everyday practice, the relevant distinction first being only that between 'ordinary' and 'extraordinary' experiences. To cope with the irregular and unknown, elaborated cognitive theories, spirit belief systems, experts (e.g. magicians, sorcerers), and rituals played a key role (see Geertz 1960; Dux 1982).

If we follow Weber's interpretation, the later evolution was characterised by two trends.

The first is an increasing intellectualisation and systemisation of spirit beliefs. Gradually, animate but volatile and unreliable spirits gave way to invisible but perennial and accountable gods. Behind the visible world, a second, invisible one emerged – the world of the gods, and, finally, of the one, almighty God; at the same time, the cleavage between immanence and transcendence became deepened. Jan Assmann (2003) has characterised this transition as a step from 'primary' to 'secondary' religions. While the primary ones include historically grown local cults and national religions, secondary religions – typically the monotheistic ones – are based on historical acts of prophecy and revelation. Though in fact building on the local religious legacies, secondary religions distanced themselves from the former, which became subject to the verdict of 'paganism'. The characteristics of secondary religions were their universal claims, their categorical distinctions between the 'true' and the 'false', and their reliance on holy scripts and written sources of revelation. To manage their encounter with God, the believers could no longer take recourse to magic practices, but had to rely on symbolically based communication via prayers, sacrifices and rituals, though magic practices often persisted informally in everyday life.

This leads to the second secular trend described by Weber: the intellectualisation of religious belief was associated with processes of social differentiation, division of labour and political centralisation. These processes culminated in the institutional separation of religion from political power and other profane spheres of society, and in the emergence of a new class of priests and religious experts managing the encounter with God in a professional way. Historically, these changes reached a preliminary climax in the so-called 'axial age' between the eighth and third centuries BCE, to cite the well-known term coined by Karl Jaspers (1949) and Shmuel Eisenstadt (1986). In Greece as well as in Palestine, Persia, India and China, new religious prophets and philosophers became influential, whose teachings, despite their vast differences, culminated in the discovery of the spiritual foundations of human existence. The new universal beliefs transcended the legitimacy of given political regimes and opened a horizon for intellectual discourse and critique based on a sharp disjunction between the mundane and a trans-mundane world.[3] A system of 'institutionally specialised' religion developed (Luckmann 1967), which monopolised the exchange of society with the 'holy cosmos' beyond the traditional association of religion with political power.

As a 'symbolic universe' (Berger and Luckmann 1966), religion gave meaning and coherence to an opaque reality, and hence became able to take a hegemonic position over society and to constitute the legitimation for centralised systems of political rule. Under such conditions, religion could take on the function of a self-representation of society in a two-fold, internal and external sense. First, religion represented the internal boundary of society, as it marked the most encompassing level of sociality beyond particular, local, kinship and national affiliations, allowing humans to relate themselves to each other *as humans*. Excommunication from the religious community, in other words, was equivalent to social exclusion. Second, by defining the utmost general level of collective identity, religion also marked the interface of society with extra-social, natural and cosmic realities. A basic distinction was set up between the realms of the knowable and observable, open to human reason, on the one hand, and of the transcendent and unknowable, being accessible only via divine revelation, on the other. As Luhmann never got tired of emphasising, defining collective identity means fixing a distinction, and a distinction always has two sides to it: an internal and an external one. This implies that the two functions of religion to identify society and to cope with transcendence are not at odds with each other, but, on the contrary, are complementary to each other.

This interpretation of religion as a symbolic self-representation of society, which I have recapitulated here only briefly, is widespread in most classic and contemporary sociological studies of religion; nevertheless, it is an extremely stylised one. In a strict sense, it applies only to the monotheistic religions of Judaism, Christianity and Islam, and even with regard to each of these religions it would require extensive modifications. Here I am concerned only with the *general* empirical limitations of the concept. A first, obvious limitation lies in the bounded character of the social universality claimed by the monotheistic religions, each of them being confined largely to the particular civilisations which they created. None of them have ever reached mankind as a whole. While Judaism can be characterised as a religion of conscious ethnic 'self-demarcation' (Assmann 2003: 30, my translation), relying on the myth of the 'Chosen People', Christianity as well as Islam took recourse to expansive missionary or military activities to promote their universal claims. As a result, they did not only generate a higher level of social integration, but intolerance and exclusion were deepened and generalised too (e.g. in Christian anti-Semitism, or in the Islamic wars against the 'unbelieving'). Moreover, the capacity of the monotheistic religions to prevent internal conflicts, factions and divisions has likewise proven very limited, as the numerous schisms in the history of Christianity as well as the history of Islam have shown.

The hegemony of religion over society, however, is contested not only with regard to social integration, but also with regard to its monopoly over the encounter of society with extra-social environments, the 'holy cosmos' according to Luckmann (1967). The institutional separation of religion is not without risk, however, because of its position in society and its legitimacy as a superior instance of social and political governance. Where religion no longer permeates everyday life in its totality, but emerges as a separate sphere, the need to draw a clear demarcation between the spheres of the sacred and of the profane arises. It becomes vital to distinguish profane knowledge, justified by its practical success, from religious faith, to be administered by the Church. At the same time, it remains important to link both spheres with each other to maintain the overall legitimacy of faith. Therefore, theology and religion came under continuous pressure to define their proper domains and to reinterpret the meaning of faith vis-à-vis mundane concerns. These needs were reinforced by the processes of functional differentiation evolving within the profane sphere itself as early as in the European Middle Ages (such as the conflict between the Pope and the Emperor arising in the Investiture Controversy of the eleventh century). The Reformation of the sixteenth century in Europe meant a further push of functional differentiation; it played a key role in redefining the position of the Church vis-à-vis the state and in giving the Christian message a more credible profile (Gorski 2000). As a consequence of these redefinitions, religious faith took on increasingly abstract, reflexive and subjective traits, with only God's 'pure' transcendence remaining in the final instance. A divine being, however, whose sovereign will is completely transcendent and unknowable (or accessible only to virtuoso believers), can no longer rule the profane world and its institutional order. Functional differentiation does not only undermine the institutional hegemony of religion over society, but it also results in an individualisation of religious faith; here Luhmann's diagnosis meets with the interpretations of Max Weber and Hans Blumenberg.

Thus, the model of institutionally specialised religion can be applied to stratified societies only with great caution. The legitimacy of religion as an ultimate framework for social and political governance was contested even under pre-modern conditions in manifold ways. This applies all the more to modern, capitalist society. Hence, we are back at the above-discussed question: do modern societies require a sub-system that is focused on the representation of collective identity and the management of existential uncertainty? And we must also ask: can society do without reflecting its own unity and – *pari passu* – its encounter with its extra-social environments?

## Notes

1 As it is well known, the culturalist focus of Parsons' theory has been taken up and taken in different directions by Jürgen Habermas' theory of communicative action (Habermas 1981) and by the neo-functionalist approach of Jeffrey Alexander (2003).
2 In this respect, both approaches show parallels to the above-discussed conception of economic ordoliberalism (Chapter 2).
3 For a recent overview on the debate on the axial age approach, see Joas (2017: 279–280).

# 6 Modernity, capitalism and religion

Apparently, Max Weber and Niklas Luhmann have good reasons for their scepticism with regard to the traditional model of institutionally specialised religion filling the function of collective identity representation for modern society. As they view it, the modern world is dominated by 'rational' knowledge – knowledge that does not come from revelation but which has be justified on rational grounds, whether they be of a cognitive or a normative kind. Rational knowledge cannot encompass the world as a totality, but is functionally specified by definition. Modern society therefore differentiates itself into a plurality of interdependent but functionally autonomous sub-systems, such as the economy, politics, law, science, art and education. In such a world of functionally specialised expertise, congregations and religious faith – including the latter's secularised derivatives, such as Talcott Parsons' and Robert Bellah's 'civil religion' – no longer have a clear place. Apparently, there is no longer any compelling *collective* need for the particular type of holistic knowledge which they can offer. This does not mean that religions will disappear from public life. However, faith is no longer anchored in tradition and collective obligation, but has become a matter of private choice (to recall Charles Taylor's argument on the matter, which we saw in Chapter 1). The churches and congregations have to accept the principles of religious pluralism and individual autonomy. It is only the individual who truly can 'bind' himself or herself, and the churches can no longer claim superior authority over autonomous individual choices. All they can do is offer advice to their believers with respect to finding a direction in their personal lives. However, even in this field they have to compete with a variety of therapeutic and social institutions, which often can offer superior professional expertise. Therefore, it is not surprising that the influence of churches and congregations on public life is declining in many advanced capitalist countries. Though they still enjoy a privileged legal and political status in some European countries, there are concerns about declining membership figures, shrinking financial resources, low attendance at services, and declining member participation in parish life: the symptoms of petrifaction cannot be denied. Though national developments are very different, the overall negative consequences of modernity for the religions seem fairly clear (Pollack and Gergely 2015).

However, the secularist diagnosis which I have summarised so far has met with harsh criticism from many sociologists of religion (e.g. Peter Berger, Peter Beyer, José Casanova, Hans Joas, Roland Robertson). The critics point to a return of religious movements on a global scale, arguing that the secularisation thesis is based on an over-generalisation of Western European experiences. For Berger, the contemporary world is 'brimming with religion' (Berger 2013: 62), which shows itself in phenomena like the worldwide advance of Pentecostalism and in the resurgence of Islam. In a similar vein, Casanova (1994) argued that a return of religious movements to the public arena began in the late 1970s. His examples are the Iranian Revolution of 1979, the advent of liberation theology in Latin America, and the prominent role of Catholicism in the Eastern European transformations after 1989. In his recent empirical studies, Casanova has focused on the growing presence of Islam on the religious scene in Western Europe (Casanova 2006).

The exact meaning of the alleged 'return' of religions, however, continues to be controversial. What obviously cannot be meant is a restoration of the pre-modern hegemony of religion over society. The principle of functional differentiation, the supremacy of science-based professional expertise over most fields of practice in modern societies cannot be undone. Even religious extremists can no longer claim the Bible or the Koran to be the ultimate source of all knowledge – if not in words, so at least in their actions, if they use mobile telephones, or if they prefer to be treated not by traditional cures, but in a modern hospital in the case of sickness. Religion can no longer claim supremacy over the totality of knowledge, but finds itself as a specialised subsystem amongst others. Much of the anti-secularist critique of Berger and other authors seems to be based on misunderstandings, as Gorski emphasises: 'Secularization theory is *not* a unified theory of religious decline. It is a *family* of theories of religious change, some of which posit religious decline, and some of which do not' (Gorski 2000: 141). The phenomenon of the revival of religions or even the birth of new religious movements in modern societies *as such* is not at odds with the secularisation concept. The point is, rather, that the apparent revival of religions is taking place under conditions deeply shaped by economic and cultural globalisation (Beyer and Beaman 2007; Simojoki 2012). As a response to globalisation, the character of religious faith itself is undergoing significant changes.

Differently from pre-modern conditions, where denominational homogeneity or at least a clear hierarchy of denominations in a territory had been the regular case, the actual situation is characterised by a strong trend towards religious pluralism. International migration movements and the circulation of ideas via modern information technologies and media are factors promoting the local diversity of religious congregations while at the same time widening their territorial reach (Graf 2004; Roy 2010). Moreover, the pluralism of religiosity is closely interconnected with the emergence of a 'market' of religions, as Thomas Luckmann observed as early as in the 1960s (Luckmann 1967). Churches and congregations no longer enjoy a natural, tradition-based monopoly over their territory, as they did in pre-modern civilisations.

They have to coexist and compete not only with other religious denominations, but also with the growing camp of the unbelieving. The market of religions requires denominations to move in a global social field, which, as a whole, is no longer constituted by any of them and is beyond their control. Emile Durkheim's definition of religion as a representation of the ultimate unity of society is at odds with the market of religions, as it is the market itself and no longer any of the religious denominations, which constitutes the overarching social framework. Moreover, social inclusion under conditions of liberal, market-based pluralism no longer depends on any religious affiliation at all, but extends to the unbelieving too. The optional character of individual religiosity forces denominations into relationships of intense emulation. To counter the declining commitment of their believers, churches and congregations feel pressed to review their identity, to sharpen their profile, and to improve their self-marketing. Evangelical communities, with rigorous standards demanding high commitment and offering close integration, often gain an edge in the competition (Graf 2004: 63). The same seems to apply to politicised and fundamentalist variants of Islam that have been spreading in the Near East and amongst immigrants in Western Europe since the late twentieth century (Roy 2010). On the other hand, there is the opposite trend of the over-adaptation of congregations to their secular environment. Not only the 'new' religions, such as New Age, Esotericism or Occultism, but even some of the established churches and congregations are adjusting their self-presentations to commercial pop and wellness cultures to enhance their attractiveness (Knoblauch 2009). In a similar vein, Bryan Turner observed that 'all forms of religion are now overlaid with consumerism and that many forms of religion have been commodified' (Turner 2011: xii). The 'prosperity gospel' of a benevolent God supporting the health and financial well-being of his believers while keeping dogmatic requirements at a minimum is not only central for mega-churches in the United States, but also for the global movement of Pentecostalism (Coleman 2000; Kern and Schimank 2013). The success of Protestantism in Brazil appears to be due largely to its emphasis on virtues which are vital for economic and social advancement, such as personal discipline and performance orientation, as Roger Bastide recognised as early as in the 1970s (Bastide 1978). In short, the apparent return of religions seems to be associated with structural changes in religiosity so deep, that doubts arise with regard to the continuity of the phenomenon itself. Can religion still bind (in the original sense of the Latin word '*religio*') individual lives, when there is no longer a clear demarcation between religious and commercial cultures and where religious 'products' can be bought and sold like ordinary goods at markets (Zinser 2006; Turner 2011)?

Indeed, it is perhaps the weakest point of the return-of-religion diagnoses that they do not differentiate sufficiently between the phenomenal and the conceptual level of analysis; due to a lack of theoretical conceptualisations, they tend to count almost everything as a religion that calls itself such. This, however, raises severe difficulties even from a mere practical point of view: if we agree that the present-day situation of religions can be adequately described by the model of a market, we should be prepared to expect fraud and deception occurring on that market too, like in any other market. Actually, there can be no doubt that there are many dubious products circulating on the religious market (think only of scientology). In order to distinguish dubious from serious products, quality controls would have to be introduced; quality controls, in turn, would require theoretically based standards of evaluation and a generally accepted theoretical concept of religion, which is largely lacking.

My argument here is that the advocates of the return-of-religions thesis, due to their one-sided focus on the phenomenal side of religious movements, are missing the point that is truly relevant for a critique of the secularist position, namely, can capitalist society persist without reflecting on its own collective unity in any way? The function of internal and external boundary management of society itself should be distinguished clearly from the concrete institutions and agencies actually performing it. Religion may be invisible, as Thomas Luckmann's (1967) well-known book title suggests; it must be also searched for where it does not manifest itself as such. If conventional, institutionally specialised religion cannot represent the collective identity of a globalised society, the conclusion may be to abandon the question of an ultimate nexus of society altogether; alternatively, the question of functional alternatives arises. The question, whether the question of the collective unity of society can be abandoned, runs through Luhmann's entire oeuvre, starting with his analysis of 'ecological communication' (Luhmann 1990) and culminating in his reflections on the concept of society in his last book (Luhmann 1998).[1] Luhmann's point – to state it in brief – is not that the issue can be simply abandoned. However, a thorough discussion of the question ends up, as he shows, in fundamental epistemological ambiguities, which now need to be considered in greater detail.

## Note

1 Recently, a much earlier version of Luhmann's final work written in 1975 has been found, and it was edited by Johannes F.K. Schmidt and André Kieserling (Luhmann 2017 [1975]).

# 7 Disembedding and the dilemma of the self-representation of Society

The concept of disembedding, of course, is known to Niklas Luhmann as well as to other sociological modernisation theorists. They even made much more extensive use of it than Polanyi, arguing that processes of disembedding evolved not only in the sphere of markets but also in other sub-systems of society such as politics, science and art. Anthony Giddens developed his very concept of modernity around this idea, pointing to the role of money and expert systems as vehicles to 'lift out' social relations from local contexts of interaction and to restructure them 'across indefinite spans of time-space' (Giddens 1990: 21). The most elaborated conceptualisation of modern society as a disembedded system is, without a doubt, Luhmann's system theory. As pointed out above (Chapter 5), Luhmann rejects the Parsonian idea of a paramount cultural value system 'integrating' modern society; instead, he argues that modern societies are confronted with the utmost complexity of the world. They can generate 'meaning' only in self-referential systemic operations which are governed by functionally specified 'codes', such as truth, power, scarcity or love. Modern society is a world-society based on functional differentiation, consisting of sub-systems which, despite their interdependence, are embedded into nothing but themselves. As Luhmann admits, the price of this conceptualisation is that society as a whole vanishes from view; to be precise, it comes into view only relationally via the differences between functionally specialised sub-systems (see also Schwinn 2001). There is, however, no way out of this dilemma. As Luhmann argues, society as a totality cannot be viewed by any observer, since observations are communicative operations which are possible only *within* society and which are dependent on the particular social and historical perspective of the observer. There is no 'external' standpoint allowing a view of society from the outside, like the man on the moon may look down on the Earth.

Nevertheless, as symbolically integrated entities, societies cannot do without reflecting on their unity in some way. Difference is not possible without unity, as Luhmann himself never gets tired of stressing in his work. The question for the unity of modern society beyond its functionally differentiated surface is a legitimate one that cannot be ignored. The answer is given by 'imaginary constructions of the unity of the system' (Luhmann 1998: 867, my translation) communicating the identity of society to itself. Luhmann calls such constructions '*Selbstbeschreibungen*' ('self-descriptions').

Pre-modern societies described their collective identities in religious terms. Here, the self-representation paradox of society is managed by the social construction of a transcendent creator and observer of the world (Luhmann 1998: 903). By taking the perspective of the creator, societies can organise and rule themselves in a coherent and legitimate way. Modern societies, by contrast, develop non-theological self-descriptions, like the ideas of nation, of class, or of modernity. The latter, however, are no less paradoxical than religious formulas, as they disclaim the unity which they are pretending by the very fact of being observations, for the observer includes and excludes himself in his portrait of society at the same time. Therefore, modern self-descriptions of society, like religious ones, cannot reclaim the status of scientific truth.[1]

The epistemological dilemma that Luhmann has pointed to is fundamental for every general social theory. This applies also to Marxian historical materialism, which suffers from Karl Marx's insufficient reflection on the dilemma. The background problem here lies with the latent Hegelian heritage in Marx's thinking. Marx is clearly aware of the character of capitalism as a 'commodified' society, that is, of the encompassing character of markets and their opaqueness to the market actors, which he highlights with his well-known concept of 'commodity fetishism'. However, the opaqueness of markets is a problem not only for the market actors, but also for the scientific observer himself. Marx fails to identify the position of a historical observer being able to verify capitalist 'laws of motion' and quantities of 'socially necessary' labour and to predict the downfall of capitalism, which he deems to be necessary. For Georg Wilhelm Hegel, the problem is not relevant due to his idealistic premises; it is vital, however, for Marx's own historical-materialist approach. Due to his incomplete detachment from his intellectual master, Marx did not provide a thorough historical explication of his epistemic premises (Kracauer 1969; Habermas 1981: Vol. II: 489; Holz 1993). Later, Georg Lukács (1970 [1923]) tried to settle the problem by imputing a superior epistemological position to the 'proletariat' as a collective 'producer' of social reality, and by justifying the superiority of Marxian historical materialism by its affiliation with the perspective of the proletariat. Lukacs' proletariat, however, turns out to be an only slightly disguised version of the Hegelian world-spirit, which had little to do with the *historical* working class and workers' movement of his time (Habermas 1981: Vol. I: 474–475).

This is not to deny Marx's assumptions about the key role of labour in the socio-economic process, which he explicated in his labour theory of value. However, Marx did not distinguish sufficiently between labour as a creative resource and its character as an objectified and measurable substance, as which he treats it in his theory of value in line with David Ricardo. He did not clarify how these contradictory meanings of the concept of 'production' are related to each other; instead, in his mature work he postulated a problematic 'law of value' resting exclusively on objectified labour. One may agree with Marx so far as labour values are determined 'somehow' within a capitalist system. However, due to the opaqueness of creative actions, the system is a black box. *How* labour values are determined within the system can never be transparent for any external observer because such an observer – to make my point again – would have to be more intelligent than the very sum of collective intelligence and creativity operating in the system itself. It is the social preponderance of innovation in combination with the self-intransparency of creative action – 'I cannot turn around quick enough to catch myself', says George Hebert Mead (1934: 174) – which makes the capitalist system incalculable as a whole, not simply the 'anarchy of the market' that is due to the private character of production, as Marx contended. Without a doubt, Friedrich von Hayek, with his analysis of markets as a process of discovery, was much clearer on this point than Marx. The concept of 'socially necessary labour' may be applicable to standard products meeting a calculable demand. However, Marx did not consider the problem of how to apply the quantitative concept of labour value to the stream of *new* products or services emerging continuously in the capitalist process. Just *because* labour a creative resource is central, the labour theory of value is inappropriate for analysing the innovative process in which technological and economic parameters themselves are being created and changed, and in which the resonance of markets to new products is no less important than the conditions of production. No supposedly 'objective' value analyses but only careful historical reconstructions of the perceptions and expectations of the relevant historical actors can help further at this point, as Jens Beckert (2016) has argued.

It is not difficult to show that it is the same problem of the opaqueness of society to itself that underlies the enigmatic character of religious representations. The problem becomes apparent in Emile Durkheim's classic analysis of religion (Durkheim 1995 [1912]). On the one hand, Durkheim characterises the system of religious beliefs and practices by its separation from the profane world, the difference between the spheres of the sacred and the profane being not only a hierarchical, but an "absolute" one, as he argues (Durkheim 1995 [1912]: 36). On the other hand, it is the key conclusion of his analysis that the reality expressed in religious practices is nothing but society: 'We have seen that this reality – which mythologies have represented in so many different forms, but which is the objective, universal, and external cause of those *sui generis* sensations of which religious experience is made – is society' (Durkheim 1995 [1912]: 421). How is it possible that the religious community experiences its own inner nexus as something so alien and distinct from everyday life?

Durkheim's point can be made clearer, if we follow Jürgen Habermas in combining the approaches of Durkheim and Mead, and translating Durkheim's somewhat vague concept of 'collective forces' into the interactionist concept of 'collective identity' (Habermas 1981: Vol. II: 11–12). As Mead has shown, identity as a reflexive relationship evolves as a result of symbolically based interaction between at least two actors. Identity is always a *social* construct, emerging not as an innate property of the single individual but in the course of communicative interaction leading the individual to identify with the perspectives that others have of himself or herself.[2] Ego can become aware of itself only via the detour of taking the perspective of alter (and *vice versa*), both thereby developing an awareness of moral obligation and of their individuality at the same time. Mead concentrated his analysis on the individual socialisation process and on the emergence of personal identities, as Habermas notes. One could hypothesise that group identities develop in an analogous way: an in-group constitutes itself, as its members mirror themselves collectively in the perspective of an out-group while *pari passu* becoming self-conscious as a distinct group. On the level of society as a totality, however, collective identity formation cannot proceed in the same way, since by definition there is no visible alter that can assume the part of a communicative mirror for ego. Society as a whole has no social counterpart; thus it cannot repeat the operation of 'taking the perspective of the other'. It cannot become aware of itself and develop a truly collective identity, just as the eye would be invisible if there were no other eyes or a mirror to reflect it.

Indeed, this seems to be nothing but a different formulation of the epistemological dilemma which Luhmann had pointed to. It is the same dilemma which religions are responding to and which explains the enigmatic character of their constructions. The defining characteristic of religious identities lies in their singularity. Whereas group, ethnic or national identities represent only one amongst other communities of a similar kind, religious identities indicate the most encompassing community, thereby also defining the ultimate criteria for social inclusion and exclusion. Because of its uniqueness, such an encompassing identity cannot form itself via the process of mutual identification between empirical collectives; rather, it requires the social construction of a supernatural collective alter. Only by taking on the perspective of the supernatural collective alter of itself is society able to become aware of its own unity beyond the limits of individual and group identities. By identifying with God, the members of society can manage their nexus in a coherent way, and develop a genuinely universal sense of moral obligation beyond particularistic affiliations. To become an integrative social force, however, the supernatural alter must be experienced as an external entity, whose socially constructed character remains hidden from its believers; in this sense, the difference between the spheres of the sacred and the profane is indeed an 'absolute' one. The presence of God is experienced as a revelation to be testified to by prophets and experts, and to be kept alive collectively in rituals.

Religious belief can be characterised as an act of human 'self-transcendence' (Joas 1997, 2017), breaking the rules of rational discourse, since what appears behind its constructions is nothing other than the community of the believers themselves. The critique of the religious projection had been the key message of nineteenth-century atheistic humanism (Ludwig Feuerbach, Karl Marx, Auguste Comte, Friedrich Nietzsche, Sigmund Freud). It had been constitutive also for the rise of sociology as a 'science' of society, claiming to understand society as a secular entity independent from religious and theological traditions. However, here we are back at Luhmann's point again: Sociological theorists fail to take account of the implicit observer position, which they reclaim for themselves in describing society as an 'autonomous', self-generating entity. Therefore, sociology has to acknowledge its own blind spots too and become aware of its own inability to successfully develop a theory of society as a totality. All that it can do is to take the position of a second-order observer, not taking society as a direct object of its observations, but observing the 'self-descriptions' which society is producing about itself. A 'theory' of society can be nothing but a theory of societal 'self-descriptions' arising in particular times and under certain historical circumstances. What self-descriptions are relevant for modern society? In the last chapter of his voluminous book, Luhmann discusses several of them: subject, nation, class, modernity and risk; however, he always does so with the aim of demonstrating their insufficiency to settle the underlying epistemological paradox. 'Reflected autology' (Luhmann 1998: 1128, my translation) remains Luhmann's last word on the theory of society.

The most promising candidate to take the role of a self-representation of modern society is lacking in Luhmann's list: the disembedded markets of modern capitalism and the liberal narrative underlying them. The reason why this is so appears clear: for Luhmann, the economy (including markets) represents only one social sub-system, amongst others, that is specialised in the function of managing scarce property rights and that is governed by the medium of money (Luhmann 1988). As he points out, the historical evolution of the economic system followed the same logic of the simultaneous specification and generalisation of codes that was characteristic of the development of the other sub-systems too. In order to secure the self-regulation of the economy, for example, the religious prohibition of interest or political interventions to guarantee 'fair' market prices had to be abandoned; on the other hand, a proper sphere of the 'economy' as distinguished from politics, religion, love and so on, had to be defined (Luhmann 1990: 101–102). Though Luhmann seems to have played with the idea of interpreting money as a quasi-religious medium representing the unity of society in his second book on religion,[3] he did not follow it further; apparently, it did not fit into the conceptual design of his theory.

It is doubtful, however, whether Luhmann's analysis of functional differentiation gives an adequate account of the market-disembedding process and the corresponding generalisation of the money code, which I am highlighting here. Luhmann's analysis is focused exclusively on the functional *autopoiesis* of the money medium underlying the evolution of markets and the economic system as a whole. What he neglects is the *historical* expansion of markets and property rights in the territorial, social, material and temporal dimensions, and the parallel expansion of the opportunity structure of money. Therefore, the analogies in the logic of functional differentiation between the economic and non-economic sub-systems, which Luhmann is pointing to, are spurious. Different from the non-economic sub-systems, the development of capitalist markets coincided with the logic of simultaneous generalisation *and* specification only on the surface. Beyond the facade of functional self-regulation, an unprecedented *empirical* universalisation of the market sphere, running counter to the functional differentiation of society, took place. At the same time, the options embodied in money became generalised to a degree that rendered any conventional functional definition of money implausible, whether departing from the problem of 'adaptation' or that of 'scarcity'.[4] If there is a 'function' of capitalised money, it is clearly not a narrowly 'economic' one, but needs to be conceptualised on a more abstract level. Perhaps the function which Luhmann ascribes to religion comes most close to it: transforming indeterminate complexity into determinate complexity (Luhmann 1992: 26). I will not go deeper into Luhmann's conceptualisations and their problems here. With regard to money, at least, Simmel's paradoxical definition of money as an 'absolute means' – a 'means' that due to its absoluteness is no longer a means and thus cannot be subsumed to any particular 'function' – seems to meet the point much better that Luhmann's concept of symbolically generalised media.[5]

No one would object to Luhmann's point that politics, science or love follow their own particular rules and codes, differing from those of the economy. Functional differentiation is essential for modern societies, though in practice the corrupting impact of money on the non-economic spheres certainly is as pervasive today as it had been in the past. What should not be overlooked, however, is that the operations even of non-economic sub-systems always need to be *financed.* Being unable to generate the financial resources they require by themselves, non-economic sub-systems depend on transfer payments, which only the economy can generate. This applies to the state, to public bureaucracies, to economic organisations, science, education, and art; in some sense, however, it even applies to love: for truly binding themselves to each other, two partners need to be personally autonomous. Personal autonomy in a modern society, however, is unthinkable without personal monetary resources. The generalisation of the opportunity structure of money – in other words – did not proceed on the same level as the formation of the other sub-systems; rather, it was basic for the process of functional differentiation itself.[6] Only due to their command over financial resources can states, organisations and families constitute themselves as autonomous social sub-systems. This is a necessary condition, not a sufficient one. The dependence of non-economic sub-systems on money is not a unilateral one, as we have seen; markets in their turn are dependent on the inputs of politics, science, education, and so on. However, the interdependence between money and non-economic media is clearly an asymmetric one. While money payments are constitutive of the economic sub-system itself as well as of the other sub-systems, this does not apply to the same degree to scientific truth, political power, or love (Deutschmann 2009b; Paul 2012; Schimank 2013, 2015). The non-economic sub-systems deliver specialised inputs to the economic sub-system, which, due to their nationally or functionally bounded character, are substitutable for each other in many cases. Markets and capitalist enterprises can work in very different institutional environments, as the varieties-of-capitalism literature has shown.[7] By contrast, the money transfers which the non-economic sub-systems receive in return are not substitutable, and they are indispensable to their very existence.

So far, I hope to have shown that disembedded markets are *not* only one social sub-system amongst others of a similar kind. Rather, it seems more adequate to conceptualise them as a 'self-description' of modern society in the sense explicated by Luhmann, indicating its latent unity beyond functional differentiation. Markets take on the function of collective self-representation, which had been the domain of religion in stratified societies. On the one hand, disembedded markets describe the most encompassing, global level of sociality; on the other, just by virtue of this description they open the view on a room of unexplored and unexplorable uncertainties beyond the socially accessible. Contrary to Durkheim's and Parsons' emphasis on civil religious values, I agree with Marx about the centrality of the commodity form for the integration of the modern world-society. The dominance of the commodity form over society is not due only to its functions for material reproduction, as orthodox Marxists pretend, but to the universality of the commodity nexus, which *by itself* is a phenomenon of religious significance (if we follow Durkheim's argument). Similar to religious transcendence, disembedded markets are a black box which, as a totality, is invisible to any observer, but can be represented only in an 'iconic' mode (Konings 2015: 15).

Not by chance, therefore, does the capital form of money have parallels with religious icons. In both cases, a characteristic paradox can be observed: The difference between the sign and the object of signification vanishes. The sign *seems to be* what it signifies, as if the sign warning of the dog would itself bite you. The capitalist reproduction process as a totality is no less opaque than the idea that God is the ground of all being; hence, the capital form of money tends to amalgamate with its object in a way that is similar to religious myths and narratives. Just as God is not only an abstract idea, but is present in holy scripts, rituals and relics, capitalised money not only symbolises wealth, but *is* wealth. Despite its immaterial character, it must be treated like a numinous substance to be transferred in precise quantities from one bank account to another. Like religious representations, capitalised money can be qualified as a 'cipher' (Luhmann 1992: 33) – that is, a symbol representing and hiding its object of signification at the same time. The paradox of *being* and *signifying* wealth at the same time can be managed only by the quantitative difference of capital with itself, as Marx had noted: 'Instead of representing relationships of commodities, (value) now enters into a private relationship with itself. It distinguishes itself as original value from surplus value, like God the Father from God the Son' (Marx 1988 [1867]: 169, my translation). The dynamic character of capitalism is thus built into the capital form of money itself. A further common characteristic of money and religion is their dependence on trust and belief. As shown above, religious belief is based on an idealised projection of a collective counterpart of society, which allows individuals to identify with this counterpart and to arrange their interpersonal relations as members of one community. Likewise, the worth of intrinsically worthless money cannot be secured without an idealised projection called 'trust'. When accepting payment, the seller does not place his or her trust in something or somebody, but solely in the notion of other actors trusting too (Ganssmann 2011; Paul 2012) – trust that appears as unconditional as the trust in God.[8]

Capital as a self-description of society is thus no less numinous than religious belief. In practice, therefore, the need arises to cope with the contingencies of capitalist markets and to develop rational explanations about their functioning. Beyond everyday knowledge, scientific models are required, making market processes appear predictable and legitimising economic policy and firm decisions in order to make economic action possible (Beckert 2016: 245–246). This is the background of the 'theological' connotations of economic theory discussed above (Chapter 1). Economic theory reconstructs the opaque reality of markets in a way that displays them as coherent, rational and legitimate. Without such a reconstruction, markets could not work in social practice, just as traditional societies could not work without the basic legitimacy provided by holy scriptures and the detailed governance by the religious and theological authorities; here, Robert Nelson's above-discussed theses (Chapter 1) find their justification.

The thesis of a functional equivalence between capitalism and religion, which has met with support even from theologians (Wagner 1985; Cox 2002), should, nevertheless, be taken with a degree of caution. Besides the parallels between both, there are also vital differences which I am going to discuss in the following chapter.

## Notes

1 Under the headline of the ontology–autology problem in social theory, Michael Beetz (2010) has made a similar point.
2 With his anthropological concept of the 'eccentric positionality' ('*exzentrische Positionalität*') of man, Helmuth Plessner (1981 [1924]) made the same point.
3 Here, Luhmann circumscribes money as a 'mysterious' form of societal 'identity' comparable with religion (Luhmann 2000: 10).
4 As shown above (Chapter 4), the property claim of capital neither extends only to 'material' goods, nor only to a given quantity of goods or services (whether material or immaterial). It also includes a claim on what *could* be produced. Imaginations, not only choices between scarce means, govern capitalist dynamics (Beckert 2016). Under such conditions, the problem of scarcity obviously can no longer be taken as a starting point from which to define the function of money, as Luhmann does in line with neoclassical economic theory (Luhmann 1988: 177–178).
5 Uwe Schimank (2013) combines the approaches of Simmel and Marx to develop an interpretation of modernity as a 'functionally differentiated capitalist society'.
6 Axel Paul stresses this point in his critique of Luhmann (Paul 2017: 217). Again, it seems that Luhmann himself had played with the same idea, as it becomes evident in the newly discovered first version of his theory of society of 1975 (Luhmann 2017: 443, 733–734).
7 Markets can flourish even in environments characterised by disorganisation and extreme corruption, as Rana Dasgupta (2014) has shown in the case of New Delhi under economic deregulation after 1991.
8 From this viewpoint, 'metallistic' approaches of monetary theory, which seek to ground the value of money in 'real' substances like gold or silver, appear to be forms of economic superstition.

# 8 Markets as an ultimate social reality?

Can disembedded markets and the capital form of money as their medium take on the function of a symbolic self-representation of capitalist society? In the case that the answer is 'yes', their status would become similar to what Peter Berger and Thomas Luckmann have called a 'symbolic universe' (Berger and Luckmann 1967), thus entering into a kind of successorship to institutionally specialised religion. As I am going to argue in this chapter, the answer is not simply 'yes', but 'yes and no': on the one hand, disembedded markets appear as the utmost universal social system, transcending and bridging even the realms of religion-based civilisations and hence performing the function of self-representation in some sense more adequately than religions. Capitalism has achieved something that none of the so-called 'world religions' had ever been able to come close to doing, namely, creating a social nexus that truly includes all of mankind. All that happens in society, including even the militant 'revival' of religions or national identities being observed today, is now occurring *within* that nexus. Capitalism has created its own global civilisation, whose impact on society does not extend only to the sphere of material reproduction, but also to the inner worlds of culture, morality and subjectivity. On the other hand, disembedded markets represent only a rudimentary, relational form of sociality, and thus fall far behind the substantial solidarity provided by religious, ethnic or kinship identities. They continue to depend on their symbiosis with the latter, as markets can work only in an environment offering a minimum of local accountability and reliability. As I am going to argue, this symbiosis is a contradictory and precarious one; it tends to produce self-reinforcing antagonisms, which are highlighted in the present-day debate on globalisation.

Defining the collective identity of the world-society means – to recall the point discussed in Chapter 5 – drawing a distinction; a distinction, however, always has an internal and an external side. Beyond the internal side of social integration, we have to consider the eternal side of managing the unknowable and non-disposable. As we have seen, the counterpart of the social universality of capitalism is its claim on the unknowable via the private appropriation of the creative capacities of labour. Creativity confines itself no longer to religious, philosophical or artistic contemplation, such as in the ancient high cultures, but takes an encompassing and practically transforming character. Thus, with regard to the 'external' side of contingency management, there is indeed some analogy between capitalism and the religions; again, however, this analogy turns out to be a bounded and ambivalent one. On the one hand, disembedded markets constitute a system of 'discovery', to use Friedrich von Hayek's term. Due to its built-in expansionary dynamics, capitalism is determined to gain new lands and to explore and develop hitherto-unknown human potentials – a dynamic that indeed has parallels with the biblical claim that God guided people into the Promised Land. On the other hand, there are two differences between capitalism and religious faith. First, religious faith is related to a wide range of mundane and cosmic contingencies, including issues such as the finite character of human life, the creation of the world, and the end of history. The capitalist discovery process, by contrast, concentrates on a much narrower realm of mundane contingencies and earthly well-being, a realm which, however, had always been vital for religious believers too (Max Weber had emphasised this point). Second, the 'management' of contingency typically has a different meaning in both systems: while the religious believer finds his fulfilment in the faithful acquiescence to God's will, capitalism finds its mission in the active transformation and mastery of the outer world, though active and transformative elements are not absent in many religious denominations too. The boundary between transcendence and immanence becomes liquid, giving capitalism its 'demonic' character, to use Paul Tillich's (1988) term. Different from religious faith, the spirit of capitalism can never reach a state of tranquillity, and cannot promise final redemption. The only possible 'redemption' that capitalism can offer lies in the *process* of creative destruction itself. Never being able to content itself with its successes, capitalism is bound to open ever-new horizons of contingence. Again, the mechanisms of the capitalist discovery process need closer consideration, which will be the subject of Chapter 9. As I am going to show, it is just the success of capitalist innovation that is undermining its own socio-structural underpinnings and that thus tends to paralyse itself. Again, we can see here how the capitalist dream of absolute wealth is destroying itself, just as it is becoming a religion for all mankind.

Here, I will concentrate on elaborating the two general aspects of societal boundary management, and thereby examine the functional equivalence thesis between capitalism and religion. I will then discuss these two aspects in turn.

## The social universality of capital and markets

The classical liberals, from Adam Smith, Jeremy Bentham and Herbert Spencer to Ludwig von Mises, Friedrich von Hayek and Karl Popper, considered markets to be the core of an 'open' society, which was free to everybody irrespective of ethnicity, race, gender, class or religion, and to be able to institute the principle of individual freedom and self-determination. Markets are a social system enabling individual interests to coincide with the interests of all others in a spontaneous way free from political domination; so far, this economic version of liberalism shares the legacy of enlightened secularism, as noted above (Chapter 3). Indeed, the tendency of markets to transcend the boundaries between nation-states, cultures and civilisations and to create a global division of labour seems beyond controversy. With the trade liberalisations of the nineteenth century and again after the Second World War, the global character of capitalism intensified further. The evolution of markets went parallel with the invention of new global communication media such as the telegraph, the telephone and the internet. At the same time, however, the emerging market-based world-society gave rise to unprecedented social polarisations and transnational economic inequalities. Therefore, it would be misleading to conceptualise the nexus of disembedded markets as an emergent form of global 'solidarity' in a Durkheimian sense, as Richard Münch (2011: 107) has suggested. This would mean watering down Emile Durkheim's strong assumptions about the institutional preconditions of contract, which certainly do not apply to present-day global capitalism, despite the existence of global organisations like the United Nations, the World Trade Organization and non-governmental organisations, whose power over national states continues to be weak. On the other hand, it would be similarly misleading to consider the global market with Polanyi and other critical theorists as a 'technocratic' system governed by nothing but the 'artificial' motive of material gain. An individual profit motive – on this point Marx had been much clearer than Polanyi – can arise only on the basis of money as an institutionalised *social medium* coordinating individual transactions. Via money, society is always present as a third partner in apparently utilitarian transactions – a point that is lacking in Polanyi's analysis (Hart 2009).

As a socially integrating device, money works in a way different from Durkheimian institutions, as had been pointed out in various ways by Max Weber and Georg Simmel. The difference can be summarised in two points. First, markets and money as their medium constitute the utmost 'impersonal' social relation, cross-cutting locally bounded norms of solidarity and brotherhood, and removing traditional privileges of insiders vis-à-vis outsiders (Weber 1972: 382; 1978: 544), while Durkheimian institutions are clearly bound to particular communities of a religious or national kind. Second, money does not integrate individual interests, like religions do, by subordinating them to an overarching collective identity and moral obligation. Though moral obligations are by no means absent in market transactions and though a minimum amount of collective trust in currencies appears to be indispensable to the success of transactions (Ganssmann 2011), money works in a relational, network-like way. Unlike a religious ethic, money is not at odds with individual vanities, but shows an almost infinite capacity to integrate heterogeneous wants, thus laying the groundwork for 'individual freedom' in society. Every transaction does not only involve the immediate partners, but an open number of mostly anonymous indirect participants appearing only in the mirror of prices and costs. By virtue of its relational character, the nexus of money and markets bypasses the logic of social inclusion and exclusion inherent in traditional ethnic, national and religious identities;[1] emotional neutrality and cool opportunism supersede the pattern of friend and foe. Free markets are open to anybody, irrespective of race, gender, nation, religion and other ascribed social characteristics. Due to the social construction of labour power as private 'property', even those who in fact own nothing are included. Thus, money and markets can overcome the class dichotomy between poor and rich, as the failure of Marxism to construct a separate 'class identity' for workers has demonstrated. Even the outsiders of society, such as criminals and terrorists, cannot do without money. Thus, if there is a medium representing the encompassing unity of modern society, the most convincing candidate to fill this function is clearly money, not states, religions or civilisations.

Another classic author who emphasised the universal nature of markets is George Herbert Mead. Mead's considerations are of particular interest from my point of view, since they concentrate on comparing religion and the economy as two basic kinds of human universality. Mead stressed that 'each of them becomes universal in its working character, not universal because of any philosophical abstraction involved in them' (Mead 1934: 289). Upon closer inspection, however, the universality of markets and the universality of religion differ in important points. The economic process is more 'superficial' and apparently 'materialistic' in its character, whereas religious cults require the individual to take the 'inner attitude' of the other believers, understanding their existential needs and helping them to save their souls. However, the economic attitude is much easier to communicate between strangers than the religious one: 'It is quite possible to understand anybody who comes to you with something of value which you want to get; if he can express himself in commercial terms, you can understand him. If he comes to you, however, with this particular religious cult, the chances are very great that you cannot comprehend him' (Mead 1934: 296). Moreover, the economic process, as it is going on, tends to overcome its superficiality, because it requires the participants to communicate with each other, to identify with potential customers and suppliers, and to anticipate their needs. Mead's conclusion is that the potential of markets to create a universal social nexus is higher than that of religion. Whereas religions often had been sources of warfare between groups and nations, the economic process can bring 'a closer and closer relationship between communities which may be definitively opposed to each other politically' (Mead 1934: 282). And he argued: 'It has been the most universal socializing factor in our whole modern society, more universally recognizable than religion' (Mead 1934: 295–296). Markets and money transcend the boundaries of religious communities, representing a form of universality that is working *in practice* and that is beyond abstract theological or philosophical reasoning.

The attitude of rivalry and mistrust that markets and money have generated at almost all times from the side of churches (Weber 1972: 352–353; Simmel 1989b [1900]: 306) can be explained largely by their universal characteristics. Money and market based individualism have a subversive influence on religious communities, as they challenge their internal coherence, as well as their external boundaries. Markets create a sphere of personal freedom which undermines the social control exerted by religious authorities; they open channels for individual mobility and social rise, including the chance to escape oppressive religious and political regimes via transnational migration. The dynamics of money-based individualisation in turn puts religious communities under pressure to adapt and to make themselves compatible with the regime of disembedded markets.

The reverse side of the universality of markets is what I have called above (Chapter 3) their 'moral minimalism'. Markets do not know solidarity, nor do show any collective accountability for personal risks (except for insurance systems, which are based on commercial principles). At the same time, markets confront actors with a vast amount of uncertainty, making individual chances of success incalculable in many cases. This applies to all dimensions of disembedding, the territorial and the social as well as the material and the temporal. Transnational commodity and service markets are subject to fluctuations largely beyond the control of national economic policies and nationally based corporate strategies, let alone individual actors. Nevertheless, collective and individual control policies are widespread: states are trying to protect national markets by imposing trade barriers or capital controls. Corporations strive to gain control over their markets by forming monopolies, cartels, or network relationships with suppliers and customers; and workers organise in unions – practices which have been analysed extensively in economic sociology following Mark Granovetter's (1985) seminal article. In most cases, markets are not 'pure' ones governed by atomistic competition, but rather they are more or less 'organised' ones subject to the control of states, corporations and networks. Moreover, market exchange gives rise to at least three basic coordination problems – the problem of the valuation of goods; the regulation of competition; and the regulation of cooperation (Beckert and Aspers 2011) – which can be solved only by the setting of rules by political institutions or sectoral business organisations. However, though such practices may provide a certain amount of local calculability, they cannot eliminate the uncertainty of markets, so far is it from their transnational or global reach. Under conditions of globally declining demand, cartels often collapse or end up in downward spirals of mutual retaliation, as it could be observed in numerous cases (e.g. oil, ship-building, steel). The volatility of commodity and service markets is reinforced by that of global financial markets with their problems of auto-reference of investment decisions and of extreme fluctuations generated by speculative moves. The incalculability of individual market chances does not come only from the sheer size of markets, but also from the volatility and the dynamic character of the market process itself. Given that amount of complexity, the knowledge of actors can never be sufficient to anticipate the conditions of their own success. As a consequence, the social norm of personal accountability, which is constitutive for a liberal society, becomes fictitious to a large degree.

The impact of social and material disembedding on the calculability of individual market chances is different, but it is even graver. Due to the separation of the material and personal factors of production from each other, economic actors find themselves divided into two classes of proprietors, one of them owning capital assets and the other one being positioned on the debt side of capital and faced with the need to sell their labour power. For the non-propertied, this means that they are confronted with an additional dimension of uncertainty beyond the general contingency of markets. Different from the owners of capital, they do not command the material means to be successful in markets. They are subject to the market in an immediate, personal sense, as the only 'asset' which they can offer is their labour power – so far there is not much to add to Marx's early theory of alienation. The commodification of labour confronts individuals with a double-bind dilemma, which Robert Merton (1968) has highlighted in his well-known analysis of anomie: while capitalism institutes financial success as a paramount social norm, it withholds the legal means to conform to this norm to the non-propertied, that is, most members of society. A widespread option for individual actors to cope with this dilemma is what Merton called 'innovation', which is the attempt to conform to the ideal of financial wealth through illegal means, the other possible options being 'ritualism' (strict conformity with legal rules while sacrificing the rewards of wealth), 'retreat', or 'rebellion'. A capitalist society of disembedded markets thus can be described largely as an anomic system, as it affords one the chance to lead a life in conformity with institutionalised aims *and* rules only to a privileged minority. The term 'anomie' (going back to Durkheim) circumscribes the impossibility for individual actors to identify with the perspectives of all others, which would be the precondition for moral integration.

One could object, along with Joseph Schumpeter and Friedrich Hayek, that the incompatibility of social norms with the factual distribution of legal means does not give rise to 'innovation' in the sense of unlawful behaviour, as Merton argued. Individual actors can cope with the double-bind dilemma of social ends and means also in a legal and socially productive way, such as in the case of economic entrepreneurship. Though entrepreneurs sometimes tend to operate at the edge of the law too, they do not formally break the law: they disrupt economic, technical and social routines when searching for unconventional ways towards market success. The dynamic and innovative nature of capitalism goes back largely to this type of economic entrepreneurship – not only of self-employed entrepreneurs, but also of employees striving for performance-based internal advance in firms.[2] Thus, one could argue that it is just the inconsistency between social norms and the lack of personal means that generates creative modes of individual adaptation and thus promotes innovation and social dynamics.

There is an element of truth in this argument because it is indeed the relative openness of capitalist society and the prospect of social advancement that is driving capitalist dynamics (I will come back to this point below in Chapter 9). The liberal argument, however, misses the point that it is not only the existence of the market *itself* that allows entrepreneurs to rise, but the parallel existence of non-market institutions and support systems, which provide necessary resources and protect actors against the risks of unlimited market exposure. The institutional guarantee of property rights by the state (North 1990) is not enough. The availability of network support by families, neighbourhood and ethnic communities, as well as risk capital providers and business 'angels' are key preconditions for successful entrepreneurship, as many empirical studies have shown (Portes and Zhou 1992; Aldrich 2005; Corsino and Soto 2005; Granovetter 2005a; Mizrachi 2005; Stamm 2013). For employees, internal labour markets, collective bargaining systems, a non-discriminating educational system, and the welfare state are vital factors that help to generate entrepreneurial ambition. Without the support of such systems, individuals with lower-class backgrounds would have little motive to invest in their qualifications and to work hard for social ascension.

To put it in a different way, the capitalist system can develop its dynamic and innovative capacities only under the condition of being *more* than a 'pure' market society. It is not the market alone, but the factual symbiosis of markets with functionally differentiated non-market institutions and networks that lays the groundwork for capitalist entrepreneurship. Wolfgang Streeck (2009, 2011) has described this as a kind of coexistence between 'Williamsonian' and 'Durkheimian' institutions, which is anything but a stable and harmonious one. Rather, due to the parasitic aspects of the relationship of markets with non-market institutions, it is prone to self-destructive feedback circles. On the one hand, only 'Durkheimian' institutions like states, associations or families can provide that minimum level of local trustworthiness, stability and solidarity in market relations that are vital for entrepreneurs. Setting and safeguarding the market as a historical institution is not something that can be left over to the market itself, but rather depends on the political and social solidarity of citizens. Moreover, even capitalist enterprises as forms of organised cooperation need interpersonal trust and cannot function solely according to the logic of market competition, as a vast literature on organisations and organisational cultures has shown (see Schein 2017). Last, but not least, markets, as a real institution, would be unthinkable without families, schools and local networks socialising children and qualifying individuals to participate in the complex social world that they create.

On the other hand, the individualising forces of globalised competition are undermining these very non-economic institutions that frame and safeguard private property. The owner of capital, being globally mobile, is in a position superior to those depending on locally bound non-market solidarities, as he or she always has the option to pack up and leave. Public infrastructure, therefore, crumbles, as tax revenues decline due to the tax evasion of the wealthy. Ever-present pressures for 'economisation' in the world's education, science and health systems as well as in popular culture and the media are undermining the functional differentiation of society (Schimank and Volkmann 2017). Aggressive innovators gain an edge not by observing market regulations, but by circumventing or breaking them. Well-established firms and industries decline just because of having settled too comfortably with their own organisational culture. Families of entrepreneurs fall apart due to rivalries between their members (Stamm 2013); networks disintegrate, as participants defect due to opportunist motives. The revolutionising impact of entrepreneurial innovation finally does not spare the social foundations of entrepreneurship themselves. With the self-destructive consequences of entrepreneurial competition, the anomic and socially polarising implications of disembedded markets are now coming to the surface (see also Michéa 2014).

The contradictions revealing themselves here have little to do with the Habermasian 'colonialisation' of the life-world. The self-destructive tendencies of entrepreneurship should not be equated with an invasion of a supposedly asocial systemic logic of markets into the communication-based life-world from the outside, as Habermas (1981: Vol. II: 447–448) does. Rather, they are related to conflicting dimensions of sociality and unanticipated consequences of action evolving just as a consequence of the global success of the liberal freedom narrative itself. Far away from reflecting only 'systemic' imperatives, disembedded markets constitute a *moral* claim of an utmost universal and pervasive character, as recent authors (Neckel 2008; Michéa 2014; Bröckling 2016) have emphasised. Today, 'entrepreneurship', 'empowerment', 'creativity' and 'self-fulfilment' have become the keywords of an ever-present media and coaching industry aiming to give advice to freelancers and employees on their way to economic success and reinforcing the disciplining effects of the market environment itself. Here, creativity is no longer framed as a free activity, but takes on the paradoxical form of an ultimate social obligation. The universalism of markets culminates in a *moral* imperative for the single actor to perfect their social self-enactment, competencies and performances. The entrepreneurial person has to prove himself or herself in a world which is no less opaque than the hidden God (*deus absconditus*) of Calvinism. Similar to the Calvinist believer, who can never be certain about his or her personal state of salvation, they can never content themselves with their past achievements. Salvation, if possible at all, can come only from the *process* of never ending self-improvement. In the regime of disembedded markets, perfect personal autonomy coincides with perfect social adaptation and governance. Under such conditions, the Kantian idea of individual freedom, being compatible with the freedom of everybody, ends up in a nightmare scenario; here, Michel Foucault's critique of neoliberalism and modern subjectivity as a form of total 'governance' finds its justification (Bröckling 2016).[3] The market narrative ignores the parallel involvement of individuals in non-market spheres, which they have to balance with each other (Honneth 2002).[4] With its encompassing, irrefutable as well as irredeemable claims, the market narrative tends to dominate the entire conduct of life; it is incompatible not only with functional differentiation, but also with what Michael Walzer has called the pluralism of the 'spheres of justice', which he deems vital for the flourishing of a free society (Walzer 1983).

Full conformity with the imperatives of the market is possible only for those who possess sufficient financial, social and cultural capital, and – hence – who are in a position to devote themselves to symbolic celebrations of entrepreneurship while avoiding its real hazards. This has begun to apply to an increasingly influential 'transnational class' that is composed of corporate, state, technical and consumerist factions (Sklair 2001; Caroll 2010) and that is capable of leading a cosmopolitan lifestyle. Living on the sunny side of globalisation, the members of this class feel comfortable with market ideologies, be it in their conservative or in their green-multiculturalist versions, which seem to fit perfectly with their social experiences. Though cosmopolitan values implicitly presuppose an appropriate personal endowment of capital in its diverse forms,[5] their cultural impact reaches far beyond the circles of the wealthy. The less wealthy are caught in a conflict between their idols and their dependence on the very non-market resources and networks at the local level that are threatened by the creative destructive forces of globalised capital. If they do not venture the hazards of an entrepreneurial existence, they may arrange themselves with market ideologies in a ceremonious way by observing the rituals of self-perfection on a formal level while factually following conventional lifestyles. Others may choose the option of 'retreat', in Merton's (1968) sense, in both cases sometimes at the price of serious personal disadvantages. Workers in traditional industrial settings may still opt for the collective organisation and defence of their interests, though deindustrialisation in many advanced industrial countries has led to a lasting decline in the power unions, and has thus largely removed this option from the table.

At the other extreme, the losers of globalisation may opt for rebellion in its various forms, ranging from the extreme left to the extreme right. While the leftist versions have lost ground in the present, right-wing forms of rebellion in the sense of a militant resuscitation of local collective identities and cultural traditions appear to be on the rise again – a development which in some sense looks similar to that which occurred in the first half of the twentieth century. As mentioned above (Chapter 4), Benjamin Barber has highlighted recent developments in the globalisation process. And he frames the push-and-pull of this process in as that between 'Jihad' and 'McWorld': 'After all, Jihad and McWorld operate with equal strength in opposite directions, the one driven by parochial hatreds, the other by universalizing markets, the one re-creating ancient subnational and ethnic borders from within, the other making national borders porous from the outside' (Barber 1996: 6). In such a constellation, the religious furor of market universalism is countered by an equally fervent invocation of local, ethnic and religious particularisms, giving the lie to the liberal dream of a mankind unified by '*doux* commerce'. As Barber argued, the relationship between McWorld and Jihad is a 'dialectical' one, with both forces not constraining but rather reinvigorating each other. In a similar vein, Michael Geyer and Charles Bright have argued that globalisation – though not destroying states – has a tendency

> to bypass politics, short-circuit the formation of national agendas, and challenge the capacity of the state for political self-organization, that is, to constitute the nation and organize complex social relations. The result of this development is not only growing disillusionment with politics, world-wide, but the proliferation and strengthening of family and kinship networks and, more generally, of identity-based (ethnic or religious) communities as substitutes for national politics in much of the world.
>
> (Geyer and Bright 2000: 64)

Today, such interpretations appear prophetic, given the spectacular successes of nationalist political movements in many European countries and in the United States, mounting popular opposition against the European Union and the Euro (Kuhn et al. 2016), and the rise of authoritarian regimes in countries like Russia and Turkey. The former optimism surrounding globalisation has given way to an increasing rift between cosmopolitan and communitarian ideologies and preferences of the electorate, which is deeply divided on issues such as the openness of national borders, the importance of supranational vs. national governance, and the relevance of universal human rights vs. local collective identities. This poses a considerable challenge to the social cohesion of Western democracies (Zürn and de Wilde 2016).[6] Moreover, the disillusionment with economic globalisation is likely lying behind much of which in the above-discussed studies has been referred to as a 'return' of religions, in particular the return of Islamic fundamentalism. The recourse to 'authentic' traditions and values to be observed here can largely be interpreted as a defensive response to the *factual* globalisation of economic and social relations. It is the background of mounting interdependence, which involuntarily shifts hitherto unnoticed or irrelevant cultural differences to the focus of attention: 'The recent globe-wide assertion of particularistic ideas is heavily contextualized by the phenomenon of increasing globality' (Robertson and Chirico 1985: 233). The gods re-emerging here are no longer the original gods but are re-invented ones, responding to the larger religion of capitalist globalisation. The demons of capitalism are replaced only by other demons of an even more dubious kind, which cannot undo capitalist globalisation and which cannot the basis of true identity and social stability. As Pankaj Mishra (2017) has shown, this is a dilemma that has not only evolved in the most recent past. The capitalist promise of absolute wealth always tended to evoke more desires and ambitions than it could satisfy. As a result, it nourished *ressentiment* on the side of the late-comers, the excluded, and the underprivileged, which took militant forms even from the very beginnings of modern capitalism in the late eighteenth century.

In the social sciences, the central issues that have been arising out of the globalisation debate since the end of the 1980s still appear to be unsettled. Above all, there is the controversy between the globalisation optimists, who point to globalisation as a social reality based on transnational markets, corporations, networks, and cultures, and the pessimists, who insist that genuine social cohesion cannot be based on markets but only on inherited collective identities. By their very nature, such identities – be they kinship ties, local communities, or nations, religions, or civilisations – are not global but particular (this includes even supranational political associations like the EU, which is still a regional phenomenon). While an optimistic tone seemed to prevail in globalisation studies until the turn of the millennium (for an overview, see Held and McGrew 2000; Lechner and Boli 2000), the trend has begun to swing in the other direction since then in scholarship as well as in politics. Today, the mainstream view in political science and sociology seems to have become sceptical of globalisation. National 'container' theories of society are now widespread, as Barrie Axford (2013) has noted in his overview.[7]

The conclusion so far is that neither the vision of market-based social universalism nor the restoration of local, national or religious identities alone can offer satisfying answers to the social tensions created by capitalist globalisation. As a model for real life – beyond the great philosophical utopias – the ideal of cosmopolitan individuality presupposes an appropriate endowment with capital in its diverse forms, which the vast majority of the population, even in the advanced industrial countries, does not command. The idea of cosmopolitan individualism, thus, cannot but vastly overtax most people, though it clearly would be premature to abandon the liberal idea altogether. Without being framed by functionally different non-market institutions at the national and local levels, markets are likely to produce irrational and destructive outcomes. It is only due to the factual plurality of institutions that markets can become manageable in practice. The very same non-market institutions, however, appear as obstacles against the freedom of competition, which is why they come under pressure to change, to adapt, or to be dismantled altogether. In this way, capitalism indeed tends to undermine its own social foundations. With non-market institutions declining, militant counter-movements at the local or national levels are likely to emerge. Thus, the universal claim of markets ends up in vicious feedback circles between global and local identities, and apparently there is no political recipe to stop their acceleration.

## Capital as a device to manage uncertainty

The promise of wealth, affluence and happiness is a central source of legitimation for capitalism, and a key driver of its dynamic. A manifestation of the capitalist dream machine is the often-cited global 'consumption culture' inventing ever new goods, artefacts and designs which become the objects of consumers' desire just because they are different from the old ones, and hence can serve as social status markers (Baudrillard 1998; Skidelsky and Skidelsky 2012). However, this is not all. As a long-term view on the industrial revolutions of capitalism shows, the transformative impact of capitalism on everyday life goes far beyond the idols of consumption. With basic inventions, such as the steam engine, the railway, the airplane, the automobile, electricity, the telegraph, the telephone, the computer and the internet, capitalism has managed to overcome the practical limitations of space and time. It has created a vast range of new lifestyle opportunities not only for small elites but for large masses of people. Journeys that took months still in the early nineteenth century, for example, take only a few hours today; worldwide communication, which had been cumbersome in pre-capitalist times, now works almost instantaneously. Individual mobility and individual connectivity have risen spectacularly; information horizons have expanded. The productivity of manual and intellectual work has been enhanced spectacularly due to industrial innovations, making work as well as life much more comfortable. The inventions in chemistry and pharmaceuticals have helped to prolong human life and to fight many diseases deemed incurable in former ages. They have also contributed to vast productivity increases in agriculture, thus averting the apparent capacity bottlenecks that would have prevented our being able to nourish a growing population – the bottlenecks which Thomas Malthus had warned of. As noted above (Chapter 4), the rise of new technologies was often accompanied by sweeping utopias, visions, and imaginations of a positive and a negative variety (Sturken et al. 2004). For those who lived at the time of these inventions, it was not always easy to believe in their natural origin, such as in the case of early users of the telegraph, who thought it was connected with supra-natural spirits through the electric wires (Sconce 2004). The industrial revolutions of capitalism have transformed human life in ways that were unprecedented and never could have been predicted by any observer. To earlier generations, the new technologies could not have appeared as anything but miracles falling from heaven. At the same time, the industrial revolutions meant a historically unprecedented amount of human intervention into the natural environment, the dangerous and destructive consequences of which have only become an issue of urgent discussion in the recent past.

There is no doubt that miracles are vital for religions too, including the monotheistic ones. Even the cursory reader of the Bible is familiar with the miracles performed not only by Jesus himself, but even by the apostles (e.g. Luke 4:31–40; 5:1–26; Acts 14:8–11; 19:11–12), and their importance as a means of enhancing the credibility of the related message. Miracles appear to play a much smaller role in the life of the Prophet Mohammed;[8] instead, the Koran offers colourful descriptions of wealth and opulence prevailing in paradise. Capitalism does not promise such heavenly pleasures: it neither offers an answer to the questions related to the finite character of human life,[9] nor provides a solution to the meaning and end of history. Instead of heavenly rewards, capitalism offers all the more reliable ways to attain earthly ones, such as health, material welfare, social status, and individual freedom, which – of course – always have been relevant for religious believers too. At the same time, the social mechanisms by which innovations are realised in capitalism are by no means entirely different from those used in religion. In both cases, charismatic leaders preaching myths and visions, and leading believers are vital.[10] Entrepreneurs and business leaders, such as Henry Ford, Bill Gates and Steve Jobs, see it as their mission to communicate their projects beyond narrow expert networks into the broader public. Comparable to religious prophets, they spark hopes, rouse confidence and point the way to progress. Mobilising the public is a decisive factor in bringing about successful innovation. Innovative visions and paradigms work like self-fulfilling prophecies: projects that appear utterly phantasmal in their initial phase (consider only the idea of the airplane around 1900), may become a realistic undertaking if the protagonists are successful in winning a critical mass of relevant actors to 'believe' and to invest in the project (Lampel 2001). Innovation myths develop in all arenas of the economy, including not only production, technology and organisation but also consumption, where the rise and fall of fashions and trends is a widely discussed phenomenon (Deutschmann 2001, 2008, 2012a; Hirschle 2012; Beckert 2016). Capitalist myths, like religious ones, can mobilise collective forces and literally 'move mountains' if they are successful.

As a means to control the creativity of human work, capital represents a powerful rival to religion, since it embodies perhaps the strongest of all utopian powers: private command over what *mankind can do*. In its approach to control mundane contingencies, capitalism even appears superior to the religions, because it is based on man's active mastery of the outer world, not only, as in the religions, on faithful acquiescence to God's will. Capitalism does not only raise promises, it can also keep them. However, the activism of the capitalist spirit also has its dark side, since it never can reach a stable state of tranquillity. While religious myths are indifferent against the historical flow of time, capitalist innovation myths tend to exhaust themselves with their implementation and therefore have to be continuously generated anew. As mentioned above (Chapter 4), human creativity is a resource that can never be defined comprehensively and can materialise itself only in a never-ending process of 'growth'. No particular paradigm of innovation can ever articulate the totality of human potentials; therefore, the career of innovations typically is made up of a sequence of phases, stretching from invention, demonstration and growth, to slowdown and maturity (Freeman and Louca 2001: 146). The mobilising impact of innovative paradigms on the economy and on society as a whole is confined to the initial phases, when the potentials of the new paradigm are still unexplored, when they can open new horizons and when they can motivate new investments. As soon as a new technology becomes established and institutionalised, slowdown sets in and profits tend to decline. To avoid the imminent danger of stagnation and recession, new inventions and myths, to be financed by new debts, need to be generated. Capitalism thus can never promise definitive redemption, but can opt only between growth and decline. It cannot escape the state of permanent self-indebtedness and settle down into a stationary state of reproduction. Capitalism is a machine to generate and to fulfil new desires; what it cannot overcome is the habit of desiring.

From this perspective, capitalist uncertainty management clearly has its limits, and profound differences with religious ideas of salvation come into view. Above all, the religious dichotomy between transcendence and immanence becomes liquid in capitalism. This brings society into a condition of permanent self-insufficiency and unrest, which Paul Tillich has circumscribed with his concept of 'the demonic'. The demonic is the destruction of form by 'the desire for infinity' (Tillich 1989: 68), and it includes not only destructive (i.e. satanic) forces but creative forces as well. A demonic being is an 'intermediate' being that is located within and, at the same time, torn apart by two different categories of life, such as between animal and human, or between human and god. Due to this 'intermediate' existence, the demon is never able to content itself with its given condition, and it is doomed to permanent unrest. In a similar sense, capitalist society can never reach a stable state of tranquillity, as Tillich argues. As opposed to the conventional religions, the capitalist spirit does not aim at the reconciliation of the believer with God. It does not face the absolute on the level of communication, prayer and sacrifice, but in an attitude of never-ending conquest and appropriation. Contingency management, therefore, takes on the character of a Sisyphean task, with contingency emerging continuously anew, as soon it is put under control.

The obvious question is this: can the Sisyphean work really go on indefinitely? Many doubts have been raised concerning this question. Above all, there are the environmentalists, who point to the devastating impact of energy-intensive economic growth on the natural environment and insist that it is urgent that the growth stop along with the consumption of energy, natural resources and $CO_2$ emissions, lest we lose the planet. While the necessity for such planet-friendly policies is largely uncontroversial today, there is much more disagreement about whether successful environmental policies are possible under capitalism or only under a 'de-growth' regime with reduced levels of consumption and production, which would presuppose an overthrow of capitalism. While there is no doubt that capitalist growth has followed an energy-intensive path in the past, there are no *a priori* reasons, why this should be the case also in the future. Advocates of so-called 'green capitalism' have argued that there is no iron law for capitalism to continue energy-intensive growth (Global Commission on the Economy and the Climate 2014). Given the foreseeable continuity of worldwide population growth, the only promising option to establish a sustainable economic regime would be to make use of the innovative potential of capitalism. In any case, an effective turn towards a sustainable economy would require vast amounts of capital investment, and, hence, of growth as well.

I will not go deeper into this still largely open debate here. Neither will I enter into a detailed discussion of recent theories of secular stagnation, which have been suggested by prominent economists, such as Larry Summers and Richard Gordon (e.g. Gordon 2014). These approaches emphasise the impact of scientific progress on growth, and they point to a slowdown of scientific inventions as a likely cause of the decline of growth rates. The counter-argument is that it is not scientific progress as such (whose course is largely unpredictable) that drives capitalist growth, but the entrepreneurial transformation of scientific inventions into marketable *innovations* (as had been Schumpeter's well-known point). The key question is not whether capitalism is able to produce enough scientific inventions (which is an unanswerable question), but whether it will be able to generate *entrepreneurs* as a particular category of social actors, who can transform scientific discoveries into marketable innovations. It is not scientific progress but entrepreneurship that could become the real bottleneck for growth. This is an empirical hypothesis open to sociological enquiry, to which I will now turn.

## Notes

1 Even the world religions (in particular Christianity and Islam) are subject to the logic of inclusion and exclusion, as, contrary to their claims, none of them have ever established a truly global nexus comparable with markets. As Friedrich W. Graf put it, 'what is true for countries applies to religions and denominations as well: there is no strong identity without a clear idea of who the enemy is' (Graf 2004: 35, my translation).

2 Voss and Pongratz (1998) have coined the term 'labour-power entrepreneur' ('*Arbeitskraft-Unternehmer*') to describe this type of entrepreneurship.

3 Even today, the republican version of liberalism (e.g. in John Rawls and Jürgen Habermas) still gets credit as a blueprint of secular justice and democracy, though the problems of this model are manifold, as the 'communitarian' critique of the liberal model has shown (Honneth 1993). A perhaps bigger problem, however, lies in the relationship between market-liberal and republican freedom narratives and their compatibility with each other.

4 Again here, the parallels with religious experience are becoming apparent: as it is impossible for the believer to fully comply with God's will, the need arises for the authentic believers to separate themselves from everyday life, to gather in monasteries, and to concentrate on spiritual experience (Riesebrodt 2007). Present-day virtuosos of business or finance practise similarly ascetic ways of life, spending day and night on meetings and travel or at their computer terminals, and nourishing themselves with fast food.

5 Craig Calhoun (2002) ironised cosmopolitan ideologies as the 'class consciousness of frequent travellers'.
6 With their terminology of 'cosmopolitanism' and 'communitarianism', the authors are referring to older philosophical debates on modern principles of justice carried on in the 1970s and 1980s between John Rawls and his 'liberal' school, and his 'communitarian' adversaries (Michael Sandel, Charles Taylor, Michael Walzer and Alasdair MacIntyre).
7 'The burden of much theorizing out of political science and sociology still has the nation state and national societies as its ontological core' (Axford 2013: 58).
8 Only Surah 3:13 reports on a battle between believers and disbelievers of Allah, where Allah intervenes to secure the victory of his militarily inferior believers.
9 Though it gradually seems to approach this level too, at least if one listens to futurologists like Ray Kurzweil or Peter Thiel, announcing that the victory over death may soon be in our grasp due to the progress of artificial intelligence and biotechnology.
10 Here, Weber's assumptions about charismatic leadership being alien to 'rational' capitalist entrepreneurship are not convincing (Kraemer 2008).

# 9 A multi-level model of capitalist dynamics

This chapter aims at a deeper sociological analysis of capitalist creative destruction, which can help to clarify the micro-foundations of economic theology and the limitations of rational choice (RC) theories. This requires a systematic analysis of the emergent interactions between institutional conditions on the macro- and meso-levels and individual actions that constitute capitalist dynamics.

From a macro-perspective, innovation-based growth is the key mechanism of capitalism for coping with social contingencies as well as with its extra-social environment. A growing economy provides the basis for the settlement of class conflicts and for social integration, as well as for the progressive mastery of nature. It is not only the economic system in a narrow sense that depends on growth, but governments as well. For the latter, growth is a crucial variable, as it determines the tax revenues required to finance the entire range of state activities, including the maintenance of material infrastructure, welfare expenditures, scientific research, defence and education. Almost all social sub-systems and most social activities depend directly or indirectly on financial resources, which only a growing economy can provide. In this sense, growth can be considered to be a social imperative in capitalist societies, though it often has destructive repercussions on society as well as on the natural environment.

Viewed from a larger historical perspective, growth is an extremely singular phenomenon, which had been confined largely to the era of disembedded markets and industrial capitalism during the last two centuries. If we take Angus Maddison's study (Maddison 2001) as a starting point, stationary reproduction with only small and gradual adaptions (and, of course, interruptions due to wars, diseases and natural disasters) had been the rule during almost all of pre-capitalist history. Even the Western European economies, which are usually considered the 'seedbed' of capitalism, grew only at a very slow pace (0.15 percent annually) during the period 1500–1820. After 1820, however, a veritable 'growth explosion' could be observed, first in Western Europe and the 'Western offshoots' of Europe (North America, Australia, New Zealand), and then successively in other world regions too. While almost stagnating in earlier times, per capita growth in the world soared to annual rates of 0.53 (1820–1870), 1.30 (1870–1913), 0.91 (1913–1950), 2.93 (1950–1973) and 1.33 (1973–1998) percent (Maddison 2001: 126). During the entire period, the world's per capita income rose by a factor of eight-and-a-half.

The growth process developed very unevenly across the world's regions; moreover, it was interrupted by recessions and severe crises. Nevertheless, it is evident that, after 1820, growth became the 'normal' mode of economic reproduction, replacing the traditional stationary pattern (Broadberry and O'Rourke 2010). Although the take-off of growth started in the western hemisphere, other world regions caught up in the late nineteenth century, detaching the growth process from its western origins. Due to the wars and economic crises of the first half of the twentieth century, growth declined significantly during this period. By contrast, the period after the Second World War was characterised by an unprecedented global boom. Since the last quarter of the twentieth century, the growth rates of the mature industrial economies of Europe, North America and Japan declined again, while the emerging economies – particularly in East Asia – became more dynamic. Today, emerging economies such as those of China, Indonesia, Thailand and Vietnam – and in recent times even the countries of sub-Saharan Africa – are showing much higher rates of growth than the mature industrial economies (4–7 percent vs. 1–2 percent; see IMF 2018). There can be no doubt that capitalist growth today has become a genuinely global phenomenon based on the worldwide integration of markets and no longer bound to any particular culture or civilisation (Deutschmann 2016b). At the same time, the unevenness of growth around the world has led to a dramatic increase in the inter-regional spread of per capita income, from 3:1 (Western Europe to Africa in 1820) to 14:1 and ultimately 19:1 (Western Europe and Western Offshoots to Africa in 1998; Maddison 2001: 126). The growth explosion coincided with a population explosion, though population growth (5.6-fold during the period 1820–1998) fell behind the growth of per capita income. While the population explosion can explain partly the rise in the absolute levels of income, it cannot account for the rise of per capita income. According to common definitions, only growth due to higher productivity, which implies a higher level of income per person, is considered to be 'true' growth.

'Productivity growth', however, is a highly abstract statistical artefact, which contains no information about the real, empirical factors underlying growth. It suggests the fiction of an increasing *physical* output of a given collection of goods per unit of time, while concealing *innovation* as the truly important factor. Growth does not result simply from a proportional increase of a given set of products, but from permanent quantitative and qualitative changes in the composition of the output, reflecting itself in a higher *valuation* of production in the markets. Innovations take many forms, including new products, new technologies, new systems of organisation and logistics, and new market explorations; their reach extends from everyday improvements to new technological paradigms revolutionising entire sectors, or even the total economic system. The permanent contest of capitalist firms for innovation (Baumol 2002) is the main factor promoting the expansion and disembedding of markets in all of their four dimensions.

Because of their multi-dimensionality, it is extremely difficult to measure the impact of innovations on the market value of the social product. Therefore, quantitative economic models such as 'y growth = x capital + u labour + v knowledge' are of little help to understand the innovative process. Of course, capital, labour and knowledge are required to generate innovations, but the real question obviously is: *what precise kind* of capital, labour and knowledge? As Joseph Schumpeter, Frank Knight and Friedrich Hayek have emphasised, such questions cannot be answered on the basis of abstract models, but only from the situational expertise of the historical actors. It is only in the recent past that intensive attempts to combine theoretical and historical analyses of capitalist growth have developed (Freeman and Louca 2001; Osterhammel 2009: 909–910; Broadberry and O'Rourke 2010). Apparently, qualitative and historical studies are more promising when it comes to explaining the success of innovations than are studies focusing on general, economic or evolutionary 'laws'.[1] Moreover, growth is not understood sufficiently when conceptualised merely as an outcome of *political* action. State intervention can promote the growth process by providing an institutional framework that favourable to innovation; however, it cannot control it. Genuine innovations cannot be made by political decisions. The state could play a key role only in 'late-comer societies', such as Japan, the Soviet Union, or China, which took over ready-made technologies invented and developed elsewhere. Last, but not least, growth does not come from intentional *individual* action alone. When consumers go shopping, or firms invest in new machines, their intention is to satisfy their wants or to improve their market position, not to make the economy grow. The popular moral critique of growth, tracing growth back to excessive consumer wants (e.g. Gross 1994; Skidelsky and Skidelsky 2012) suffers from shortcut methodological individualism.

Thus, neither the macro-, nor the micro-perspective *alone* is sufficient to analyse growth. The most promising approaches from a sociological viewpoint are those conceptualising growth as a social emergent that develops from largely unintentional interactions between the macro-and micro-levels of society. As argued above (Chapter 8), innovation is based on creativity; creativity, however, is a genuinely *individual* capacity that develops in an unforeseeable way and should not be equalised with rational action. The uncertainty inherent in capitalist dynamics goes back largely to the incalculability of entrepreneurial innovations and their economic and social consequences. An appropriate way to analyse macro–micro interactions in a social system is dynamic multi-level analysis (DMA), which aims to clarify the feedback processes between individual actions and their structural conditions (Coleman 1990; Esser 1993).[2] Usually DMA proceeds in three main steps (Esser 1993, 1999): first, a reconstruction of the social situation of the actors, which in its turn is to be carried on from the two-fold perspective of the scientific observer, on the one hand, and of the actors themselves, on the other one (the 'logic of the situation', according to Hartmut Esser); second, a theoretically based interpretation of individual action in the given situation (the 'logic of selection'); and third, an explanation of the newly constituted collective situation from the aggregated effects of individual actions (the 'logic of aggregation'). The three steps can be iterated to reconstruct the long-term dynamics of social processes. DMA thus allows one to view the feedback process between the institutional and social framing of individual action, its emergent effects, and its unintended collective consequences.

In my analysis of growth, I will follow this approach. To anticipate the line of argument: capitalist growth is a collective emergent based on the aggregate effects of innovative actions and entrepreneurial projects; entrepreneurial creativity, however, is motivated largely by the prospect of market-based social advancement. To become a force of growth, the capitalist polarisation of classes needs to be socially framed in a way that makes it appear *individually surmountable*. The innovative capacity of capitalism depends largely on its potential to generate entrepreneurial careers that are capable of crossing the class dichotomy *individually* while leaving it intact *collectively*. The creative performances of entrepreneurs and workers, in turn, nourish the profitability of capital and, with it, the expansion of markets and macro-economic growth. The profit of capital, thus, does not come simply from the quantitative amount of surplus labour, as Marx contended. What is vital, rather, is the creative capacity of labour (as defined above in Chapter 4). I am arguing, along with Joseph Schumpeter and Werner Sombart, that profit comes from new products as well as from technical and logistical combinations, which are based on the innovative performances of entrepreneurs. Profit is a premium on the temporary monopoly which the successful entrepreneur enjoys. Moreover, as I emphasise, beyond Schumpeter and Sombart, the creative commitment of employees and their thousands of 'small' ideas in implementing innovations is vital for profitability and growth too – in this respect, Marx was right. Capitalist growth, in other words, is the aggregate effect of the quest of entrepreneurs and employees to cope creatively with the institutional and structural inconsistencies of their situations. The continuation of the Sisyphean task depends on the capacity of capitalism to generate entrepreneurs and entrepreneurial careers, which, however, is not likely to persist. Rather, as I am going to show, it tends to undermine itself not only due to diminishing population growth, but also due to unintended collective consequences of structural upward mobility. The biggest challenge for capitalism, thus, lies in its own success.

## Logic of the situation

### *Structural conditions*

The logic of the situation circumscribes the structural conditions of society relevant to explaining capitalist growth, as well their cultural and subjective framing. Again, my starting point is the disembedding process of markets, Polanyi's 'Great Transformation', which began to develop on a large scale around the turn of the nineteenth century. As I have argued above (Chapter 2, Chapter 4), the process of disembedding was the process of markets becoming universal in their territorial, social, material and temporal dimensions. Markets expanded across national borders; they started to permeate social relations, creating a class dichotomy between those owning wealth and those owning nothing but their labour power. With regard to the structural conditions of growth, the capitalist class dichotomy, with capital as the positive pole and labour as the negative pole of wealth, deserves particular attention. It is only the prospect of profit that motivates capital owners to invest their capital. Without profit, there would be no reason for the owners of capital to expose their property to the risks of circulation and to enter into the productive process at all. With workers possessing the means of production themselves and with the incomes of capital and labour coinciding, there would be no need for growth and little danger of recession. At the same time, there would be less market pressure for efficiency enhancement and innovation, though both would remain possible. The counterpart to the exclusive attribution of property rights over the material factors of production to a separate class of owners is the exclusive 'ownership' of the human factors by those owning nothing. The historical precondition for the emergence of formally free labour was (and continues to be) the expropriation of the rural workforce from their land, as I have maintained above (Chapter 4) in agreement with Marx. From an ecological perspective, a further precondition was (and is) a rapidly growing population based on the agricultural revolution and giving rise to a large young labour force competing intensively for gainful employment and market success.

Moreover, it is the ambivalent, double-bind character of capitalist property relations that appears to be relevant here. On the one hand, the class dichotomy seems to be collectively closed due to the superior market power of wealth owners. This means a primary inequality with regard to social opportunities (i.e. social rise), which is acerbated by the transmission of fortunes in families and the factual amalgamation of capitalist class positions with inherited pre-capitalist status hierarchies (Beckert 2004). On the other hand, the class dichotomy appears individually open, as the affiliation of individuals to classes is not fixed formally by social origin or ascription, such as in pre-modern status hierarchies, but depends solely on factual ownership of marketable resources. Individual advancement from the working into the wealthy classes appears possible, either within the individual life course, or at least within a few generations. Due to the global character of markets, such careers may no longer occur only within national boundaries; rather, they can also follow transnational paths. The capitalist class dichotomy turned out not to be as hermetically closed for workers as Marx had expected. At least temporarily, and due not least to the impact of social-democratic reforms, it took on the character of an incentive structure for social advancement. Actually, this meant a historically new type of social rise, entrepreneurial advancement, based not on vested privileges, educational privileges or bureaucratic rules, but on individual success through the market. It is important here not to make a sharp distinction between self-employed entrepreneurs in a legal sense and employees striving for market success and social advancement within firms.

Though social advancement across the class dichotomy is possible, its actual chances are often thin. The basic message coming from the structural context, thus, is an ambivalent one. The class dichotomy appears to be open and closed *at the same time*; its formal openness gives rise to *aspirations* for social climbing, making people struggle for success despite the factual inequality of social chances. Arlie Hochschild has aptly illustrated this constellation with her metaphor of social climbers waiting patiently in a line leading up a hill and striving to reach the sanctuary of the American Dream located on the top of the hill (Hochschild

2016: 136). In other words, to enter paradise, praying and singing are not enough, as in the case of the traditional religious believer; one has to work hard for ascension. Thus, despite the social polarisation between capital and labour, the liberal dream of freedom materialises to some degree; however, it does so at the price of instituting a struggle for social advancement as a social imperative for the majority of the population.

Inequality of wealth is a structural precondition for entrepreneurship; without inequality, there would be no incentive for the struggle for advancement. To leave room for upward mobility, however, the class dichotomy should not be too rigid and unequal, as is shown by a quantitative analysis performed by Lippman and colleagues (2005) of the relationship between inequality and entrepreneurship. Based on an internationally comparative analysis of the data of the Global Entrepreneurship Monitor (GEM), the authors found a significant positive correlation between the level of (national) wealth inequality and the frequency of early entrepreneurship (in terms of the workforce share of persons engaged in founding or managing start-up firms). To identify genuine entrepreneurship, the GEM survey distinguishes between 'necessity-based' and 'opportunity-based' entrepreneurship (GEM 2014). While in the first case the motive to start a business lies in the sheer absence of alternative bases of subsistence, the main motive in the second case has to do with perceived economic chances. As it turned out in Lippman and colleagues' (2005) study, the frequency of necessity-based entrepreneurship tends to increase linearly with wealth inequality. By contrast, the correlation of wealth inequality with opportunity-based entrepreneurship shows a curvilinear pattern, with nascent entrepreneurship rising with inequality but declining again beyond a medium level of inequality. As the authors conclude, it appears that only 'moderate levels of inequality do help opportunity-based entrepreneurship to flourish. Countries with high levels of inequality do not experience as much opportunity entrepreneurship, because people lack the resources and information required to take advantage of opportunities essential for such activity' (Lippman et al. 2005: 15). This confirms the importance of intermediate social layers with regard to generating 'genuine', opportunity oriented entrepreneurship. A highly polarised social distribution of wealth fosters necessity-based entrepreneurship, but is detrimental to genuine, opportunity-based entrepreneurship. Entrepreneurship as an option for social advancement via the exploration of innovative opportunities is most likely to occur under conditions of moderate wealth inequality and the existence of financially stable middle classes.

To mediate the process of entrepreneurial rise, and to render it economically productive, however, further institutional conditions beyond the class-based distribution of property rights are required. The innovation contest may be carried on by violence and illegal means, as in the case of many emerging and developing countries. Workers may be not truly 'free' due to extreme poverty, or due to informally continuing master–servant relationships. As I argued above (Chapter 4), the disembedding process can become economically productive only under the paradoxical condition of a parallel 're-embedding' of markets into additional institutional structures at the local, regional and national levels, such as industrial relations, labour laws, education, and social security systems.

Recent institutional theories of growth, again, have emphasised the relevance of these structures. For Douglass North (1990), the key factors for promoting growth are a meritocratic culture and a strong state being able to guarantee private property rights and to contain political corruption. In a similar vein, Daron Acemoglu and James Robinson stressed the importance of 'inclusive' political institutions setting incentives for economic entrepreneurship, in contrast to 'extractive' institutions existing solely for the enrichment of small circles of elites (Acemoglu and Robinson 2012). Xavier Sala-i-Martin and Elsa Artadi developed a more elaborate model built on three groups of institutional factors relevant for growth, which they called 'basic requirements', 'efficiency enhancers' and 'innovation and sophistication factors' (Sala-i-Martin and Artadi 2004). 'Basic requirements' include elementary material infrastructure, a minimum level of personal and legal security, macro-economic stability, and a workforce with a basic education. The category of 'efficiency enhancers' circumscribes conditions such as an efficient regulation of labour, commodity and financial markets, an ability to adopt and implement new technologies, and an elaborated system of secondary education. 'Innovation and sophistication factors' include an advanced research infrastructure at the corporate and the societal level and a superior level of human capital and academic education. While cross-cutting national, cultural and civilisational differences, Sala-i-Martin and Artadi's model aims to describe different degrees of competitiveness and growth potential at the national and the company level. Basically, three kinds of economies are distinguished: developing ('factor-driven') economies can offer not more than the basic requirements for growth; emerging ('efficiency-driven') economies rate high with regard to 'basic requirements' and 'efficiency enhancers'; and industrial ('innovation-driven') economies show high scores in all three dimensions.

The institutional structures identified by North and Sala-i-Martin and Artadi, however, do not basically change the ambivalent character of the incentive structure embodied in the capitalist class dichotomy. The guarantee of private property rights, for example, has a different meaning for capital owners and for employees. While capital owners are interested primarily in 'negative' guarantees, such as protection against force and fraud; low taxes; and a fair and efficient public administration, such provisions are not sufficient for employees. What is no less important for them are state interventions to guarantee positive 'social rights' (to use T.H. Marshall's well-known terminology; see Marshall 1950), including the institutionalisation of collective-bargaining systems, public education, social insurance schemes, and social aid. Without such support systems, employees would be subject immediately to the hazards of markets and would have little incentive to invest in their qualifications and to work hard for social advancement. The wealth owners, in their turn, oppose the high tax and social insurance burdens created by the welfare state, which they view as an illegitimate curtailment of their property rights and of the employer's prerogative. Thus, the state finds itself caught up in a conflict of interests: whichever definition of property rights is applied, state interventions will always be both supportive and detrimental to the growth process at the same time.

A similar dilemma can be observed in the field of labour market institutions and qualification systems. It is a commonplace of labour market theory that labour markets are not homogeneous, but are divided into different segments with diverging levels of institutional regulation. A well-known segmentation model distinguishes between 'secondary' and 'primary' labour markets, the latter in their turn being divided into occupational, internal and 'network' labour markets (Marsden 1999). While secondary markets are lightly regulated, characterised by low levels of pay and skill, external flexibility, and rigid job definitions, primary markets are highly institutionalised, distinguishing themselves by high pay and qualification levels, internal flexibility, and long-term career and qualification prospects (Gordon et al. 1982; Sengenberger 1987; Marsden 1999). It is not the first, but the second type of labour market which is dominant in innovative and technologically advanced firms. Primary (network, internal as well as occupational) labour markets offer greater chances for employees to learn, to develop skills and innovative ideas, and to advance, thus contributing to the 'dynamic capabilities'" (Teece et al. 1997) of firms. At the same time, primary labour markets are burdening firms with high fixed costs, thus creating incentives to externalise employment, to cut wages and to downsize bureaucracies. Deregulation and downsizing, however, tend to be detrimental to employee commitment, and are likely to endanger firms' innovative potential.

Another similar dilemma has to do with gender roles and family structures. For Schumpeter, the traditional pattern of gender roles, with women concentrating on domestic duties and men taking on the role of breadwinner, constituted an indirect precondition for an entrepreneurial career. It is only an intact family and the will to build a dynasty that can motivate the entrepreneur and give meaning to his projects, even beyond his death. Without the background of his family and his wife staying at home, the entrepreneur would feel no strong commitment to his mission. Therefore, entrepreneurship would crumble as soon as women were to detect their own market potential (Schumpeter 2003 [1942]: 156–157). Yet, women started to enter into that process even in Schumpeter's time. Today, the traditional gender arrangement, preventing – as it is being criticised – one half of the population from taking their chances, has largely vanished. Though women are still underrepresented in self-employment and nascent entrepreneurship (OECD 2013), the social norm of entrepreneurial advance applies to men and women alike.[3] However, women in their turn are in need of family support too when devoting themselves to entrepreneurial careers – at least as long as they do not renounce having children. A possible solution to the dilemma is to outsource homework to externally hired service workers, with the result of a further commercialisation of the family sphere. For the less affluent, the only possible remedy again lies in the state and public childcare facilities.

Beyond the issue of gender roles, historical research has often pointed to the importance of family support and family networks for nascent entrepreneurs' success (Croner 1962; Kocka 1975, 1982; Gall 2000; Berghoff 2004; Nasaw 2006; Lesczenski 2008; Stamm 2013). The family is important as a provider of capital, for marriages are often arranged with a view to potential business synergies. Core tasks of firm governance, such as the provision of capital, management, and the exploration of new business fields, are assigned frequently to relatives or close friends; trust and trustworthiness are vital when it comes to managing the challenges associated with entrepreneurship. Even in highly industrialised countries, family firms constitute the dominant type of enterprise (Granovetter 2005b: 441). Beyond the family, ethnic, religious and gender affiliations are important preconditions for establishing trust-based relationships. Empirical studies on start-up teams in the United States have revealed a strong inclination towards social homogeneity,[4] and despite all campaigns to promote 'diversity', little seems to have changed in the underrepresentation of women, Hispanic Americans and African Americans in the management of American firms (Dobbin and Kalev 2016). Social homogeneity, however, does not only provide opportunities, but also traps, as it can block innovative potential and it can lead to a selective perception of market opportunities. Despite the importance of network support for nascent entrepreneurs, it is equally important for them to distance themselves from excessive in-group claims. Entrepreneurs need to maintain a 'balance between coupling and decoupling' (Granovetter 2005b), that is, to build trustful relationships with external partners and customers without losing their network support – a balance, which often comes down to trying to 'square the circle'.

Again, all of this confirms the hypothesis of the 'double-bind' character of capitalist institutions: while the distribution of economic, social and cultural capital is polarised and strongly uneven at the collective level, the class structure appears open at the individual level. Individual advancement aspirations, thus, are encouraged and blocked at the same time. From this background, the following question seems vital: how do individuals *perceive* their actual chances of entrepreneurial advancement? Here, we arrive at the second step in the reconstruction of the logic of the situation, namely, the analysis of cultural and subjective framings.

### *Cultural and subjective framings*

The structural conditions of the capitalist economy as analysed by scientific observers will certainly not be completely different from how they are perceived by the historical actors themselves. Nevertheless, the perceptions of the latter cannot be expected to be a one-to-one copy of the first. As Hartmut Esser (1999) argues, the analysis of perceptions and their cultural framings require its own separate enquiry, one that goes beyond the analysis of class structures. Observations are always selective, and the selectivity of the scientific observer is likely to be different from that of the actor himself or herself. The scientific observer in turn will have to take this difference into account when analysing the actor's perceptions from a reflexive perspective (Schütz 1971: 6–7). As Alfred Schütz argues, a main difference between scientific and everyday knowledge is that the latter is much more subject to the consistency imperatives of practical action; hence it is less tolerant of contradictions and ambiguities. In comparison to the scientific observer, the life-world actor is much more pressed to homogenise his or her views and to disregard all aspects that do not fit into their chosen framework. Obviously, these insights are relevant with regard to structural conditions of action in capitalist class societies too. Since these conditions, as we have seen, have a contradictory character and are subject to a 'double bind', it cannot be expected that they will reflect themselves one-to-one in the practical consciousness of actors, be they capitalists, entrepreneurs, managers or employees. Rather, the subjective perceptions and their cultural framings will show a trend towards selective homogenisation, depending on the relative position of actors in the class dichotomy. Moreover, as the class dichotomy is internally stratified according to criteria of education, occupation, ethnicity, gender, and so on, corresponding differences in subjective framings are to be expected too.

Under which conditions is the 'double-bind' of capitalist class relations likely to reflect itself in entrepreneurial frames of individual action? There can be no doubt that entrepreneurial orientations are influenced not only by class positions, but also by a variety of other social and cultural contexts, including religious ones. For instance, the individual orientation towards financial success, as a precondition of entrepreneurship, certainly is not a simple reflection of class structurs, but also depends on overarching cultural traditions. In his seminal work on the rise of capitalism, Werner Sombart showed how the 'capitalist spirit' of the early merchant classes developed historically under the conditions of the urban culture in Western European cities well before the Great Transformation of the early nineteenth century and before the emergence of the modern capitalist class dichotomy. Religious beliefs, such as the ethics of ascetic Protestantism, had been only one factor behind this cultural transformation amongst others (Sombart 2002: 151–152). The emergence of capitalist entrepreneurship, nevertheless, would have been unthinkable without the religious and moral changes in the seventeenth and eighteenth centuries that gave rise to a 'disciplinary' society (Tawney 1926; Taylor 2007: 90–91); in this respect, Max Weber's interpretation of ascetic Protestantism as a catalyst for capitalist entrepreneurship remains central. In advanced capitalism, however, the influence of genuine religious motivations on entrepreneurship is much more uncertain, as Weber himself had emphasised. Contemporary researchers analysing the motives of nascent entrepreneurs, too, found it difficult to differentiate between genuinely religious motivations and other motivations (Dodd and Gotsis 2007).

Robert Merton's classic analysis of the concept of 'anomie' (Merton 1968: 127–128) offers an alternative starting point from which to explore the socio-cultural background of entrepreneurship in advanced capitalism. According to Merton's model, individuals find themselves in anomic situations if they lack access to the legitimate means of reaching institutionalised social goals. Since they share these goals, they have no choice but to opt to use illegitimate means to achieve them, or at least to pursue their goals around the edges of the law (the pattern of 'innovation'). Merton's analysis focuses on 'deviance' in the sense of illegal behaviour. However, the 'innovation' pattern can be extended also to deviant behaviour in an economic sense: entrepreneurship as discussed above. Just as Merton's innovative actor cannot succeed without breaking or creatively re-interpreting the law, the entrepreneur cannot advance and achieve his or her aim of profit without disrupting or creatively re-arranging given economic routines.

According to Merton's model, the supreme social goal in capitalist societies is financial wealth. A conflict between the goal and the available means will surely not occur at the level of the top rich, the elites and the upper middle classes. Here, neither the goal nor the access to means appear problematic; thus, 'conformity' in Merton's sense seems to be the most likely pattern. Innovation as a pattern of economic action is equally unlikely to emerge at the bottom of the class dichotomy, that is, on the level of the socially marginalised and the lower strata of the working class. Though they experience the double-bind of capitalist class relations, the members of the underclass are hardly susceptible to the illusion of social advance, 'ritualism' 'retreat', or 'rebellion' being the most likely patterns. People in traditional working class milieus, too, usually do not see realistic options to solve the means–end conflict individually. Rather, they tend to develop a defensive stance about their interests, which they try to pursue collectively.

By contrast, middle-class individuals, including not only the self-employed, but also white-collar and qualified blue-collar workers, tend to view their personal chances in a more positive light. To bridge the gap between ambitious personal objectives and limited resources, they are more inclined towards 'innovative' ways of adaptation. This does not only include an extraordinary work ethic, but also ambitious styles of consumption enacted by social climbers trying to anticipate the social status they are striving after (McCracken 1988; Calder 1999; Deutschmann 2012b). The pattern of economic innovation is most likely to occur in the middle and lower middle classes, which include immigrants striving for social integration and success. This conclusion is in line with the above-cited quantitative findings of Lippman and colleagues (2005) about the correlation between social inequality and entrepreneurship. While the inconsistency between goals and accessible means is felt most clearly in the middle layers of society, the confidence in one's own capabilities to overcome social barriers tends to be high enough. This conforms with the empirical observation that entrepreneurs – as a rule – do not come from the lower working classes. Self-recruitment notwithstanding, entrepreneurs often have a petty-bourgeois or middle-class background (Sombart 1955[1902]: 19–20; Bendix and Howton 1978; Kaelble 1978, 1983; Berghoff 2004; Mokyr and Voth 2010: 28–29). Moreover, as mentioned above, the entrepreneur is not necessarily a self-employed person. He or she can be also an 'intrapreneur', building their career on innovative performances in their job as an employee, and advancing in internal, vocational or project labour markets (Kanter 2000; Marsden 1999; Voss and Pongratz 1998). Even employees, who have abandoned the goal of upward mobility for themselves, may put their hopes on the success of their children. This corresponds to the phenomenon of the *embourgeoisement* of the working class after the Second World War, which had been a key theme of industrial sociology in the 1960s and 1970s (for the United Kingdom, see Goldthorpe et al. 1968; for Germany, see Mooser 1983). As Schumpeter had maintained, entrepreneurs are not a class, but a category of individuals motivated by the prospect of social advancement.

## Logic of action

The social framing of capitalist entrepreneurship varies considerably between regions, sectors, nations and cultures. The original ambiguity of the institutional constellation, however, cannot be neutralised completely on the level of cultural framings. Rather, it reproduces itself in an internal inconsistency in the frame itself. The entrepreneur is faced with a complex world of promises, chances and risks, which can almost never offer a guaranteed path to success. Uncertainty is a key characteristic not only of the situation of the entrepreneur, but also of the situation of the capital owner making investment decisions, be these investments in the form of loans or shares. While the entrepreneur usually needs an advance of capital or credit to finance his or her projects and thus will try to communicate his visions and plans in a promising light, the capital owner has to assess the chances that his or her capital will flow back with profit. How do economic actors actually cope with conditions of uncertainty, as they are prevalent in capitalist markets?

As argued above (Chapter 4), rational choice (RC) theories cannot be of great help here, as entrepreneurial action fails to meet the former's analytical premises. Neither is the actor fully aware about his or her own preferences, nor are the outcomes of potential action known and open to evaluation. The actor himself or herself is deeply involved in the perplexing, contradictory nature of the situation. He or she first has to disentangle himself or herself from the context and to come to a consistent definition of the situation as a precondition for developing an adequate strategy. RC concepts appear too narrow to understand and conceptualise such processes; instead, pragmatist concepts appear more promising (Beckert 2002; Lester and Piore 2004; Deutschmann 2009a, 2011a; Stark 2009). As noted above, this is not to deny the relevance of RC theories in general. However, RC theories cannot be applied to the innovative process as a whole, but only to its final stage, with a stable and socially accepted definition of the situation and clearly articulated options for action already having been achieved.

According to Schumpeter (1991 [1947]: 411), entrepreneurs need to act 'creatively', not only 'adaptively'. What does that mean exactly? To enter the market, the entrepreneur first has to build his or her 'niche' (White 2005), that is, a unique profile of competencies, which can bring him or her as close as possible to the position of a (temporary) monopolist. If there is a 'logic' to the process of building niches, it is not one of rational choice but of 'enquiry', to use John Dewey's (1938) terminology (as cited above in Chapter 4). The actor will 'test' different possible definitions of the situation by comparing himself or herself with the competition; only gradually will he or she be able to establish a consistent position in the market that will allow him or her to take part in the competitive process. The entrepreneur does not simply exploit the chances given to him or her in the given situation; what happens, rather, is a process of *mutual adaptation* between the actors, their situation and their perceptions. In practice, this means a tough contest between rival projects, challengers and incumbents, often carried out with means at the edge of or even beyond the law and ending with the elimination of not a few of the players (Welskopp 2017). The common view of markets being guided by rules of competition is not very convincing, since it does not take account of the emergence of new market players, which is hardly governed by any rules except for the Darwinist principle of the survival of the fittest. The very notion of competition would make little sense if competition were to be perfect. Price competition hardly offers a sufficient basis for new players to succeed in the market. Their products must be also qualitatively different – qualities which need to be discovered and tested in prior processes of niche-building. Product idiosyncrasies give rise to market imperfections and information asymmetries, which in the case of success can be exploited by the producers to gain an edge over their competitors (Thielemann 2010: 167). Not only the products, but also the underlying skills and organisational capabilities of the producing firm need to be unique in some way (Teece et al. 1997; Teece 2009). The reality of markets, thus, is characterised not simply by competition, but by a mixture between monopoly and competition, 'monopolistic competition', as Edward Chamberlin (1956 [1933]) has put it.

While it might be possible to manage a *given* set of niches in a rational way, the emergence of a *new* niche creates a situation that cannot be anticipated by any of the participants. Niches are, as White (1981) has shown, relational phenomena, as the position of every actor in a given market depends on his or her relations to all other market actors. Hence, the building of a new niche tends to change the entire set of relations between the participants, thus invalidating the very basis of *ex ante* calculations. The niche or monopoly that the entrepreneur is striving to establish might not necessarily come from economic innovation; it may also come from social innovation in a wider sense, such as from exploiting personal contacts and network 'holes' (Burt 2000), or from inconsistencies in institutional regulations (Streeck 2011). In his analysis of the careers of the very rich of his time, C. Wright Mills concluded that these careers could be characterised neither as bureaucratic nor as entrepreneurial; rather, the key to success had been the accumulation of personal advantages (Mills 1957: 114). The entrepreneurial promotion of new combinations is not a game determined by rules of fairness and economic rationality, but is the outcome of struggles aiming to build niches and monopoly positions.

Richard Lester and Michael Piore and David Stark have highlighted niche-building processes in illuminating case studies (Lester and Piore 2004; Stark 2005; see also Ruef 2005). As the authors argue, innovation does not fit into the conventional analytical management approach of presupposing a given problem definition and allowing for a rationally ordered sequence of solution steps. Rather, it is an activity directed towards finding solutions for problems which are still unknown. Consumer wants, for example, are not treated simply as a given, but as developing in a process of 'joint discovery' between supplier and customer (Lester and Piore 2004: 78). The suppliers are not faced with a clear-cut task, but with contradictory expectations, such as the website designers in one of Stark's case studies who had to serve the wants of their customers and to re-interpret them at the same time. Hence, suppliers have to move permanently between contradictory criteria of relevance. The search for the unknown is based on an interpretive assessment of diverse fields of knowledge, with 'interpretation', not 'analysis', being the dominant mode of proceeding. Entrepreneurship is 'the ability to keep multiple evaluative principles in play and to exploit the resulting frictions of their interplay' (Stark 2009: 15).

In the first stages of the innovative process, risks are incalculable, as are potential profits. Competition will concentrate on the qualitative dimensions of products. If the niche-building is successful, and the new product gets established in the market, the risks tend to diminish and to become calculable; with intensifying price competition, however, profits will dwindle too. In the final phase of the product cycle, the product will reach its highest level of sophistication. At the same time, competition is likely to become 'perfect', transparent and calculable, with the consequence, however, of profits beginning to vanish (see also Deutschmann 2008: 72–73).

## Logic of aggregation

Innovation is a genuinely individual capacity, as I argued above in agreement with Dewey (1938). It is only the individual – not groups or organisations – that, due to his or her simultaneous presence in the symbolic as well as in the physical world, can become creative in the sense of generating something genuinely new *in practice*. Only creative individual action can intentionally surmount technical and social routines. However, were innovation to exhaust itself in idiosyncratic actions of individuals, it would indeed end up in collective anomie, as Merton (1968) argued. By building his niche, the innovator strives to consolidate his or her own position at the price of generating uncertainty for others. This dilemma can be managed only if innovation becomes communicated and institutionalised in a dynamic way. Innovation is always a social process, which, though being based on creative individual action, depends also on communication and cooperation (Kanter 2000; Dopfer 2006). Social skills (Fligstein 2001) that one can use to find financiers, partners and customers are vital. Not all entrepreneurs are genuine innovators: many prefer to jump on running trains or drive in a convoy. As the vast research literature on innovation has shown, the diffusion of innovations is communicatively framed in various spatial, social and temporal ways. These frames reduce the complexity of entrepreneurial and investment decisions to a degree that makes coordinated action possible. Here, I am focusing on the communicative frames that arise in the innovative process itself, which are to be distinguished from pre-existing institutional frames, which I discussed above in this chapter.

Innovations always start with process or product inventions; however, it is a long way from inventions to new products and technologies actually finding resonance in the market and entering into customers' daily routines. At its initial stages, the development prospects of the original invention, including its potential uses and applications, are largely unpredictable (Nye 2004). The actual path of the innovation depends on conditions emerging in the process itself, in particular in the communication of the invention, the mobilisation of relevant actors in diverse social arenas, and the cooperative networks between these actors. To conceptualise the communication of innovations, the concept of 'technological paradigm' (Dosi 1982, 1988; Choi 1993; Bijker 1995; Peine 2006) and the concept of 'vision' (Dierkes et al. 1996; Rammert 2000; Nye 2004; Sturken et al. 2004) have become common topics in the literature. With the concept of 'technological paradigm, the authors refer to the well-known work of Thomas Kuhn, suggesting that the logic of scientific paradigms described by Kuhn can be applied to the development of economic innovations. 'Paradigms' are composed of a real and a symbolic element. The real element is an artefact representing a prototypical solution to a technical or logistical problem and bearing the potential for further improvement. The first prototype of a fast-running petrol engine constructed by Gottlieb Daimler, which is displayed in the Mercedes-Benz-Museum in Stuttgart, may serve as a prominent example of this. The symbolic element is 'a set of heuristics – "Where do we go from there?" "Where should we research?" "On what sort of knowledge should we draw?"' (Dosi 1988: 224). In the case of the Daimler engine, the symbolic element is represented by the Mercedes star, which indicates the sucessful use of the company's engines on earth, on water and in the air. Paradigms are projections which link the present with the future, give direction to the search for the 'new', and enable and motivate cooperation between producers in heterogeneous fields, thus securing the 'social embedding' (Halfmann 1997) of the innovative process.

To make the innovation a success, however, cooperation between researchers, experts and producers is a necessary but not a sufficient condition. In order to 'valorise' the innovation (Canzler and Marz 2011) and to secure its acceptance in the market, communication with the larger milieu of potential users and customers is vital too. To circumscribe the symbolic framing of larger market communication, the concept of 'vision' has become popular. 'Visions' are narratives about the new product emerging in the early stages of the innovative process; they may be generated intentionally by the producers themselves, or by third parties such as scientists, journalists, intellectuals or writers. Visions depict an imaginary future of the new technology and new life-worlds associated with it (such as the 'information society' around the internet, or the 'green' mobility associated with electric cars), presenting these future worlds as desirable or inevitable. These projections do not have the status of objective predictions but rely on their performative effects:[5] 'As public relations people are well aware, when investors and consumers believe such stories, they can become self-fulfilling' (Nye 2004: 160). If the feedback between paradigms and visions becomes successful in the sense of convincing a critical mass of actors about the promises of the new technology, a 'path' of innovation will be generated (Garud and Karnoe 2001; Beckert 2016).

To safeguard the continuity of innovative dynamics, visions and myths need to be continuously created anew. No single vision can represent the entire potential of human creativity; thus visions tend to exhaust themselves in the process of their implementation, thereby giving room for the emergence of new ones. In the literature, various phase models of the innovative cycle have been developed (Anderson and Tushman 1990; Tolbert and Zucker 1996; Rammert 2000; Freeman and Louca 2001; Schreyögg et al. 2003; Meyer and Schubert 2007; for the field of finance, see Kraemer 2016). Summing up these models, four stylised phases can be distinguished. The first is the phase of *path creation* (Garud and Karnoe 2001; Windeler 2003), where the basic discoveries are made and corresponding new visions and paradigms are developed. Visions and utopias, giving meaning to the invention and showing ways to explore its potential, play a crucial role in this phase. The personal creativity of inventors and entrepreneurs is equally important, as is their ability to win the cooperation of other relevant actors. The risks of the project are high in this phase, as are the potential gains.

If the pioneers are successful in winning over a critical mass of partners, motivating them to believe in and to invest in the paradigm, the second phase of *path consolidation* begins. This phase is characterised by the self-reinforcing positive feedback effects of the initial paradigm. To join the train now appears promising no longer only for insiders, but for larger circles of investors. With more actors joining and investing, a snowball effect of further opportunity develops. What first appeared as a risky speculation can now become a realistic project due to the cumulative effects of cooperative efforts and investments. An increasing variety of applications of the basic invention are being developed, which gives rise to a lasting market expansion (for the case of electricity, see Nye 2004).

The third phase is that of *institutionalisation*, where the paradigm gets established as a general technological standard. The technology or product now has become widespread, and has reached a high degree of sophistication and reliability; at the same time, it has largely lost its original innovative aura. Competition shifts from the level of product quality to that of price and cost. Further improvements are largely confined to cosmetic refinements; the market has become largely transparent and calculable; and profits have started to dwindle.

The fourth and final phase is that of *lock-in*, where the potential of the original invention reaches its exhaustion; any further development seems to be blocked, and market competition increasingly becomes ruinous. This is the phase of crisis, which however bears the potential of generating a new path. What appears as a dead end for the majority of actors can be perceived by some as a chance to come up with new ideas. Thus, the possibility of a new cycle arises.

Innovations occur in all fields of the economy from finance to technology and from production to organisation and consumption. At the same time, they differ considerably in their reach: Christopher Freeman and Carlota Perez distinguish between 'incremental innovations', 'radical innovations', 'changes in the technology system' and 'changes in the techno-economic paradigm' (Freeman and Perez 1988). Whereas the impact of incremental innovations is confined to the local or to the firm level, radical innovations and changes in the technology system give rise to industry- and sector-level structural changes. Changes in the techno-economic paradigm are governed by so-called 'meta-paradigms', which can transform the structure of the entire economy. Not only is the economy in a narrow sense involved in such big transformations, but so is the larger frame of social institutions, including industrial relations, education, science, politics and law. New meta-paradigms are associated with overall changes in 'regimes' or 'spirits' (Boltanski and Chiapello 2007) of capitalism. Drawing largely on Nikolai

Kontratieff's theory of long waves, Christopher Freeman and Francisco Louca identify five such 'meta-paradigms' and corresponding ages in the history of capitalism: (1) the age of cotton, iron, and water power, starting with the British Industrial Revolution in the late eighteenth century; (2) the age of iron railways, steam power and mechanisation; (3) the age of steel, heavy engineering and electrification; (4) the age of oil, automobiles, motorisation and mass production; and (5) the contemporary age of information and communication technology (Freeman and Louca 2001).

As mentioned above, the success of innovative paradigms can never be calculated in advance, but depends on experiences emerging in the process itself and on the response of actors to these experiences. As a result, new cooperative relationships between inventors, customers and financiers, which help to implement the project, may develop (or not). As entrepreneurs need to finance their projects, new visions and paradigms cannot be successful without financial promotion, be it by shareholders, credit issuers or business angels. Again, the key relevance of credit becomes evident here. To be continued, capitalist dynamics requires a permanent inflow of additional credit-financed demand motivated by the visions and profit expectations associated with innovations. Without such an inflow, the system will stagnate and recede, though it is not the inflow of credit *alone* that keeps the system moving. The point is that capitalist growth depends on relating *different* kinds of contingencies to each other: the contingencies of entrepreneurial creativity, socially mediated by the circulation of economic myths, on the one hand, and the contingencies of credit, on the other.[6] The positive response that myths may find in the markets (or not) will ultimately ratify the original investment decisions and make the economy grow (or not); failure can be due to conditions on the financial as well as on the non-financial side. There is no inherent drive towards any state of equilibrium between these financial and non-financial contingencies: like a bicycle, the capitalist system can only move forward or fall over.

## Structural background of financialisation[7]

The approach I have developed so far can be summarised in five propositions. First, capitalist dynamics go back to the performative, self-fulfilling effects of innovation myths and the parallel expansion of credit. Second, the social force behind the generation of myths are entrepreneurs striving to build up niches to consolidate their market positions. Third, the quest of entrepreneurs for market success and social advance in turn is structurally based in the double-bind of capitalist class relations, which are collectively closed and individually open at the same time. Fourth, the social perception of the double bind of the class dichotomy as an incentive for social advancement tends to be most pronounced in the intermediate social layers of society, in particular the lower middle classes. Fifth, by working hard and running up debts for their social advancement, entrepreneurs are developing innovative ways of social adaptation. Successful innovation, in turn, will secure the profitability of the capital and, with it, the social position of the wealthy classes. The collective success of innovations is the precondition for making the economy grow as a whole, while the individual success of entrepreneurial projects can never be guaranteed in advance.

The ideal constellation for a capitalist system to flourish, then, would be a dichotomous, but socially open distribution of wealth, on the one hand, and a growing population with masses of young and poor but ambitious social climbers, on the other. Such conditions indeed have occurred repeatedly in the history of modern capitalism, such as in Britain during the Industrial Revolution, in the United States with its continuous waves of immigration during the nineteenth and early twentieth centuries, in the West German 'economic miracle' after the Second World War, and today perhaps in China, India, South Africa and Brazil and other emerging countries. Nevertheless, it would be naïve to assume that this is the normal case, and that there is something like a built-in equilibrium in capitalist growth. Indeed, there is no ideal path of smooth development, but only, as I am going to argue now, a basic dilemma, which capitalist dynamics muddles through: on the one hand, growth will be hampered by a stagnating or decreasing population, or by a socially closed class structure allowing for *too little* upward mobility. On the other hand, *too much* upward mobility will be detrimental to growth as well.

An ageing and decreasing population, as it is to be observed today in many advanced capitalist countries, will result in a relative or absolute decline in the social reservoirs of entrepreneurship. Capitalist growth presupposes a growing population and large *young* cohorts, as entrepreneurial mentalities are a privilege of the young developing plans for their life and striving for success and social advancement. As entrepreneurship is highly concentrated in young cohorts (Kelley et al. 2011: 32), an ageing population will have a negative effect on growth. Entrepreneurship, however, can be blocked not only by demographic factors, but also by rigidly closed social class structures demotivating social climbers, such as it had been the case in the semi-feudal property relationships prevailing for a long time in Latin America and many other emerging countries. If nascent entrepreneurs do not get social support, or even meet resistance due to political corruption, social discrimination, or despotic political power structures, the growth potential will be hampered in a two-fold way. On the one hand, entrepreneurs will be discouraged and deprived from vital means and resources, such as access to education, network support, and credit, with the likely consequences of resignation or political conflict, but, on the other hand, the privileged will be protected against competition and feel even less motivated to engage in innovative activities.

At the same time, however, growth is not likely to sustain itself, should *too many* people be successful in social advancement. If the capitalist growth machine is working efficiently, the result will be an upward shift in the social structure, that is, a relative expansion of the elites and higher middle classes at the cost of the lower classes. Indeed, this is what seems to have happened in the mature economies of Western Europe, North America and Japan in the second half of the twentieth century. As a consequence of the social 'elevator effect', as Ulrich Beck (1986: 122) characterised the shift, economic growth rates too went up initially. At the same time, however, the structural tension between the classes diminished and the incentive structure for entrepreneurial advancement eroded. The financial rentier became progressively dominant over the entrepreneur. On the one hand, the elevator effect made the rich layers of society grow. Even the upper middle classes – the 'patrimonial middle classes', as Thomas Piketty (2014) termed them – accumulated substantial amounts of financial wealth, let alone the top rich, whose wealth grew to unprecedented levels. The volume of rent-seeking assets soared accordingly, paving the way for mutual funds, pension funds, and investment banks to serve the needs of a larger and larger clientele. However, financial assets always depend on debts as their necessary counterpart, with the value of assets depending precisely on the availability of solvent debtors servicing the claims of capital. Due to the elevator effect, the social reservoir of potential debtors coming from the lower classes and still being eager to advance and to run debts for their career shrunk. And this effect was exacerbated by the stagnation or decline of the population. Moreover, the chances of subsequent climbers deteriorated, as the intergenerational transmission of fortunes cemented the financial and educational privileges of earlier climbers and their offspring. For those not belonging to the privileged networks and lacking access to credit, resources and education, their chances dwindled. Nascent real economy entrepreneurs, when they asked banks for credit, often could not compete with the apparently superior profitability of financial investments. At the same time, firm-internal entrepreneurs felt frustrated by the tough cost regime and the short-term profit targets characteristic of financialised firms. As a consequence, the gospel of social advancement, and, with it, of growth, lost its credibility even for many qualified young entrepreneurs (Blossfeld et al. 2005).

The descendants of the successful may still be career-oriented, but they no longer have a stringent motive for entering into the hazards of a genuinely *entrepreneurial* career; instead, they are likely to prefer careers in organisations or public bureaucracies. Higher education indeed is becoming an increasingly important precondition for qualifying employees and entrepreneurs for the innovative process. However, it does not necessarily pave the way to more genuine entrepreneurship, as it also opens ways to alternative, more comfortable elite positions without real entrepreneurial responsibility. In short, it is the very success of the capitalist growth machine that reveals itself in the collective upward trend of social mobility. However, the social elevator effect tends to create a structural imbalance in the capital markets, as a growing volume of financial assets meets less and less debtors servicing the claims of capital. Thus, the conditions required for sustained growth are progressively undermined.

A possible countervailing factor against structural upward mobility is immigration, which, indeed, seems to have mitigated the dilemma in some cases, for example in the United States in the nineteenth century. With constantly arriving immigrants filling in the shrinking lower layers of the host society, the detrimental economic effects of structural upward mobility on growth could be counterbalanced. It seems, however, premature to expect a simple repetition of the American experiences of the nineteenth century in contemporary advanced capitalist economies. To enter into entrepreneurial careers, migrants today need to command advanced levels of general, professional and cultural skills – a condition, which present-day immigrants coming from poor backgrounds cannot fulfil. The share of nascent entrepreneurs, indeed, tends to be higher amongst immigrants than amongst natives. However, immigrant entrepreneurship is largely confined to certain segments of the economy already overcrowded, such as gastronomy, import–export and trade, and personal services. Immigrant entrepreneurs are largely absent in more sophisticated areas, such as software and digital technologies (OECD 2013). At the same time, international competition in the fields of qualified employment and 'high-potential' careers is tough. Thus, one should not expect too much from immigrant entrepreneurs rejuvenating the shrinking potentials of domestic entrepreneurship in present-day advanced capitalist economies. As the GEM surveys have shown, the level of early-stage entrepreneurial activity as well as the social attractiveness of the entrepreneurial role is much lower in mature capitalist economies than in emerging economies.[8] The authors of the report make the following conclusion:

> In the wealthier economies, with relatively good infrastructure, education and other basic and efficiency factors, shaping attitudes may be more critical because entrepreneurs are more likely to enter this role because of choice. At the same time, with status rated higher than perceptions about entrepreneurship as a career, it appears that people in these economies may admire entrepreneurs more than they want to become one.
>
> (Kelley et al. 2011: 21)

While non-financial entrepreneurship and real growth are declining, financial entrepreneurship and wealth are on the rise. What is developing, then, is a mismatch between the growing volume of financial assets, on the one hand, and declining non-financial investment opportunities, on the other. Financial innovators are trying to fill in the gap by inventing new outlets for idle financial capital, investing capital no longer directly into shares and credit, but into 'bets' on the price development of other financial titles, such as derivatives, securitisations and swaps. Capital is no longer mediating the contingencies of real entrepreneurship, but is switching towards a self-referential mode of operation driven by ever-increasing financial leverage. Indeed, this seems to have happened since the last decades of the twentieth century, particularly in the advanced capitalist economies.[9] Key developments were a tremendous nominal increase of financial wealth; an exploding circulation of new financial products; the rising power of shareholders at the corporate level, and a secular shift in capitalist dynamics towards 'financialisation' (Windolf 2005; Epstein 2005; Krippner 2005; Reinhart and Rogoff 2009; Lounsbury and Hirsch 2010; Deutschmann 2011b; Heires and Nölke 2014; Kornrich and Hicks 2015). As we know, many of the financial innovations did not prove sustainable and ended up being wiped out in the crash of 2008–2009. Central banks and nation-states had to intervene with historically unprecedented rescue packages to avoid the imminent collapse of the global economy. Only by continuing policies of quantitative easing (QE), flooding the banking system with liquidity, and lowering not only real but even nominal interest rates below zero, did they manage to maintain a state of precarious stabilisation. This is the status quo up to the present day; nobody knows how long it can continue.

To conclude, present-day advanced capitalist economies seem to be exposed to the second horn of the dilemma mentioned above, that is, the consequences of too many people having advanced socially in the past. A capitalist system, however, can never content itself with its own success, and cannot reach a stable state of general affluence; rather, it is bound to restore the polarisation of capital and labour, of wealth and poverty, continuously anew as a precondition for mobilising new dynamic forces. Capitalism mobilises people by promising affluence for everybody. However, should the majority of social climbers actually reach the sanctuary of the American Dream at the top of the hill – to take up again Arlie Hochschild's above-mentioned metaphor – the dream will vanish. Crisis will set in, as there will be no longer enough debtors to service the claims of capital. Indeed, since the late twentieth century the advanced capitalist countries have experienced increasingly severe crises, which have led to a marked resurgence in unemployment and social inequality. In the United States, Britain and other European countries, a tiny and extremely rich new financial aristocracy, monopolising financial wealth as well as controlling education, politics and media, has emerged (Haseler 2001; Philipps 2003; Hertz 2006; Murray 2012; Piketty 2014; Sayer 2015). At the same time, real growth has continued to decrease, as has social upward mobility (Byrne 2005; Grabka and Frick 2008). The move back to the first horn of the dilemma seems to have begun already. However, to fully restore the polarisation of capital and labour, a major global crash wiping out the still huge amount of ailing assets hidden in bank balances would have to occur. Keeping the traumatic experiences of the 1930s still in mind, central banks and nation-states, however, seem to be utterly determined to prevent such a crash. Though the present QE policies of central banks and nominally negative interest rates may prevent a marked downturn of the economy, they cannot make it grow either. Stagnation, however, means a permanent crisis which is likely to stir up not only social polarisations, but also ethnic and national particularisms. The key problem with capitalism is that it is incapable of putting its own success on a sustainable footing.

## Notes

1 This applies also to evolutionary economic approaches, as it focuses on the identification of *general* mechanisms of economic evolution, thereby drawing on Darwinist models of natural selection (e.g. Nelson and Winter 1982; for an overview, see Witt 2006). The problem with these approaches is not only their lack of historical specification, but also their susceptibility to naturalistic analogies. Evolutionary economists seem to show little understanding of the intentional and symbolically based nature of human action.

2 James Coleman and Hartmut Esser combine their versions of the DMA approach with an RC concept of action. However, as the fruitfulness of DMA does not depend crucially on linking it with an RC concept, I will not follow Coleman and Esser on this point.

3 As it is well known, however, the actual employment pattern in industrialised countries is still far away from being gender-neutral, as women continue to be overrepresented in the lower and middle layers of the employment system, particularly in public service and part-time jobs. So far, the traditional gender arrangement has remained intact tacitly, and thus Schumpeter's dire predictions have not fully come to pass.

4 'Men and women were both disproportionately likely to form same-sex teams, comparing to their underlying distribution in the population of nascent entrepreneurs. They also found a pronounced tendency for co-ethnics to join together, rather than forming teams across ethnic lines, and for occupational homophily' (Aldrich 2005: 461).
5 In an earlier work (Deutschmann 2008: 55–56), I suggested the concept of 'economic myths' to circumscribe the performative effects of innovative visions, referring to the concept of 'rationality myths' developed by the neo-institutionalist school in organisational sociology (John Meyer, Brian Rowan, Paul DiMaggio, Walter Powell). In a similar vein, Jens Beckert (2016: 173) speaks of 'fictional expectations' to circumscribe the driving forces of innovative processes.
6 This also marks the difference between growth and mere speculation, where the contingency of credit is arranged in a self-referential way.
7 This section contains a summary of the argument, which I have presented more extensively in earlier publications (see Deutschmann 2009, 2011a, 2011b).
8 Total early entrepreneurship (TEA), indicating the ratio of persons engaged in founding and managing new enterprises to active workforce, amounted in 2013 to an average of 21.4 percent in developing economies, 14.4 percent in emerging economies, and only 7.9 percent in mature economies (GEM 2014).
9 According to analyses performed by the McKinsey Global Institute, global financial depth (ratio of total financial assets to GDP) rose from 256 percent in 1995 to 355 percent in 2007. In the advanced economies (United States, Japan, Western Europe), financial depth was significantly above the global average. Almost two-thirds (62 percent) of the overall increase in financial depth was due to rising equity market valuations and the growing leverage and size of the financial sector itself. Only 28 percent went back to the financing of households and corporations (McKinsey 2013: 17).

# 10 Conclusions

Almost no approach has been more successful in shaping recent discourses in economic sociology than the concept of 'socially embedded' economic action coined by Karl Polanyi (1944) and Mark Granovetter (1985). In her opening remarks to a Polanyi symposium held in 2002, Greta Krippner pointed to some paradoxical consequences of the use of the concept. As she argued, the focus on 'social' factors enabling market transactions, such as political institutions, networks, or trust, had the implicit consequence of 'preserving intact the asocial market construct' (Krippner 2004: 111). Contrary to its own critique of the self-misunderstanding of neoclassical economics as a kind of 'physical' science (Mirowski 1989), economic sociology still seems to have no serious intention of entering into an analysis of private property as such (i.e. apart from organisations, networks, trust, and so on) as the core institution of markets. As an involuntary consequence of the embeddedness perspective, economic sociology helped to preserve the neoclassical view of the economy as a sphere of 'instrumental', 'utilitarian' and 'material' calculations.

As one could add to Krippner's point, another conceptual implication of embeddedness lies in a parochial or – at least – a nation-state-focused understanding of society. If the presence of society in markets exhausts itself in the influence of locally based social norms, network ties or – at most – national political institutions, the underlying concept of society cannot be anything but a particularistic one. Certainly, the embeddedness concept has opened up new views on the local complexity of market transactions. What has been lost from sight, however, is the *universal* dimension of markets, which stretch across local and national borders and which connects actors with each other at the global level. Without a doubt, economic sociology has profited much from social anthropology with its focus on economic transactions in and between the small communities of primitive societies. However, the countervailing perspective of universal history, with its view on societies developing encompassing forms of communication and intercourse, should not be neglected either. 'Society' should not be understood merely as an *aggregate* of locally based socio-culturally integrated communities, but as a system that develops its identity from 'within', aiming at the 'world-society' as its ultimate horizon. In their widely renowned theories of 'axial civilisations', Karl Jaspers (1949) and Shmuel Eisenstadt (1986) have highlighted the role of religions in constructing such universal forms of human interdependence. However, it is not only religions, but also markets that should be considered in this context. It has been the main intention of this study to elaborate the character of disembedded markets as a universal form of sociality – a form which by no means is alien to the universality of religions, but which continues it and even surpasses it.

There is no need here to recapitulate the well-known contributions of Max Weber to the sociology of religion and his analysis of ascetic Protestantism as a pacemaker for capitalism. The rise of global capitalism was certainly no historical accident, with the latter falling from heaven and becoming at odds with the basic principles of the human condition. To the contrary, the society of global capitalism embodies in some sense the very universalistic legacy which the critics of capitalism refer to themselves: the liberal idea of civil society, which – certainly not without reason – has been interpreted as a secularised version of the Christian idea of human universality. Today's global capitalism goes back to the intellectual heritage of the market narrative invented by eighteenth-century Scottish moral philosophers, and it can be interpreted as a consequence of its overwhelming success. The spread of markets and the market narrative around the world, and into all dimensions of society, achieved something that not only Christianity but also Islam have striven for in vain: the creation of a truly global society encompassing all nations, religions and civilisations. Any critique of capitalism that is based on a 'disavowal' (Konings 2015: 90) of this legacy misses the point. What is required, rather, are careful historical reconstructions of the process in which the market narrative became turned into practice and of the unanticipated consequences occurring in that process. The liberal utopia, like any great social vision, cannot be expected to manifest itself on a one-to-one basis when becoming a force of real social transformation. Benjamin Nelson states the following at the end of his analysis of the historical transformations of the Mosaic prescriptions about usury:

> The road from clan comradeship to universal society is beset with hazards. When two communities merge and two sets of others become one set of brothers, a price is generally paid. The price … is an attenuation of the love, which had held each set together. It is a tragedy of moral history that the expansion of the area of the moral community has ordinarily been gained through the sacrifice of the intensity of the moral bond, or, to recall the refrain of this sketch, that all men have become brothers by becoming equally others.
>
> (Nelson 1969: 136)

Indeed, universal 'otherhood' would seem to be the price for mankind becoming a single coherent society. As I have argued in this book, 'otherhood should not be equated with immorality. Even disembedded and self-regulated markets are clearly *social* systems, not natural or technical ones. They are based on the institution of private property, the medium of money; they are governed by the 'abstract' and culturally indifferent norm of personal liability. The characteristics of this system were analysed from two perspectives: disembedded markets as a universal social system and as an interface between society and its non-social environments. Moreover, I have discussed the epistemological problems arising from such conceptualisations.

As a universal social system, markets stand above civilisations, nations and local communities; in this respect, their role can be compared with the encompassing hegemony of institutionally specialised religion over society in the 'axial' civilisations.[1] At the same time, disembedded markets are not self-sufficient (again similar to institutionally specialised religion), as they depend on their coexistence with morally more inclusive institutions and social structures, the reach of the latter being, however, confined to the regional, national or local levels. These institutions and structures do not simply 'embed' markets, as they are in their turn 'embedded' into the more encompassing system of global markets. As I have argued throughout the book, this relationship of bilateral 'embeddedness' is not a harmonious, but a contradictory and potentially antagonistic one. The very social structures securing the quality and reliability of economic transactions at the regional and local levels are being undermined and disrupted by the forces of transnational competition. The vicious circle evolving here may end up in a militant revival of local religious or national identities, which can be interpreted as an involuntary reaction to the experience of global interconnectedness. Benjamin Barber has highlighted this dilemma with his model of 'Jihad vs. McWorld'. In a similar vein, Wolfgang Streeck spoke of a self-destructive interaction between 'Durkheimian' and 'Williamsonian' institutions. Most recently, Pankaj Mishra characterised the revolt of those excluded from the capitalist promises of freedom and prosperity as a mobilisation of *ressentiment* (Mishra 2017: 159). These approaches promise to throw light on present-day social and political conflicts, as well as on unsettled controversies in the globalisation debate. Obviously, global "otherhood" alone cannot offer a viable model of society, as men cannot live in a world consisting solely of markets. In this sense, Polanyi certainly is right in his verdict over the liberal model as a 'stark utopia'. However, given the advanced level of present-day globalisation, his plea for political counter-movements aiming at a restoration of nationally controlled economies also appears to be 'utopian'.

Is there a way out of the vicious circles between global markets and local identities that aims at a state of at least peaceful coexistence between both? We may be able to find that way out if we turn to the second perspective on disembedded markets as an interface between society and its non-social environments. As a self-description of society, disembedded markets constitute the demarcation of society vis-à-vis the non-social, as I have tried to show. They do not only form society's perspective on itself, but also the interface of society with its non-social environments, including not only nature but also spiritual transcendence or the 'telic' system, as the late Talcott Parsons (1951) called it with reference to Robert Bellah. The disembedding of markets indeed has a lasting impact on the relationship of society with its non-social environments, as it constitutes a private property claim on nature as well as on the creative potential of work. It is neither possible nor necessary here to recapitulate the vast literature on the ecological impact of capitalism and on the devastations of the natural environment due to the application of capitalist technology. The focus here has been on the capitalist growth imperative, which is the main factor behind the expansion and disembedding of markets and behind significant environmental changes. As I have tried to show, capitalism can indeed be understood as a secularised version of Christian eschatology, as it strives to bring down paradise all the way down to the earth. No longer is the absolute perceived as a supreme and self-sufficient reality, but as a field to be explored and conquered in a this-worldly process of never-ending 'creative destruction'. To make the system move, and to promote the private exploitation of the creativity of work, ever-new economic visions need to be created and implemented. In this sense, capitalism has become an encompassing social reality governing individual actions not only by setting external constraints, but also by providing meaning and personal orientation. It is a system caught up in a never-ending drive to redeem its indebtedness to itself by moving into new territories. Despite its spectacular technical and material achievements, it can never manage to reach a stable state of tranquillity.

This does not mean that capitalist growth can go on infinitely. To the contrary, there are clear limits, which are due not only to the foreseeable stagnation and decline of the population, but to mounting ecological threats as well. A key problem lies also, as I have tried to show, in the endogenous deterioration of the socio-structural conditions of entrepreneurship built into the macro–micro feedback loops of capitalist growth. What destabilises capitalism as a social order is its very success in promoting market-based social advancement. The promise of wealth makes people strive for social advancement, affluence and success. For decades, liberal and social-democratic parties have successfully propagated equality of social chances as a key receipt for social integration, and they continue to do so. However, what would happen if these promises materialised on a large scale? Social integration in capitalism depends on growth, and growth depends on the structural tensions created by the polarisation of classes. With continuing structural upward mobility, and expanding middle and upper classes, these tensions, and incentives for subsequent entrepreneurs to arise, will diminish. The class polarisation will become top-heavy, with an increasing accumulation of financial wealth at the top and declining chances for those at the bottom. The class structure will cease to function as an incentive structure for social advancement, and, hence, for growth. The present-day phenomenon of 'financialisation' in the advanced industrial economies can be understood from this background. The decoupling of the financial sector from real entrepreneurship means a state of permanent crisis, which in turn can become a factor fuelling the vicious circle between global markets and local identities.

Thus, capitalism seems to be exposed not only to one but two 'vicious circles', in the sense of the very expansionary drive of markets that gives rise to countervailing, self-undermining forces. The territorial universalisation of markets provokes countervailing forces that strengthen collective identities at the national and local levels, and the innovative dynamics of capitalism tend to undermine the social foundations of entrepreneurship. There is some evidence that the two antagonistic circles do not operate in isolation from each other but are intertwined, as had been observed already by Max Weber: 'As a rule, time periods and countries dominated by "pure" class conditions are also characterized by economic roll over, while any slow-down of economic transformations will result in an immediate revival of status ties, and a restauration of social "honour"' (Weber 1972: 539, my translation). The present-day condition of capitalism seems to confirm the interconnectedness of the two vicious circles, as it is characterised by an exhaustion of the innovative circle and an escalation of national and cultural antagonisms *at the same time*. Joseph Schumpeter's pessimistic predictions about the future of capitalism and entrepreneurship seem to have found a late justification. At the same time, the idea Schumpeter played with – that nationally based state socialism could provide a way out – can be clearly ruled out today.

Again: is there a way out? Let me, at this point, come back again to Arlie Hochschild's above-cited (Chapter 9) metaphor about social climbers, which she extracted as a 'deep story' from her interviews with frustrated US middle-class workers and Tea Party followers in Louisiana:

> You are patiently standing in a long line leading up a hill, as in a pilgrimage. You are situated in the middle of this line, along with others who are also white, older, Christian, and predominantly male, some with college degrees, some not. Just over the brow of the hill is the American Dream, the goal of everyone waiting in line. Many in the back of the line are people of colour – poor, young and old, mainly without college degrees. It is scary to look back; there are so many behind you, and in principle you wish them well. Still, you've waited a long time, worked hard, and the line is barely moving. You deserve to move forward a little faster. You're patient, but weary. You focus ahead, especially on those at the very top of the hill. … Look! You see people *cutting in line ahead of you.* You're following the rules. They aren't. As they cut in, it feels like you are being moved back. How can they just do that? How are they? Some are black. Through affirmative action plans, pushed by the federal government, they are given preference for places in colleges and universities, apprenticeships, jobs, welfare payments and free lunches.
>
> (Hochschild 2016: 136–137)

Hochschild's deep story gives a concise reconstruction of the perceptions and motives underlying the eruption of racist and nationalist stereotypes amongst the white middle classes, which could be observed in the Tea Party movement and in the 2016 presidential campaign of Donald Trump. It is obvious, as she emphasises, that the mobilisation of such stereotypes cannot really help to solve the underlying social problems. However, the deep story involuntarily also shows us why the liberal strategy of social inclusion, which the author herself is advocating, cannot work either. Given the huge concentration of wealth on the top of the hill, the line will become only longer and larger, and it will slow down even more should everybody (irrespective of sex, race, religion, ethnicity, and so on) be enabled to join the line. The competition between the aspirants in the line will become all the more fierce and destructive.

Thus, if we stick to Hochschild's metaphor, the only way out of the dilemma would be questioning the agenda of the game itself: finding ways to flatten the hill, to put the sanctuary of the American Dream down to the earth and to make it accessible to everybody. What would this mean? At present, there is no lack of debate about the future of capitalism. Are we facing a possible 'end' of capitalism, as Streeck (2016) suggests? Should we enter into a new debate about socialist ideas (Wright 2010; Honneth 2015)? Sociology is not philosophy of history, and its competence to discuss such questions is limited. Still, many of the debates about a post-capitalist future are characterised by a narrow focus on the advanced economies. Apparently, they do not take the global character of capitalism seriously, as they are neglecting the fact that there are still many developing and emerging countries in Africa, in the Near and Middle East, and in Latin America suffering less from capitalism itself than from an *insufficient level* of capitalist development. For many of the problems of these countries, such as excessive population growth and poverty, no realistic solution seems to be available except some path to capitalist development, perhaps even the Chinese one. Thus, any debate about the future of capitalism should keep the differences between developing, emerging, and advanced countries in mind. For many of the developing and emerging countries, 'degrowth' is clearly not a formula for solving their problems in the near future.

The situation in the advanced economies is different. Here, the challenge is to think over the institutional shape of a society which continues to offer freedom and social opportunities at the individual level, *but must no longer grow as a collective*. It would be superficial to ascribe the capitalist growth imperative solely to excessive consumer wants or to greedy and egoistic personal habits, as a vast anti- and post-growth literature is doing. Sermons against egoism and consumerism alone will not suffice. What appears more promising is a debate about a society that consciously accepts its own mundane limitations and refrains from the demonic quest for the endless exploitation of human creativity. The point is not how to unfetter the 'productive forces' of society even more, as Marxists are arguing in accordance with liberals. To the contrary, it is vital to find ways to confine the forces of production in a socially legitimate and ecologically efficient way. The modern project of transferring the paradise to earth certainly cannot be cancelled. However, the project must be given a shape that takes account of the mundane and natural constraints of human life, and which puts an end to the *institutionalised imperative* of unceasing desires. There is no lack of general philosophical ideas about this; however, there is little clarity about the institutional and political implications of such a solution, which I am going to discuss now in my concluding remarks.

As I have argued above (Chapter 9), the logic of capitalist growth can be analysed sufficiently only within a multi-level approach that takes account of the shaping of social action by institutions and, in particular, by private property. The capitalist growth imperative has its institutional basis in the extension of private property rights to the conditions of production ('material disembedding'), with the material and human conditions of production constituting *separate* categories of ownership. It is this particular design of private property rights that gives rise to the need of capital to grow and to produce a separate yield for capital. In order to remove the growth imperative of capitalism, there would be no need to dismantle the market and the institution of private property altogether. What would be required, however, is a *different design of private property rights*, with the abolition of divided property rights over production and land as a key step in the design process. With stakeholders owning the means of production jointly, money-based property claims would no longer extend directly to the *potential* of labour, but only to its products or to pre-contractually defined personal services. This would not mean curbing human creativity; however, it would put an end to the capitalist *commodification* of creativity as the key driver of growth. With net revenues flowing to stakeholders in their entirety, there would be no need for profit and growth, though growth would nevertheless be possible. Given the consent of stakeholders, production could be continued under conditions of stagnation, and even under conditions of declining revenues.

Certainly, the distinction between capital and labour cannot be undone overnight. What makes sense, nevertheless, is a discussion about the legitimacy of attributing property rights over production to different social classes under advanced capitalist conditions. Capital as a distinct form of property falls into three main categories: industrial technology and means of production, land, and finance. Here, we meet one of the top sanctuaries of orthodox economic theory, which is the postulate that any rational allocation of economic means is impossible without an autonomous capital account and a separate calculation of the efficiency of capital. Though not being wrong altogether, the postulate needs to be made more specific, as I have tried to show. It is not the instalment of machinery and technical equipment *as such* that generates the profit of firms, but the dispositive and innovative work of entrepreneurs and managers (who, regrettably, are almost completely absent in orthodox economic theory). Moreover, it is not only entrepreneurs and managers who are relevant, but likewise employees investing in new ideas and securing the implementation and market success of innovations on the shop-floor level ('intrapreneurs' in management parlance). Management handbooks tell us that the true capital of firms is located not in the hardware of their technical and material infrastructure, but in their software, that is, in their knowledge and in the explicit and implicit competencies of their staff. This applies in particular to modern firms employing digitalised industrial and service technologies. Though advanced digital technologies seem to have the potential to automate an unprecedented amount of complex production, service and administrative tasks (Lanchester 2015; Frey and Osborne 2017), it remains controversial whether this will lead to a corresponding reduction of employment. The consequence may be not to make work redundant, but to concentrate it even more on newly generated, highly skilled non-routine operations (Bonin et al. 2015). More than ever in the past, the new and the irregular are becoming the domains of human intervention. Firm hierarchies are becoming decentralised; the qualification levels and the operative autonomy of workers have increased as a consequence; and the functional preponderance of labour over capital will increase even more.

A positive contribution of capital to production and profit-generation can be identified in the case of the owner-entrepreneur, where the owner personally engages in dispositive or managerial work and takes care of the success of the firm. The owner-entrepreneur continues to be relevant in (mostly middle or small) family firms, which still constitute the majority of companies in the advanced capitalist economies, though their contribution to value creation and employment is clearly less than proportional. The situation in the dominant sectors of the global economy is different: here, despite persisting national differences in corporate governance, capital has confined itself largely to the role of a profit-seeking principal, while it has delegated the factual organisation of production to managers and employees. The factual retreat of financialised capital from the control of production which can be observed today is anything but a new phenomenon. It can be interpreted as the culmination point of a long-term historical process starting already with the 'managerial revolution' (Chandler 1977) of the early twentieth century, when managers took control over firms, while owners drew back to a passive role, confining themselves largely to the collection of dividends. The 'counter-revolution' of shareholders, which started in the United States in the 1970s, did not restore the productive functions of capital ownership; to the contrary, as analyses of the consequences of financialisation for firms have shown, the main concern of the institutional investors, whose control over firms tightened, concentrated on the extraction of higher revenues for their clientele (Windolf 2005; Lazonick and O'Sullivan 2000; Lounsbury and Hirsch 2010; Lazonick 2017). To secure the cooperation of top managers, the investors allowed manager salaries and bonuses to rise spectacularly. Yet, the appalling experiences of shareholder activism and of Anglo-American hedge funds should not be overgeneralised, for the degree of company financialisation as well as its impact on income inequality appears to be lower in 'coordinated' market economies (to use the terminology of the well-known 'varieties of capitalism' approach) such as Germany, France or Sweden than in 'liberal' market economies such as the United States or the United Kingdom (Faust 2017; Robertson and Kwon 2017). Nevertheless, with mounting financialisation and with firms themselves becoming a tradeable commodity, industrial capital ownership is clearly taking on 'parasitic' (Sayer 2015) traits, contributing little to productivity and innovation and engaging in minimal capital risk so that their investors may have flexible exit options. This is not to say that industrial innovation no longer takes place in the large, global corporations. However, innovation here increasingly takes the form of oligopolistic competition between a small number of internet companies (such as Apple, Google, Facebook, Amazon and Microsoft) striving for monopolistic control over data and social infrastructure – a trend which meets with increasing public criticism due to its totalitarian potential (for an overview, see Dolata 2017).

The legitimacy of land as a distinct form of capital investment is no less dubious as it had been since the early times of industrial capitalism. Adam Smith and David Ricardo interpreted the rent of the landowner as a deduction from wealth, not as a reward for contributing to its creation. Different from entrepreneurial profit, the income of the rentier is based not on productive work, but solely on his monopoly over the 'fictitious commodity' of land, which allows him to extract rents from the rest of society. Free real estate markets do not only hamper the accumulation of productive capital by inflating differential rents and living costs, but they also have a devastating effect on the natural environment. Thus, there are little objections even from a liberal standpoint against the transfer of land into public ownership or against a land-value tax siphoning off speculative profits on land, an idea that was already intensively discussed in the nineteenth century (George 1879).

The finance form of capital has not really been much of a success story either. In the late twentieth and early twenty-first centuries, the working of free market forces in liberalised financial markets resulted, due to the spread of derivative financial products, in the build-up of a speculative bubble of historically unprecedented dimensions. The collapse of the bubble, which was imminent in 2008–2009, was prevented only by unconventional 'rescue' and 'quantitative easing' policies of governments and central banks. As these policies were implemented on a large scale, central bank interest rates went down to and even below zero. Finance capital today is no longer an outcome of self-regulated market processes, but depends on permanent injections of central bank money. As asset inflation is being guaranteed politically, finance capital is no longer scarce, but in huge oversupply. To some degree, John Maynard Keynes' vision of a long-term 'socialisation' of investment (Keynes 1978: 378) with the consequence of bringing down interest rates to zero has come into being. In so far as they are still private, financial markets have largely become an arena of speculation. The traditional definition of finance as a mediator for real production has become outmoded. Where real firms or start-ups, nevertheless, are trying to finance their investments by bank credit instead of internal funds, they are often having difficulties due to the higher attractiveness of financial projects for the banks. Under such conditions, the idea of transferring the privilege of money creation from private banks to national banks is likely to meet with increasing support. Similar to the case of land, the justification for maintaining a large private finance sector appears weak. As the case of finance demonstrates again, through radicalising itself the capitalist dream of absolute wealth is losing its transformative power. Imagine that, by some accident, the entire superstructure of inflated assets and derivative products would disappear at one stroke, with the exception only of primary balances of states, households and firms. Would that really do much harm to the rest of society outside the finance sector?

A capitalist order, where the factor of capital exhausts itself largely in speculative real estate and finance projects while no longer being rooted in real entrepreneurship, can no longer claim legitimacy. Instead of promoting innovation, capital seems to move between excesses of (politically safeguarded) financial speculation and the parasitic exploitation of land and industrial resources. Increasingly, the capitalist class is taking on the character of a quasi-feudal rentier class (Neckel 2010), taking advantage of its monopoly over the means of production to extract rents from the rest of society. Capitalist growth no longer indicates a rising *aggregate* level of wealth, but reduces itself to a zero-sum game, with the profits of the wealthy equalling the losses of the non-wealthy. In some sense, the American Dream destroys itself, as if the hill it is located on (according to Hochschild's deep story) would be closed to the public and access reserved to a small elite of super-rich people. The question is indeed: can society still 'afford the rich' (Sayer 2015)?

No one would recommend removing the legal separation between capital and labour at one stroke. Nevertheless, policies and institutional models aiming to dismantle it step by step are worth considering. Possible policies would include an expansion of public control over real estate markets, a re-regulation of the global financial system, and, moreover, a relocation of the money-creation function of private banks to central banks. Employee share-ownership programmes (which already exist in many European firms, albeit only to a small degree) could be enlarged, including the perspective of exclusive employee ownership over companies. Likewise, policies to strengthen the industrial and commercial middle classes, in combination with strong systems of industrial co-determination, deserve to be discussed. The cooperative as a model of economic organisation may gain new life in the industrial as well as in the banking and consumer fields (Brockmeier and Fehl 2007). Without the separation of capital and labour and with net revenues falling entirely to stakeholders, as is the case in the cooperative model, the economy would no longer need to grow, but could remain in a stable stationary state. Though this arrangement is not meant to curb market competition and the Faustian drive of the economy altogether, it probably would slow down the pace of innovation. However, under conditions of a stagnating or declining population and a technologically sophisticated economy, this would certainly not do much harm. Moreover, it might be good for a society that has let technology take itself over in ways that nobody had ever wanted. On the other hand, a re-arrangement of property rights over production, attributing ownership over production collectively to stakeholders, would offer significant advantages in terms of social fairness, equality and stability. Money would lose its numinous quality as capital and become a profane exchange medium. The slowdown of economic growth could also have a beneficial effect on the natural environment.

Today, there is no need to warm up to Marx's communist vision of universal individuality, reconciling men (and women) with each other as well as with nature in a spontaneous way, which he developed as a positive counterpart to capitalist alienation in his early writings (Marx 1968).[2] Just as the immediate immersion in God remains a gift that is reserved to religious virtuosos and cannot be practised by the ordinary believers, Marx's romantic idea of human universality cannot immediately offer a way to organise everyday social and economic life. With regard to this point, system-theoretical insights about the key importance of functional differentiation for social universality appear more convincing than Marx's critique of alienation. Contrary to what the young Marx believed, humans cannot unite globally as natural beings, but only on the basis of highly formalised and functionally specified social structures. In this sense, practised social universality is possible only at the price of 'alienation'. Legitimate critique of market fundamentalism should not brush aside the biggest historical achievement of markets, namely their *universalism.* At the same time, global market integration meets its limits in the need of framing markets by national and local institutions, which Polanyi had emphasised. In a similar vein, 'communitarian' approaches (Amitai Etzioni, Michael Sandel, Charles Taylor, Michael Walzer) have pointed to the importance of intermediate nationally, regionally and locally based collective identities for maintaining a balanced relationship between markets and different social 'spheres of justice' (Walzer 1983).

However, how do we overcome the present-day hegemony of disembedded markets over society? Marx was probably on the right track when he considered a change in property relationships as a key for overcoming the evils of capitalism. However, to avoid the tyranny of market fundamentalism, there is – as I have tried to show – no need to abolish the institution of private property altogether and to replace it by a *politically* controlled system. The disastrous experiences with 'real socialism' should be kept in mind; given the present level of global economic integration, the model of state socialism appears to be even more anachronistic. What appears vital, rather, are private property rights reforms that aim to integrate social control over the human and material conditions of production. Moreover, the limits not only of material, but also of territorial and social disembedding will require a new, thorough discussion; here, I am reminded of Dani Rodrik's (2011) well-founded plea for political limitations on transnational market liberalisation. A selective redesign and re-embedding of private property rights would help to curb the capitalist growth imperative. The vanishing of the growth imperative, in turn, would strengthen intermediate communities and help to establish subsidiary relationships between transnational markets and national and local communities.[3]

## Notes

1 Following this idea, Wolfgang Schluchter has suggested the interpretation of modernity as a new form of 'axial' civilisation, according to the conceptualisations of Jaspers and Eisenstadt (Schluchter 2016).

2 In the later phases of his life, Marx seems to have thought more pragmatically about social reform, as Gareth Stedman Jones has shown in his recent biography (Jones 2016).

3 This seems to be also the key point of 'market socialism' conceptions discussed in the 1990s (e.g. Weisskopf 1993).

# References


Acemoglu, Daron, and Robinson, James A. (2012). *Why Nations Fail: The Origins of Power, Prosperity and Poverty*. London: Profile Books.

Admati, Anat, and Hellwig, Martin (2014). *Des Bankers neue Kleider: Was bei Banken wirklich schiefläuft und was sich ändern muss*, 2nd Edition. München: Finanzbuch.

Agamben, Giorgio (2011). *The Kingdom and the Glory: For a Theological Genealogy of Economy and Government*. Stanford: Stanford University Press.

Akerlof, George A., and Shiller, Robert J. (2015). *Phishing for Fools: The Economics of Manipulation and Deception*. Princeton: Princeton University Press.

Aldrich, Howard (2005). 'Entrepreneurship', in Richard Swedberg and Neil Smelser, ed., *Handbook of Economic Sociology*, 451–477. Princeton: Princeton University Press.

Alexander, Jeffrey C. (2003). *The Meanings of Social Life: A Cultural Sociology*. Oxford: Oxford University Press.

Anderson, Philip, and Tushman, Michael L. (1990). 'Technological Discontinuities and Dominant Designs: A Cyclical Model of Technological Change'. *Administrative Science Quarterly* 35(4), 604–633.

Arrighi, Giovanni, and Silver, Beverly (1999). *Chaos and Governance in the Modern World System*. Minneapolis: University of Minnesota Press.

Arrow, Kenneth J., and Debreu, Gerard (1954). 'Existence of an Equilibrium for a Competitive Economy'. *Econometrica* 22(3), 265–290.

Asbach, Olaf (2014). 'Politik, Handel und international eOrdnung im Denken der Aufklärung', in Olaf Asbach, ed., *Der moderne Staat und 'le doux commerce': Politik, Ökonomie und internationale Beziehungen im politischen Denken der Aufklärung*, 13–38. Baden-Baden: Nomos.

Assmann, Jan (2003). *Die Mosaische Unterscheidung oder der Preis des Monotheismus*. München: Hanser.

Axford, Barrie (2013). *Theories of Globalization*. Cambridge: Polity Press.

Backhaus, Jürgen (2005). 'Evolution of Legal Rules: Hayek's Contribution Reconsidered', in *Entrepreneurship, Money and Coordination: Hayek's Theory of Cultural Evolution*, ed., Jürgen Backhaus, 73–106. Cheltenham: Edward Elgar.

Barbalet, Jack (2008). *Religion and Profits: The Protestant Ethic and The Spirit of Capitalism in Context*. Cambridge: Cambridge University Press.

Barber, Benjamin (1996). *Jihad vs. McWorld: How Globalization and Tribalism Are Reshaping the World*. New York: Ballantine Books.

Bastide, Roger (1978). *The African Religions of Brazil: Toward a Sociology of the Interpenetration of Civilizations*. Baltimore: Johns Hopkins University Press.

Baudrillard, Jean (1998). *The Consumer Society: Myths and Structures*. London: SAGE.
Baumol, William J. (2002). *The Free Market Innovation Machine*. Princeton: Princeton University Press.
Beck, Ulrich (1986). *Risikogesellschaft: Auf dem Weg in eine andere Moderne*. Frankfurt/M: Suhrkamp.
Beck, Ulrich (1992). *Risk Society: Towards a New Modernity*. London: SAGE.
Beckert, Jens (2002). *Beyond the Market: The Social Foundations of Economic Efficiency*. Princeton: Princeton University Press.
Beckert, Jens (2004). *Unverdientes Vermögen: Soziologie des Erbrechts*. Frankfurt/M: Campus.
Beckert, Jens (2010). 'Institutional Isomorphism Revisited: Convergence and Divergence in Institutional Change'. *Sociological Theory* 28(2), 150–166.
Beckert, Jens (2011). 'Imagined Futures: Fictionality in Economic Action', MPIfG Discussion Paper, August. Cologne: Max Planck Institute for the Study of Societies.
Beckert, Jens (2016). *Imagined Futures: Fictional Expectations and Capitalist Dynamics*. Cambridge, MA: Harvard University Press.
Beckert, Jens, and Aspers, Patrick, eds. (2011). *The Worth of Goods: Valuation and Pricing in the Economy*. Oxford: Oxford University Press.
Beetz, Michael (2010). *Gesellschaftstheorie zwischen Autologie und Ontologie: Reflexionen über Ort und Gegenstand der Soziologie*. Bielefeld: Transcript.
Bell, Daniel (1974). *The Coming of Post-Industrial Society*. New York: Harper Colophon.
Bendix, Reinhard, and Howton, Frank W. (1978). 'Soziale Mobilität und die amerikanische Wirtschaftselite', in Hartmut Kaelble, ed., *Geschichte der sozialen Mobilität seit der industriellen Revolution*, 221–247. Königstein/Ts.: Athenäum.
Benjamin, Walter (1985). "Kapitalismus als Religion", in Walter Benjamin, *Gesammelte Schriften*, ed. Rolf Tiedemann and Hermann Schweppenhäuser, Vol. VI, 100–103, Frankfurt/M: Suhrkamp.
Berger, Peter (2013). 'Religion as a Transnational Force', in Hans Georg Soeffner, ed., *Transnationale Vergesellschaftungen: Verhandlungen des 35. Kongresses der Deutschen Gesellschaft für Soziologie in Frankfurt/M 2010*, 59–71. Wiesbaden: Springer.
Berger, Peter, and Luckmann, Thomas. (1966). *The Social Construction of Reality: A Treatise in the Sociology of Knowledge*. New York: Doubleday.
Berghoff, Hartmut (2004). *Moderne Unternehmensgeschichte*. Paderborn: UTB.
Bergmann, Werner (1992). 'The Problem of Time in Sociology: An Overview of the Literature on the State of Theory and Research on the "Sociology of Time", 1900–1982'. *Time and Society* 1(1), 81–134.
Beyer, Peter, and Beaman, Lori, eds. (2007). *Religion, Globalization and Culture*. Leiden: Brill.
Biernacki, Richard (1995). *The Fabrication of Labor: Germany and Britain 1640–1914*. Berkeley: University of California Press.
Bijker, Wiebe E. (1995). *Of Bicycles, Bakelites and Bulbs: Towards a Theory of Sociotechnical Change*. Cambridge, MA: MIT Press.
Binswanger, Hans Christoph (2015). 'Der Glaube an die "unsichtbare Hand"', in Georg Pfleiderer, Peter Seele and Harald Matern, ed., *Kapitalismus – Eine Religion in der Krise II: Aspekte von Risiko, Vertrauen, Schuld*, 171–184. Baden-Baden: Nomos.
Binswanger, Matthias (1996). 'Money Creation, Profits and Growth: Monetary Aspects of Economic Evolution', in Ernst Helmstaeder, ed., *Behavioural Norms, Technical Progress, and Economic Dynamics*, 413–447. Ann Arbor: University of Michigan Press.
Block, Fred (2003). 'Karl Polanyi and the Writing of "The Great Transformation"', *Theory and Society* 32 (3), 275–306.

Block, Fred, and Somers, Margaret F. (2014). *The Power of Market Fundamentalism: Karl Polanyi's Critique*. Cambridge, MA: Harvard University Press.

Blossfeld, Hans-Peter, Klijzing, Erik, Mills, Melinda and Kurz, Karin (2005). *Globalization, Uncertainty and Youth in Society*. London: Routledge.

Blumenberg, Hans (1996 [1966]). *Die Legitimität der Neuzeit*. Frankfurt/M: Suhrkamp.

Boltanski, Luc, and Chiapello, Eve (2007). *The New Spirit of Capitalism*, trans. Gregory Elliott. New York: Verso.

Bonin, Holger, Gregory, Terry and Zieran, Ulrich (2015). 'Übertragung der Studie von Frey/Osborne auf Deutschland', ZEW Kurzexpertise No. 57. Mannheim: Zentrum für Europäische Wirtschaftsforschung (ZEW). http://ftp.zew.de/pub/zew-docs/gutachten/Kurzexpertise_BMAS_ZEW2015.pdf.

Braudel, Fernand (1992). *Civilization and Capitalism in the 15–18th Century, Vol. II: The Wheels of Commerce*. Berkeley: University of California Press.

Broadberry, Stephen, and O'Rourke, Kevin, eds. (2010). *The Cambridge Economic History of Modern Europe, Vol. I: 1700–1870*. Cambridge: Cambridge University Press.

Bröckling, Ulrich (2016). *The Entrepreneurial Self: Fabricating a New Type of Subject*. London: SAGE.

Brockmeier, Thomas, and Fehl, Ulrich, eds. (2007). *Volkswirtschaftliche Theorie der Kooperation in Genossenschaften*. Göttingen: Vandenhoek & Ruprecht.

Brodbeck, Karl-Heinz (2001). 'Die fragwürdigen Grundlagen des Neoliberalismus: Wirtschaftsordnung und Markt in Hayeks Theorie der Regelselektion'. *Zeitschrift für Politik* 48, 49–71.

Brubaker, Roger (2012). 'Religion and Nationalism: Four Approaches'. *Nations and Nationalism* 18(1), 2–20.

Burt, Ronald S. (2000). 'The Network Entrepreneur', in Richard Swedberg, ed., *Entrepreneurship: The Social Science View*, 281–307. Oxford: Oxford University Press.

Byrne, David (2005). *Social Exclusion*. New York: Open University Press.

Calder, Lendol (1999). *Financing the American Dream: A Cultural History of Consumer Credit*. Princeton: Princeton University Press.

Calhoun, Craig J. (2002). 'The Class Consciousness of Frequent Travelers: Toward a Critique of Actually Existing Cosmopolitanism'. *South Atlantic Quarterly* 101(4), 869–897.

Canzler, Weert, and Marz, Lutz (2011). 'Wert und Verwertung neuer Technologien: Das Beispiel der Wasserstoff- und Brennstofftechnologien'. *Leviathan* 39(2), 223–246.

Casanova, José (1994). *Public Religions in the Modern Society*. Chicago: University of Chicago Press.

Casanova, José (2006). 'Einwanderung und der neue religiöse Pluralismus'. *Leviathan* 34 (2): 182–207.

Caroll, William K. (2010). *The Making of a Transnational Capitalist Class: Corporate Power in the 21th Century*. New York: Zed Books.

Castells, Manuel (2000). *The Information Age: Economy, Society and Culture, Vol. I: The Rise of the Network Society*, 2nd Edition. Oxford: Blackwell.

Chamberlin, Edward H. (1956 [1933]). *The Theory of Monopolistic Competition: A Re-Orientation of the Theory of Value*. Cambridge, MA: Harvard University Press.

Chandler, Alfred DuPont, Jr. (1977). *The Visible Hand: The Managerial Revolution in American Business*. Cambridge, MA: Harvard University Press.

Choi, Young Back (1993). *Paradigms and Conventions: Uncertainty, Decision Making and Entrepreneurship*. Ann Arbor: University of Michigan Press.

Christensen, Clayton (1997). *The Innovator's Dilemma: When New Technologies Cause Great Firms to Fail*. Boston: Harvard Business School Press.

Coleman, James (1990). Foundations of Social Theory. Cambridge, MA: The Belknap Press of Harvard University Press.
Coleman, Simon (2000). *The Globalization of Charismatic Christianity: Spreading the Gospel of Prosperity*. Cambridge: Cambridge University Press.
Corsino, Louis, and Soto, Maricella (2005). 'Socializing the Ethnic Market: A Frame Analysis', in Lisa A. Keister, ed., *Entrepreneurship*, 233–256. Oxford: Elsevier.
Cox, Harvey (2002). 'Mammon and the Culture of the Market: A Socio-Theological Critique', in Richard Madsen, Ann Swidler, William Sullivan, Steve Tipton and Robert Bellah, ed., *Meaning and Modernity: Religion, Polity, Self*, 274–283. Berkeley: University of California Press.
Croner, Fritz (1962). *Soziologie der Angestellten*. Köln: Kiepenheuer&Witsch.
Dasgupta, Rana (2014). *Capital: A Portrait of Twenty-First Century India*. Edinburgh: Canongate.
Davis, Gerald F. (2009). *Managed by the Markets: How Finance Reshaped America*. Oxford: Oxford University Press.
Deutschmann, Christoph (1985). *Der Weg zum Normalarbeitstag: Die Entwicklung der Arbeitszeiten in der deutschen Industrie bis 1918*. Frankfurt/M: Campus.
Deutschmann, Christoph (1996). 'Money as a Social Construction: On the Actuality of Simmel and Marx'. *Thesis Eleven* 47(1), 1–19.
Deutschmann, Christoph (2001). *Die Verheißung des absoluten Reichtums: Zur religiösen Natur des Kapitalismus*, 2nd Edition. Frankfurt/M: Campus.
Deutschmann, Christoph (2002). *Postindustrielle Industriesoziologie: Theoretische Grundlagen, Arbeitsverhältnisse und soziale Identitäten*. Weinheim: Juventa.
Deutschmann, Christoph (2008). *Kapitalistische Dynamik: Eine gesellschaftstheoretische Perspektive*. Wiesbaden: VS.
Deutschmann, Christoph (2009a). 'Soziologie kapitalistischer Dynamik', MPIfG Working Paper, May. Köln: Max Planck Institute for the Study of Societies.
Deutschmann, Christoph (2009b). 'Geld als universales Inklusionsmedium moderner Gesellschaften', in Rudolf Stichweh and Paul Windolf, ed., *Inklusion und Exklusion: Analysen zur Sozialstruktur und sozialen Ungleichheit*, 223–240. Wiesbaden: VS.
Deutschmann, Christoph (2011a). 'A Pragmatist Theory of Capitalism'. *Socio-Economic Review* 9(1), 83–106.
Deutschmann, Christoph (2011b). 'Limits to Financialization: Sociological Analyses of the Financial Crisis'. *European Journal of Sociology* 52(3), 347–389.
Deutschmann, Christoph (2012a). 'Capitalism, Religion and the Idea of the Demonic', MPIfG Discussion Paper, February. Köln: Max Planck Institute for the Study of Societies.
Deutschmann, Christoph (2012b). 'Die Dynamik des Konsums und die moralische Integration moderner Gesellschaften'. *Leviathan* 40(4), 517–535.
Deutschmann, Christoph (2015). 'Disembedded Markets as a Mirror of Society: Blind Spots of Social Theory'. *European Journal of Social Theory* 18(4): 368–389.
Deutschmann, Christoph (2016a). 'Entzauberung des Geldes: Max Weber und der heutige Finanzmarkt-Kapitalismus', in Thomas Schwinn and Gert Arbeit, ed., *Alte Begriffe – Neue Probleme: Max Webers Soziologie im Lichte aktueller Problemstellungen*, 149–170. Tübingen: Mohr und Siebeck.
Deutschmann, Christoph (2016b). 'Multiple Futures or One Future? The Capitalist Growth Imperative'. *Comparativ: Zeitschrift für Globalgeschichte und vergleichende Gesellschaftsforschung* 26(2), 17–28.
Dewey, John (1958 [1925]). *Experience and Nature*. New York: Dover Publications.
Dewey, John (1938). *Logic: The Theory of Inquiry*. New York: Rinehart and Winston.

Dierkes, Meinolf, Hoffmann, Ute and Marz, Lutz (1996). *Visions of Technology: Social and Institutional Factors Shaping the Development of New Technologies*. Frankfurt/M: Campus.

van Dijk, Jan A.G.M. (1999). 'The One-Dimensional Network Society of Manuel Castells'. *New Media and Society* 1(1), 127–138.

Djelic, Marie-Laure and_Quack, Sigrid, eds. (2003). *Globalization and Institutions: Redefining the Rules of the Economic Game*. Cheltenham: Edward Elgar.

Dobbin, Frank, and Kalev, Alexandra (2016). 'Why Diversity Programs Fail'. *Harvard Business Review* 97(7), 52–60.

Dodd, Nigel (2014). *The Social Life of Money*. Princeton: Princeton University Press.

Dolata, Ulrich (2017). 'Apple, Amazon, Google, Facebook, Microsoft. Market Concentration-Competition-Innovation Strategies', SOI Discussion Paper, January. Stuttgart: University of Stuttgart Institute for Social Sciences.

Dopfer, Kurt (2006). 'The Origins of Meso-Economics: Schumpeter's Legacy'. Papers on Economics and Evolution. Jena: Max Planck Institute of Economics.

Dörre, Klaus (2009). 'Die neue Landnahme: Dynamiken und Grenzen des Finanzmarktkapitalismus', in Klaus Dörre, Stephan Lessenich and Hartmut Rosa, ed., *Soziologie-Kapitalismus-Kritik: Eine Debatte*, 21–86. Frankfurt/M: Suhrkamp.

Dosi, Giovanni (1982). 'Technological Paradigms and Technological Trajectories: A Suggested Interpretation of the Determinants and Directions of Technical Change'. *Research Policy* 11(3), 147–162.

Dosi, Giovanni (1988). 'The Nature of the Innovative Process', in Giovanni Dosi, Christopher Freeman and Richard Nelson, ed., *Technical Change and Economic Theory*, 221–238. London: Pinter.

Drakopolou, Sarah Dodd, and Gotsis, George (2007). 'The Interrelationships between Entrepreneurship and Religion'. *International Journal of Entrepreneurship and Innovation* 8(2), 93–104.

Durkheim, Emile (1982 [1895]). *The Rules of Sociological Method*. New York: The Free Press.

Durkheim, Emile (1995 [1912]). *The Elementary Forms of Religious Life*. New York: The Free Press.

Durkheim, Emile (2014 [1893]). *The Division of Labour in Society*. New York: The Free Press.

Dux, Günter (1982). 'Der Grund der Religion', in Günter Dux, ed., *Die Logik der Weltbilder: Sinnstrukturen im Wandel der Geschichte*, 147–180. Frankfurt/M: Suhrkamp.

Eisenstadt, Shmuel N., ed. (1986). *The Origins and Diversity of Axial Age Civilizations*. Albany, NY: State University of New York Press.

Eisenstadt, Shmuel N. (2000). 'Multiple Modernities'. *Daedalus* 129(1), 1–19.

Elster, Jon (1985). *Sour Grapes: Studies in the Subversion of Rationality*. Cambridge: Cambridge University Press.

Engster, Frank (2014). *Das Geld als Maß, Mittel und Methode: Das Rechnen mit der Identität der Zeit*. Berlin: Neofelis.

Epstein, Gerald A., ed. (2005). *Financialization and the World Economy*. Cheltenham: Edward Elgar.

Esposito, Elena (2007). *Die Fiktion der wahrscheinlichen Realität*. Frankfurt/M: Suhrkamp.

Esposito, Elena (2010). *Die Zukunft der Futures: Die Zeit des Geldes in Finanzwelt und Gesellschaft*. Heidelberg: Carl Auer.

Esser, Hartmut (1993). *Soziologie: Allgemeine Grundlagen*. Frankfurt/M: Campus.

Esser, Hartmut (1999). *Soziologie: Spezielle Grundlagen, Vol. I: Situationslogik und Handeln*. Frankfurt/M: Campus.

Faust, Michael (2017). 'Die Konstellationen externer Einflussnahme beim börsennotierten Unternehmen', in Michael Faust, Jürgen Kädtler and Harald Wolf, ed., *Finanzmarkt-Kapitalismus? Der Einfluss von Finanzialisierung auf Arbeit, Wachstum und Innovation*, 269–333. Frankfurt/M: Campus.

Ferguson, Niall (1998). *The World's Banker: The History of the House of Rothschild*. London: Weidenfeld & Nicolson.

Fleischmann, Christoph (2010). *Gewinn in alle Ewigkeit: Kapitalismus als Religion*. Zürich: Rotpunktverlag.

Fligstein, Neil J. (2001). 'Social Skill and the Theory of Fields'. *Sociological Theory* 19 (2), 105–125.

Foley, Duncan (2006). *Adam's Fallacy: A Guide to Economic Theology*. Cambridge, MA: Harvard University Press.

Freeman, Christopher, and Perez, Carlota (1988). 'Structural Crises of Adjustment, Business Cycles and Investment Behaviour', in Giovanni Dosi, Christopher Freeman, Richard Nelson, ed., *Technical Change and Economic Theory*, 38–65. London: Pinter.

Freeman, Christopher, and Louca, Francisco (2001). *As Time Goes By: From the Industrial Revolution to the Information Revolution*. Oxford: Oxford University Press.

Frey, Carl Benedikt, and Osborne, Michael A. (2017). 'The Future of Employment: How Susceptible Are Jobs to Computerization?' *Technological Forecasting and Social Change* 114(C), 254–280.

Friedman, Milton, and Schwartz, Anna J. (1963). *A Monetary History of the United States 1867–1970*. Princeton: Princeton University Press.

Fukuyama, Francis (1992). *The End of History and the Last Man*. New York: The Free Press.

Galiani, Ferdinando (1751). *Della moneta – libri quinque*. Napoli.

Galiani, Ferdinando (1999). *Über das Geld*, trans. and ed. Werner Tabarelli. Düsseldorf: Verlag Wirtschaft und Finanzen.

Gall, Lothar (2000). *Krupp: Der Aufstieg eines Industrieimperiums*. Berlin: Siedler.

Ganssmann, Heiner (2011). *Doing Money: Elementary Monetary Theory from a Sociological Standpoint*. London: Routledge.

Garud, Raghu, and Karnoe, Peter (2001). 'Path Creation as a Process of Mindful Deviation', in Raghu Garud and Peter Karnoe, ed., *Path Dependence and Creation*, 1–40. Mahwah, NJ: Lawrence Erlbaum.

Geertz, Clifford (1960). *The Religion of Java*. Chicago: University of Chicago Press.

GEM (2014). 'Global Entrepreneurship Monitor 2013 Global Report', ed. José Ernsto Amorós and Niels Bosma. Utrecht: Global Entrepreneurship Association.

Genschel, Philipp, and Schwarz, Peter (2011). 'Tax Competition: A Literature Review'. *Socio-Economic Review* 9(2), 339–370.

George, Henry (1879). *Progress and Poverty: An Inquiry into the Causes of Industrial Depressions and the Increase of Wants with Increase of Wealth: The Remedy*. Garden City, NY: Doubleday, Page & Co.

Geyer, Michael, and Bright, Charles (2000). 'World History in a Global Age', in David Held and Anthony McGrew, ed., *The Global Transformation Reader: An Introduction to the Globalization Debate*, 61–67. Cambridge: Cambridge University Press.

Giddens, Anthony (2002). *The Consequencs of Modernity*. Stanford: Stanford University Press.

Global Commission on the Economy and Climate (2014). 'Better Growth Better Climate – Synthesis Report'. Washington, DC: Global Commission on the Economy and Climate.

Go, Julian, ed. (2012). *Political Power and Social Theory*. Bingley, UK: Emerald.

Goldthorpe, John H., Lockwood, David, Bechhofer, Frank andPlatt, Jennifer (1968). *The Affluent Worker: Industrial Attitudes and Behaviour*. Cambridge: Cambridge University Press.

Goodchild, Philip (2007). *Theology of Money.* London: SCM Press.

Gordon, David, Reich, Michael and Edwards, Richard (1982). *Segmented Work, Divided Workers: The Historical Transformation of Labor in the U.S.* New York: Cambridge University Press.

Gordon, Richard (2014). 'The Demise of U.S. Economic Growth'. NBER Working Paper, February. Washington, DC: National Bureau of Economic Research.

Gorski, Philip S. (2000). 'Historicizing the Secularization Debate: Church, State and Society in Late Medieval and Early Modern Europe, ca. 1300 to 1700'. *American Sociological Review* 65(1), 138–167.

Grabka, Markus, and Frick, Joachim (2008). 'Schrumpfende Mittelschicht: Anzeichen einer dauerhaften Polarisierung der verfügbarem Einkommen?' *DIW Wochenbericht* 75 (10), 101–108.

Graeber, David (2011). *Debt: The First 5,000 Years*. New York: Melville House.

Graf, Friedrich Wilhelm (2004). *Die Wiederkehr der Götter: Religion in der modernen Kultur*, 3rd Edition. München: Beck.

Grampp, William D. (1965). *Economic Liberalism, Vol. II: The Classical View.* New York: Random House.

Granovetter, Mark (1985). 'Economic Action and Social Structure: The Problem of Embeddedness'. *American Journal of Sociology* 91(3), 481–510.

Granovetter, Mark (2005a). 'The Economic Sociology of Firms and Entrepreneurs', in Richard Swedberg, ed., *New Developments in Economic Sociology, Vol. II*, 160–197. Cheltenham: Edward Elgar.

Granovetter, Mark (2005b). 'Business Groups and Social Organization,' in Neil Smelser and Richard Swedberg, ed., *The Handbook of Economic Sociology*, 2nd Edition, 429–450. Princeton: Princeton University Press.

Gross, Peter (1994). *Die Multioptionsgesellschaft.* Frankfurt/M: Suhrkamp.

Habermas, Jürgen (1971). 'Karl Löwiths stoischer Rückzug vom historischen Bewußtsein', in Jürgen Habermas, ed., *Philosophisch-politische Profile*, 116–140. Frankfurt/M: Suhrkamp.

Habermas, Jürgen (1981). *Theorie des kommunikativen Handelns*. 2 Vols. Frankfurt/M: Suhrkamp.

Halfmann, Jost (1997). 'Die Implementation von Innovationen als Prozess sozialer Einbettung', in Daniel Bieber, ed., *Technikentwicklung und Industriearbeit: Industrielle Produktionstechnik zwischen Eigendynamik und Nutzerinteressen*, 87 110. Frankfurt/M: Campus.

Halperin, Sandra (2016). 'Modernity and the Embedding of Economic Expansion'. *European Journal of Social Theory* 19(2), 172–180.

Hann, Chris, and Hart, Keith, eds. (2009). *Market and Society: The Great Transformation Today.* Cambridge: Cambridge University Press.

Hart, Keith (2009). 'Money in the Making of World Society', in Chris Hann and Keith Hart, ed., *Market and Society: The Great Transformation Today*, 91–105. Cambridge: Cambridge University Press.

Hartmann, Michael (2016). *Die globale Wirtschaftselite: Eine Legende*. Frankfurt/M: Campus.

Harvey, David (2003). *The New Imperialism*. Oxford: Oxford University Press.

Haseler, Stephen (2001). *The Super-Rich: The Unjust World of Global Capital.* Basingstoke: Macmillan.

Hayek, Friedrich A. (1945). 'The Use of Knowledge in Society'. *American Economic Review*, 35(4), 519–530.

Hayek, Friedrich A. (1948). *Individualism and Economic Order.* Chicago: University of Chicago Press.

Hayek, Friedrich A. (1960). *The Constitution of Liberty*. Chicago: University of Chicago Press.

Hayek, Friedrich A. (1990). *Denationalization of Money – The Argument Refined: An Analysis of the Theory and Practices of Concurrent Theories*, 3rd Edition. London: The Institute of Economic Affairs.

Heires, Marcel, and Nölke, Andreas, eds. (2014). *Politische Ökonomie der Finanzialisierung*. Wiesbaden: Springer.

Held, David, and McGrewAnthony, eds. (2000).*The Global Transformations Reader. An Introduction into the Globalization Debate*. Cambridge: Polity Press.

Helleiner, Eric (1995). 'Explaining the Globalization of Financial Markets: Bringing States Back In'. *Review of International Political Economy* 2(2), 315–341.

Hertz, Tom. (2006). 'Understanding Mobility in America'. Washington, DC: Center for American Progress.

Herzog, Lisa (2013). *Inventing the Market: Smith, Hegel, and Political Theory*. Oxford: Oxford University Press.

Hien, Josef and Joerges, Christian (2017). 'Das aktuelle europäische Interesse an der ordoliberalen Tradition'. *Leviathan* 45(4), 459–493.

Hill, Lisa (2001) 'The Hidden Theology of Adam Smith', *European Journal of the History of Economic Thought*, 8(1), 1–29.

Hirschle, Jochen (2012). *Die Entstehung des transzendenten Kapitalismus*. Konstanz: UVK.

Hirschman, Albert O. (1977). *The Passions and the Interests: Political Arguments for Capitalism before its Triumph*. Princeton: Princeton University Press.

Hirst, Paul, and Thompson, Grahame (1999). *Globalization in Question*, 2nd Edition. Cambridge: Polity Press.

Hochschild, Arlie Russell (2016). *Strangers in Their Own Land: Anger and Mourning on the American Right*. New York: The New Press.

Hochschild, Arlie Russell, and Ehrenreich, Barbara, eds. (2002). *The Global Woman: Nannies, Maids and Sex Workers in the New Economy*. New York: Metropolitan Books.

Holthaus, Stefan (2015). *Zwischen Gewissen und Gewinn: Die Wirtschafts- und Sozialordnung der 'Freiburger Denkschrift' und die Anfänge der Sozialen Marktwirtschaft*. Münster: LIT.

Holz, Klaus (1993). *Historisierung der Gesellschaftstheorie: Zur Erkenntniskritik marxistischer und kritischer Theorie*. Pfaffenweiler: Centaurus.

Honneth, Axel, ed. (1993). *Kommunitarismus: Eine Debatte über die moralischen Grundlagen moderner Gesellschaften*. Frankfurt/M: Campus.

Honneth, Axel, ed. (2002). *Befreiung aus der Mündigkeit: Paradoxien des gegenwärtigen Kapitalismus*. Frankfurt/M: Campus.

Honneth, Axel (2015). *Die Idee des Sozialismus: Versuch einer Aktualisierung*. Frankfurt/M: Suhrkamp.

Horn, Karen (2011). 'Diesseits von Angebot und Nachfrage: Einige Anmerkungen zur Überdehnung des Gegensatzes von Markt und Moral', HWWI Policy Paper 57. Hamburg: Hamburgisches Weltwirtschaftsinstitut (HWWI).

Huntington, Samuel (1996). *The Clash of Civilizations and the Remaking of World Order*. New York: Simon & Schuster.

Huntington, Samuel (2000). 'The Clash of Civilizations?' in *The Globalization Reader*, ed., Frank J. Lechner and John Boli, 27–33. Malden, MA: Blackwell.

IMF. (2018). *World Economic Outlook 2018*. Washington, DC: International Monetary Fund. https://www.imf.org/en/publications/weo.

Ingham, Geoffrey (2004). *The Nature of Money*. Cambridge: Polity Press.

Jaspers, Karl (1949). *Vom Ursprung und Ziel der Geschichte*. München: Piper.

Joas, Hans (1992). *Die Kreativität des Handelns*. Frankfurt/M: Suhrkamp.

Joas, Hans (1997). *Die Entstehung der Werte*. Frankfurt/M: Suhrkamp.

Joas, Hans (2017). *Die Macht des Heiligen: Eine Alternative zur Geschichte von der Entzauberung*. Berlin: Suhrkamp.

Jones, Gareth Stedman (2016). Karl Marx: Greatness and Illusion. London: Allen Lane.

Kaelble, Hartmut (1978). 'Soziale Mobilität in den USA und Deutschland 1900–1960: Ein vergleichender Forschungsbericht', in Hartmut Kaelble, ed., *Geschichte der sozialen Mobilität seit der industriellen Revolution*, 109–126. Königstein/Ts: Athenäum.

Kaelble, Hartmut (1983). *Soziale Mobilität und Chancengleichheit im 19. Und 20. Jahrhundert*. Göttingen: Vandenhoek & Ruprecht.

Kanter, Rosabeth Moss (2000). 'When a Thousand Flowers Bloom: Structural, Collective, and Social Conditions for Innovation in Organization', in Richard Swedberg, ed., *Entrepreneurship: The Social Science View*, 167–210. Oxford: Oxford University Press.

Kelley, Donna J., Bosma, Niels and Amorós, José Ernesto (2011). *Global Entrepreneurship Monitor 2010 Annual Global Report*. London: Global Entrepreneurship Research Association.

Kern, Thomas, and Schimank, Uwe (2013). 'Megakirchen als religiöse Organisationen: Ein dritter Gemeindetyp jenseits von Sekte und Kirche?' In Christof Wolf and Matthias Koenig, ed., *Religion und Gesellschaft: Sonderheft 53 der Kölner Zeitschrift für Soziologie und Sozialpsychologie*, 285–310. Wiesbaden: Springer VS.

Keynes, John Maynard (1978). *The Collected Writings of John Maynard Keynes, Volume VII: The General Theory of Employment, Interest and Money*, ed. Elizabeth Johnson and Donald Moggridge. Cambridge: Royal Economic Society.

Kindleberger, Charles, and Aliber, Robert (2005). *Manias, Panics and Crashes: A History of Financial Crises*. London: Palgrave Macmillan.

Kley, Roland (1992). 'F. A. Hayeks Idee einer spontanen sozialen Ordnung: Eine kritische Analyse'. *Kölner Zeitschrift fur Soziologie und Sozialpsychologie* 44(1), 12–34.

Knafo, Samuel (2013). *The Making of Modern Finance: Liberal Governance and the Gold Standard*. London: Routledge.

Knoblauch, Hubert (2009). *Populäre Religion: Auf dem Weg in eine spirituelle Gesellschaft*. Frankfurt/M: Campus.

Kocka, Jürgen (1969). *Unternehmensverwaltung und Angestelltenschaft am Beispiel Siemens 1847–1914*. Stuttgart: Enke.

Kocka, Jürgen (1975). *Unternehmer in der deutschen Industrialisierung*. Göttingen, Gcmany: Vandcnhock & Ruprccht.

Kocka, Jürgen (1982). 'Familie, Unternehmer und Kapitalismus', in Heinz Reif, ed., *Die Familie in der Geschichte*, 163–182. Göttingen: Vandenhoek & Ruprecht.

Koddenbrock, Kai (2017). 'What Money Does: An Inquiry into the Backbone of the Capitalist Political Economy', MPIfG Discussion Paper, September.Köln: Max Planck Institute for the Study of Societies.

Koenig, Matthias (2011). 'Jenseits des Säkularisierungsparadigmas? Eine Auseinandersetzung mit Charles Taylor', *Kölner Zeitschrift für Soziologie und Sozialpsychologie* 63(4), 649–673.

Konings, Martijn (2015). *The Emotional Logic of Capitalism: What Progressives Have Missed*. Stanford: Stanford University Press.

Kornrich, Sabino, and Hicks, Alex (2015). 'The Rise of Finance: Causes and Consequences of Financialization'. *Socio-Economic Review* 13(3), 411–415.

Koselleck, Reinhart (2003). *Zeitschichten: Studien zur Historik*. Frankfurt/M: Suhrkamp.

Koselleck, Reinhart, ed. (2003). 'Zeitverkurzung und Beschleunigung: Eine Studie zur Sakularisation', in Reinhart Koselleck, ed., *Zeitschichten: Studien zur Historik (stw 1656)*, 177–202. Frankfurt/M: Suhrkamp.

Koslowski, Peter (1998). *Ethik des Kapitalismus*, 6th Edition. Tübingen: Mohr Siebeck.
Koslowski, Peter, ed. (2000). *The Theory of Capitalism in the German Economic Tradition: Historism, Ordo-Liberalism, Critical Theory, Solidarism*. Berlin: Springer.
Kracauer, Siegfried (1969). *History: The Last Things before the Last*. New York: Oxford University Press.
Kraemer, Klaus (2008). 'Charisma im ökonomischen Feld', in Andrea Maurer and Uwe Schimank, ed., *Die Gesellschaft der Unternehmen – Die Unternehmen der Gesellschaft: Gesellschaftstheoretische Zugänge zum Wirtschaftsgeschehen*, 63–77. Wiesbaden: VS.
Kraemer, Klaus (2016). 'Propheten der Finanzmärkte: Zur Rolle charismatischer Ideen im Börsengeschehen', in Thomas Schwinn and Gert Albert, ed., *Alte Begriffe-Neue Probleme: Max Webers Soziologie im Licht aktueller Problemstellungen*, 311–338. Tübingen: Mohr und Siebeck.
Krippner, Greta R. (2005). 'The Financialization of the American Economy'. *Socio-Economic Review* 3(2), 173–208.
Krippner, Greta R., et al. (2004). 'Polanyi Symposium: A Conversation on Embeddedness'. *Socio-Economic Review* 2(1), 109–135.
Kuhn, Oliver (2015). 'Kredit und Krise: Zum Zusammenhang von Geld, Kredit und Krise'. *Leviathan* 43(3), 410–441.
Kuhn, Theresa; van Elsas, Erika, Hakhverdian, Armen, and van der Brug, Wouter (2016). 'An Even Wider Gap in an Even Closer Union: Rising Inequalities and Euroskepticism in 12 West European Democracies 1975–2009'. *Socio-Economic Review* 14(1), 27–45.
Lampel, Joseph (2001). 'Show-and-Tell: Product Demonstrations and Path Creation of Technological Change', in Raghu Garud and Peter Karnoe, ed., *Path Dependence and Creation*, 303–328. Mahwah, NJ: Lawrence Erlbaum.
Lanchester, John (2015). 'The Robots Are Coming'. *London Review of Books* 37(5), 3–8.
Laum, Bernhard (1924). *Heiliges Geld: Eine historische Untersuchung über den sakralen Ursprung des Geldes*. Tübingen: Mohr und Siebeck.
Lazonick, William (1991). *Business Organization and the Myth of the Market Economy*. Cambridge: Cambridge University Press.
Lazonick, William (2017). 'Innovatives Unternehmen oder Sweatshopökonomie', in Michael Faust, Jürgen Kädtler and Harald Wolf, ed., *Finanzmarktkapitalismus? Der Einfluss von Finanzialisierung auf Arbeit, Wachstum und Innovation*, 155–224. Frankfurt/M: Campus.
Lazonick, William, and O'Sullivan, Mary (2000). 'Maximizing Shareholder Value: A New Ideology for Corporate Governance'. *Economy and Society* 29(1), 13–35.
Lechner, Frank J., and Boli, John, eds. (2000). *The Globalization Reader*. Malden, MA: Blackwell.
Lenger, Friedrich (2018). *Globalen Kapitalismus denken: Historiographie-, theorie- und wirtschaftsgeschichtliche Studien*. Tübingen: Mohr und Siebeck.
Lepore, Jill (2014). 'The Disruption Machine: Why the Gospel of Innovation Gets Wrong'. *The New Yorker*, June 23.
Lesczenski, Jörg (2008). *August Thyssen 1842–1926: Lebenswelt eines Wirtschaftsbürgers*. Düsseldorf: Klartext.
Lessenich, Stefan (2016). *Neben uns die Sintflut: Die Externalisierungsgesellschaft und ihr Preis*. München: Hanser.
Lester, Richard K., and Piore, Michael J. (2004). *Innovation – The Missing Dimension*. Cambridge, MA: Harvard University Press.
Lie, John (1991). 'Embedding Polanyi's Market Society'. *Sociological Perspectives* 34(2), 219–235.

Lippman, Stephen, Davis, Amy and Aldrich, Howard E. (2005). 'Entrepreneurship and Inequality', in Lisa A. Keister, ed., *Entrepreneurship*, 3–32. Amsterdam: Elsevier.

Lounsbury, Michael, and Hirsch, Paul M., eds. (2010). *Markets on Trial: The Economic Sociology of the U.S. Financial Crisis*. Bingley: Emerald.

Löwith, Karl (2004). *Weltgeschichte und Heilsgeschehen: Die theologischen Voraussetzungen der Geschichtsphilosophie*. Stuttgart: Metzler. ( Original: 1949. *Meaning in History: The Theological Implications of the Philosophy of History*. Chicago: University of Chicago Press).

Luckmann, Thomas (1967). *The Invisible Religion*. London: Macmillan.

Luhmann, Niklas (1975). 'Weltzeit und Systemgeschichte', in Niklas Luhmann, ed., *Soziologische Aufklärung*, 103–133. Opladen: Westdeutscher Verlag.

Luhmann, Niklas (1984). *Soziale Systeme: Grundriss einer allgemeinen Theorie*. Frankfurt/M: Suhrkamp.

Luhmann, Niklas (1988). *Die Wirtschaft der Gesellschaft*. Frankfurt/M: Suhrkamp.

Luhmann, Niklas (1990). *Ökologische Kommunikation: Kann die moderne Gesellschaft sich auf ökologische Gefährdungen einstellen?*Third Edition. Opladen: Westdeutscher Verlag.

Luhmann, Niklas (1992). *Funktionen der Religion*, Third Edition. Frankfurt/M: Suhrkamp.

Luhmann, Niklas (1998). *Die Gesellschaft der Gesellschaft, Vol. I*. Frankfurt/M: Suhrkamp.

Luhmann, Niklas (2000). *Die Religion der Gesellschaft*. Frankfurt/M: Suhrkamp.

Luhmann, Niklas (2017 [1975]). *Systemtheorie der Gesellschaft*. Frankfurt/M: Suhrkamp.

Lukács, Georg (1970 [1923]). *Geschichte und Klassenbewusstsein: Studien über marxistische Dialektik*. Neuwied: Luchterhand.

Lutz, Burkhard (1984). *Der kurze Traum immerwährender Prosperität: Eine Neuinterpretation der industriell-kapitalistischen Entwicklung im Europa des 20. Jahrhunderts*. Frankfurt/M: Campus.

Maddison, Angus (2001). *The World Economy: A Millennial Perspective*. Paris: OECD Development Centre.

Malets, Olga (2017). 'Globalization, Governance and the Nation-State: An Overview'. *Economic Sociology* 18(2), 16–24.

Manow, Philip (2001). 'Ordoliberalismus als ökonomische Ordnungstheologie'. *Leviathan* 29(2), 179–198.

Marsden, David (1999). *A Theory of Employment Systems: Micro Foundations of Societal Diversity*. Oxford: Oxford University Press.

Marshall, T.H. (1950). *Citizenship and Social Class and Other Essays*. Cambridge: Cambridge University Press.

Marx, Karl (1968). 'Ökonomisch-philosophische Manuskripte aus dem Jahr 1844', in Karl Marx and Friedrich Engels, *MEW Ergänzungsband, Schriften, Manuskripte, Briefe bis 1844*, 467–588. Berlin: Dietz.

Marx, Karl (1988 [1867]). *Das Kapital: Kritik der Politischen Ökonomie, Band I*. Berlin: Dietz.

Mayntz, Renate ed. (2012). *Crisis and Control: Institutional Changes in Financial Market Regulation*. Frankfurt/M: Campus.

McCracken, Grant D. (1988). *Culture and Consumption*. Bloomington: Indiana University Press.

McCraw, Thomas K., ed. (1997). *Creating Modern Capitalism: How Entrepreneurs, Companies and Countries Triumphed in Three Industrial Revolutions*. Cambridge, MA: Harvard University Press.

McKinsey (2013). 'Financial Globalization: Retreat or Reset? Global Capital Markets 2013'. San Francisco: McKinsey Global Institute.

Mead, George Herbert (1934). *Mind, Self and Society from the Standpoint of a Social Behaviourist*. Chicago: University of Chicago Press.

Meier, Heinrich (2012). *Die Lehre Carl Schmitts: Vier Kapitel zur Unterscheidung Politischer Theologie und Politischer Philosophie.* Stuttgart: Metzler.
Merton, Robert K. (1968). *Social Theory and Social Structure*, Enlarged Edition. New York: The Free Press.
Meyer, John W. (2009). *World Society: The Writings of John Meyer*, ed. Georg Krücken and Gili S. Drori. Oxford: Oxford University Press.
Meyer, Uli, and Schubert, Cornelius (2007). 'Integrating Path Dependency and Path Creation in a General Understanding of Path Consolidation: The role of Agency and Institutions in the Stabilization of Technological Innovations'. *Science, Technology and Innovation Studies* 3(1), 23–44.
Michéa, Jean Claude (2014). *Das Reich des kleineren Übels: Über die liberale Gesellschaft*. Berlin: Matthes & Seitz.
Mills, C. Wright (1957). *The Power Elite*. New York: Liberty Book Club.
Mirowski, Philip (1989). *More Heat than Light: Economics as Social Physics*. Cambridge: Cambridge University Press.
Mishra, Pankaj (2017). *Age of Anger: A History of the Present*. London: Allen Lane.
Mizrachi, Beverly (2005). 'The Henna Maker: A Moroccan Immigrant Woman Entrepreneur in an Ethnic Revival', in Lisa A. Keister, ed., *Entrepreneurship*, 257–278. Oxford: Elsevier.
Mokyr, Joel, and Voth, Hans-Joachim (2010). 'Understanding Growth in Europe, 1700–1870: Theory and Evidence', in Stephen Broadberry and Kevin O'Rourke, ed., *The Cambridge Economic History of Europe, Vol. I 1700–1870*, 7–42. Cambridge: Cambridge University Press.
Mooser, Josef (1983). 'Auflösung der proletarischen Milieus: Klassenbildung und Individualisierung in der Arbeiterschaft vom Kaiserreich bis in die Bundesrepublik Deutschland: Analysen und Daten über die Anhebung der sozialen Lage der Arbeiter und die Aufstiegsmobilität der Arbeiter nach dem 2. Weltkrieg in Westdeutschland'. *Soziale Welt* 34(3), 270–306.
Münch, Richard (2011). *Das Regime des Freihandels: Entwicklung und Ungleichheit in der Weltgesellschaft*. Frankfurt/M: Campus.
Murray, Charles (2012). *Coming Apart: The State of White America, 1960–2010*. New York: Crown Forum.
Nasaw, Andrew (2006). *Andrew Carnegie*. New York: Penguin Books.
Neckel, Sighard (2008). *Flucht nach vorn: Die Erfolgskultur in der Marktgesellschaft*. Frankfurt/M: Campus.
Nelson, Benjamin (1969). *The Idea of Usury: From Tribal Brotherhood to Universal Otherhood*, 2nd Edition. Chicago: University of Chicago Press.
Nelson, Richard, and Winter, Sidney (1982). *An Evolutionary Theory of Economic Change*. Cambridge, MA: Harvard University Press.
Nelson, Robert H. (2001). *Economics as Religion: From Samuelson to Chicago and Beyond*. University Park, PA: Pennsylvania State University Press.
North, Douglass (1990). *Institutions, Institutional Change and Economic Performance*. Cambridge: Cambridge University Press.
Nutzinger, Hans G., and Hecker, Christian (2008). 'Gererechtigkeit in der Ökonomie – ein unlösbarer Widerspruch?'. *Leviathan* 36(4), 543–575.
Nye, David E. (2004). 'Technological Prediction: A Promethean Problem', in Marita Sturken, Douglas Thomas, and Sandra Ball-Rokeach, ed., *Technological Visions: The Hopes and Fears that Shape New Technologies*, 159–176. Philadelphia: Temple University Press.
OECD (2013). *The Missing Entrepreneurs: Policies for Inclusive Entrepreneurship in Europe*. Paris: OECD Publishing.

OECD (2016). 'Labour Force Participation Rates (Indicators)'. Organisation for Economic Co-operation and Development. doi:10.1787/8a801325-en.

Osterhammel, Jürgen (2009). *Die Verwandlung der Welt: Eine Geschichte des 19. Jahrhunderts*. München: Beck.

Ostrom, Elionor (1990). *Governing the Commons: The Evolution of Institutions for Collective Action*. Cambridge: Cambridge University Press.

Parsons, Talcott (1951). *The Social System*. New York: The Free Press.

Parsons, Talcott (1999). 'Religion in Postindustrial America: The Problem of Secularization', in Bryan S. Turner, ed., *The Talcott Parsons Reader*, 300–320. Oxford: Blackwell.

Paul, Axel (2010). 'Die Unverfügbarkeit des Geldes und die Rolle der Zentralbanken', in Jens Beckert and Christoph Deutschmann, ed., *Wirtschaftssoziologie: Sonderheft 49 der Kölner Zeitschrift für Soziologie und Sozialpsychologie*, 243–265. Wiesbaden: VS.

Paul, Axel (2012). *Die Gesellschaft des Geldes: Entwurf einer monetären Theorie der Moderne*, 2nd Edition. Wiesbaden: VS.

Paul, Axel (2017). *Theorie des Geldes zur Einführung*. Hamburg: Junius.

Peck, Jamie (2013). 'Disembedding Polanyi: Exploring Polanyian Economic Geographies'. *Environment and Planning* 45(7), 1536–1544.

Peine, Alexander (2006). *Innovation und Paradigma: Epistemische Stile in Innovationsprozessen*. Bielefeld: Transcript.

Perelman, Michael (2000). *The Invention of Capitalism: Classical Political Economy and the Secret History of Primitive Accumulation*. Durham, NC: Duke University Press.

Philipps, Robert (2003). 'Stakeholder Legitimacy'. *Business Ethics Quarterly* 13(1), 25–41.

Piketty, Thomas (2014). *Capital in the Twenty-First Century*. Cambridge, MA: The Belknap Press of Harvard University Press.

Plessner, Helmuth (1981 [1924]). *Die Stufen des Organischen und der Mensch*. Berlin: Walter de Gruyter.

Polanyi, Karl (1944). *The Great Transformation: The Political and Economic Origins of Our Time*. London: Rinehart & Company.

Polanyi, Karl (1947). 'Our Obsolete Market Economy: "Civilization Must Find a New Pattern"'. *Commentary* 3, 109–128.

Polanyi-Levitt, Kari (2013). *From the Great Transformation to the Great Financialization: On Karl Polanyi and Other Essays*. Halifax: Fernwood Publishing.

Pollack, Detlef (1995). 'Was ist Religion? Probleme der Definition'. *Zeitschrift für Religionswissenschaft* 3, 163–190.

Pollack, Detlef, and Gergely, Rosta (2015). *Religion in der Moderne: Ein internationaler Vergleich*. Frankfurt/M: Campus.

Popitz, Heinrich (1997). *Wege der Kreativität*. Tübingen: Mohr und Siebeck.

Portes, Alejandro, and Zhou, Min (1992). 'Gaining the Upper Hand: Economic Mobility among Domestic and Immigrant Minorities'. *Ethnic and Racial Studies* 15(4), 491–522.

Priddat, Birger (2013). 'Benign Order und Heaven on Earth – Kapitalismus als Religion?' in Peter Seele and Georg Pfleiderer, ed., *Kapitalismus – Eine Religion in der Krise I: Grundprobleme von Risiko, Vertrauen, Schuld*, 25–136. Baden-Baden: Nomos.

Priddat, Birger (2015). 'Schuld und Schulden: über eine abendländische Transformation', in Georg Pfleiderer, Peter Seele and Harald Matern, ed., *Kapitalismus – Eine Religion in der Krise II: Aspekte von Risiko, Vertrauen, Schuld*, 141–170. Baden-Baden: Nomos.

Rammert, Werner (2000). *Technik aus soziologischer Perspektive, Vol. II: Kultur-Innovation-Virtualität*. Opladen: Westdeutscher Verlag.

Reinhart, Carmen M., and Rogoff, Kenneth S. (2009). *This Time is Different: Eight Centuries of Financial Folly*. Princeton: Princeton University Press.

Riesebrodt, Martin (2007). *Cultus und Heilsversprechen: Eine Theorie der Religionen.* München: Beck.

Roberts, Anthony, and Kwon, Roy (2017). 'Finance, Inequality and the Varieties of Capitalism in Post-Industrial Democracies'. *Socio-Economic Review* 15(3), 511–538.

Robertson, Anthony, and Kwon, Roy (2017). 'Finance, Inequality and the Varieties of Capitalism in Post-Industrial Democracies'. *Socio-Economic Review* 15(3), 511–538.

Robertson, Roland (1995). 'Glocalization: Time-Space and Homogeneity-Heterogeneity', in *Global Modernities*, ed., Mike Featherstone, Scott Lash and Roland Robertson, 24–44. London: SAGE.

Robertson, Roland, and Chirico, JoAnn (1985). 'Humanity, Globalization and Worldwide Religious Resurgence: A Theoretical Exploration'. *Sociology of Religion* 46(3), 219–242.

Robinson, William I. (2004). *A Theory of Global Capitalism: Production, Class, and State in a Transnational World.* Baltimore: Johns Hopkins University Press.

Rodrik, Dani (2011). *The Globalization Paradox: Why Global Markets, States and Democracy Can't Coexist.* Oxford: Oxford University Press.

Roethlisberger, Fritz W., and Dickson, William J. (1939). *Management and the Worker.* Cambridge, MA: Cambridge University Press.

Rosa, Hartmut (2005). *Beschleunigung: Die Veränderung der Zeitstrukturen in der Moderne.* Frankfurt/M: Suhrkamp.

Roudomelof, Victor (2016). 'Theorizing Glocalization: Three Interpretations'. *European Journal of Social Theory* 19(3), 391–408.

Roy, Olivier (2010). *Heilige Einfalt: Über die politischen Gefahren entwurzelter Religionen.* München: Siedler.

Ruef, Martin (2005). 'Origins of Organizations', in Lisa A. Keister, ed., *Entrepreneurship*, 63–100. Amsterdam: Elsevier.

Rüstow, Alexander (2001). *Die Religion der Marktwirtschaft.* Münster: LIT.

Sachweh, Patrick, and Münnich, Sascha, eds. (2017). *Kapitalismus als Lebensform? Deutungsmuster, Legitimation und Kritik in der Marktgesellschaft.* Wiesbaden: VS.

Sahlins, Marshall (1972). *Stone Age Economics.* Chicago: Aldine-Atherton.

Sala-i-Martin, Xavier, and Artadi, Elsa (2004). 'The Global Competitiveness Index', in Michael Porter, Klaus Schwab and Augusto López-Carlos, ed., *The Global Competitiveness Report 2004–2005.* Oxford: Oxford University Press.

Sandel, Michael (2012). *What Money Can't Buy: The Moral Limits of Markets.* New York: Farrar, Strauss and Giroux.

Sassen, Saskia (2007). *A Sociology of Globalization.* New York: W.W. Norton & Company.

Sayer, Andrew (2015). *Why We Can't Afford the Rich.* Bristol: The Policy Press.

Schein, Edgar (with Peter Schein) (2017). *Organizational Culture and Leadership*, 5th Edition. Hoboken, NJ: Wiley.

Schimank, Uwe (2013). *Gesellschaft.* Bielefeld: Transcript.

Schimank, Uwe (2015). 'Modernity as a Functionally Differentiated Capitalist Society'. *European Journal of Social Theory* 18(4), 413–430.

Schimank, Uwe, and Volkmann, Ute (2008). 'Ökonomisierung der Gesellschaft', in Andrea Maurer, ed., *Handbuch der Wirtschaftssoziologie*, 382–393. Wiesbaden: VS.

Schimank, Uwe, and Volkmann, Ute (2017). *Das Regime der Konkurrenz: Gesellschaftliche Ökonomisierungsdynamiken heute.* Weinheim: Beltz.

Schluchter, Wolfgang (2016). 'Die Moderne – eine neue Achsenzeitkultur?', in: Thomas Schwinn and_Gert Albert, ed., *Alte Begriffe – Neue Probleme: Max Webers Soziologie im Lichte aktueller Problemstellungen*, 187–208. Tübingen: Mohr und Siebeck.

Schmitt, Carl (1934). *Politische Theologie: Vier Kapitel zur Lehre von der staatlichen Souveränität*. München: Duncker und Humblot.

Schreyögg, Georg, Sydow, Jörg and Koch, Jochen (2003). 'Organisatorische Pfade – Von der Pfadabhängigkeit zur Pfadkreation?' in Georg Schreyögg and Jörg Sydow, ed., *Strategische Prozesse und Pfade: Managementforschung 13*, 257–294. Wiesbaden: Gabler.

Schultze, Gerhard (1993). *Die Erlebnisgesellschaft: Kultursoziologie der Gegenwart*. Frankfurt/M: Campus.

Schumpeter, Joseph A. (1934 [1911]). *The Theory of Economic Development: An Inquiry into Profits, Capital, Credit, Interest and the Business Cycle*. London: Transaction Publishers.

Schumpeter, Joseph A. (2003 [1942]). *Capitalism, Socialism and Democracy*. New York: Harper and Brothers.

Schumpeter, Joseph A. (1991 [1947]). 'Comments on a Plan for the Study of Entrepreneurship', in Richard Swedberg, ed., *The Economics and Sociology of Capitalism*, 406–428. Princeton: Princeton University Press.

Schütz, Alfred (1971). 'Wissenschaftliche Interpretation und Alltagsverständnis menschlichen Handelns', in Ilse Schütz, ed., *Gesammelte Aufsätze Bd. 1: Das Problem der sozialen Wirklichkeit*, 3–54. Den Haag: Martinus Nijhoff.

Schwinn, Thomas (2001). *Differenzierung ohne Gesellschaft*. Weilerswist: Delbrück.

Sconce, Jeffrey (2004). 'Medium and Media', in Marita Sturken, Thomas Douglas and Sandra Ball-Rokeach, ed., *Technological Visions: The Hopes and Fears that Shape New Technologies*, 48–70. Philadelphia: Temple University Press.

Sengenberger, Werner (1987). *Struktur und Funktionsweise von Arbeitsmärkten: Die Bundesrepublik Deutschland im internationalen Vergleich*. Frankfurt/M: Campus.

Simmel, Georg (1989a [1890]). 'Über sociale Differenzierung', in *Aufsätze 1887 bis 1890: Über sociale Differenzierung: Die Probleme der Geschichtsphilosophie*, 109–297. Frankfurt/M: Suhrkamp.

Simmel, Georg (1989b [1900]). *Gesamtausgabe, Band 6: Philosophie des Geldes*. Frankfurt/M: Suhrkamp.

Simmel, Georg (1992 [1898]). 'Zur Soziologie der Religion', in Heinz-Jürgen Dahme and David P. Frisby, ed., *Gesamtausgabe, Vol. 5: Aufsätze und Abhandlungen 1894–1900*, 266–286. Frankfurt/M: Suhrkamp.

Simojoki, Henrik (2012). *Globalisierte Religion: Ausgangspunkte, Maßstäbe und Perspektiven religiöser Bildung in der Weltgesellschaft*. Tübingen: Mohr und Siebeck.

Simon, Herbert (1976 [1945]). *Administrative Behaviour*, 3rd Edition. New York: Simon & Schuster.

Skidelsky, Robert, and Skidelsky, Edward (2012). *How Much Is Enough? Money and the Good Life*. New York: Other Press.

Skinner, Andrew (1999). 'Introduction', in Adam Smith, *The Wealth of Nations, Books I–III*, 8–96. Revised Edition. London: Penguin.

Sklair, Leslie (2001). *The Transnational Capitalist Class*. Oxford: Wiley Blackwell.

Smith, Adam (1991 [1759]). *The Theory of Moral Sentiments*, ed. David D. Raphael. Oxford: Clarendon.

Smith, Adam (1999 [1776]). *The Wealth of Nations: Books I–III*. London: Penguin.

Sombart, Werner (1955 [1902]). *Der moderne Kapitalismus: Historisch-systematische Darstellung des gesamteuropäischen Wirtschaftslebens von seinen Anfängen bis zur Gegenwart, Vol. III, Part I: Das Wirtschaftsleben im Zeitalter des Hochkapitalismus*. Berlin: Duncker & Humblot.

Sombart, Werner (2002). *Nationalökonomie und Kapitalismustheorie: Ausgewählte Schriften*, ed. Alexander Ebner and Helge Peukert. Marburg: Metropolis.

Stalder, Felix (2006). *Manuel Castells: The Theory of the Network Society.* Cambridge: Polity Press.

Stamm, Isabel (2013). *Unternehmerfamilien: Der Einfluss des Unternehmens auf Lebenslauf, Generationenbeziehungen und soziale Identität.* Opladen: Budrich.

Stark, David (2009). *The Sense of Dissonance.* Princeton: Princeton University Press.

Stearns, Peter (1975). *Lives of Labor: Work in a Maturing Industrial Society.* New York: Holmes and Meier.

Strange, Susan (1986). *Casino Capitalism.* Oxford: Blackwell.

Strange, Susan (1996). *The Retreat of the State: The Diffusion of Power in the World Economy.* Cambridge: Cambridge University Press.

Streeck, Wolfgang (1990). 'Status and Contract as Basic Categories of a Sociological Theory of Industrial Relations', in David Sugerman and Gunther Teubner, ed., *Regulating Corporate Groups in Europe*, 105–145. Baden-Baden: Nomos.

Streeck, Wolfgang (2009). *Re-Forming Capitalism: Institutional Change in the German Political Economy.* Oxford: Oxford University Press.

Streeck, Wolfgang (2011). 'Taking Capitalism Seriously: Towards an Institutional Approach to Contemporary Political Economy'. *Socio-Economic Review* 9(1), 137–168.

Streeck, Wolfgang (2012). 'On Fred Block, Varieties of What? Should We Still Be Using the Concept of Capitalism?', in Julian Go, ed., *Political Power and Social Theory*, 311–321. Bingley, UK: Emerald.

Streeck, Wolfgang (2013). *Gekaufte Zeit: Die vertagte Krise des demokratischen Kapitalismus.* Frankfurt/M: Suhrkamp.

Streeck, Wolfgang (2016). *How Will Capitalism End? Essays on a Failing System.* London: Verso.

Sturken, Marita, Douglas, Thomas and Ball-Rokeach, Sandra, eds. (2004). *Technological Visions: The Hopes and Fears that Shape New Technologies.* Philadelphia: Temple University Press.

Tawney, Richard H. (1926). *Religion and the Rise of Capitalism: A Historical Study.* London: John Murray.

Taylor, Charles (2007). *A Secular Age*, Cambridge, MA: Harvard University Press.

Teece, David J. (2009). *Dynamic Capabilities and Strategic Management: Organizing for Innovation and Growth.* Oxford: Oxford University Press.

Teece, David J., Pisano, Gary and Shuen, Amy (1997). 'Dynamic Capabilities and Strategic Management'. *Strategic Management Journal* 18(7), 507–533.

Tenbruck, Friedrich (1981). 'Emile Durkheim oder die Geburt der Gesellschaft aus dem Geist der Soziologie'. *Zeitschrift für Soziologie* 4(10), 333–350.

Thielemann, Ulrich (2010). *Wettbewerb als Gerechtigkeitskonzept: Kritik des Neoliberalismus.* Marburg: Metropolis.

Thompson, Edward P. (1963). *The Making of the English Working Class.* New York: Pantheon Books.

Tillich, Paul (1988). 'Das Dämonische: Ein Beitrag zur Sinndeutung der Geschichte (1926)', in Robert P. Scharlemann, ed., *Hauptwerke Vol. 5: Religiöse Schriften*, 99–124. Berlin: De Gruyter.

Tillich, Paul (1989). 'The Demonic: A Study in the Interpretation of History', in Jacquelyn Ann K. Kegley, ed., *Paul Tillich on Creativity*, 63–91. London: University Press of America.

Tolbert, Pamela, and Zucker, Lynne G. (1996). 'The Institutionalization of Institutional Theory', in Stuart G. Clegg, Cynthia Hardy and Walter R. Nord, ed., *Handbooks of Organizational Studies*, 175–190. London: SAGE.

Türcke, Christoph (2015). *Philosophie des Geldes*. München: Beck.

Turner, Bryan S. (2011). *Religion and Modern Society: Citizenship, Secularization and the State*. Cambridge: Cambridge University Press.

Van der Zwan, Natascha (2014). 'Making Sense of Financialization'. *Socio-Economic Review* 12(1), 99–129.

Viner, Jacob (1972). *The Role of Providence in the Social Order: An Essay in Intellectual History*. Princeton: Princeton University Press.

Viner, Jacob (1978). *Religious Thought and Economic Society*. Durham, NC: Duke University Press.

Vogl, Joseph (2010). *Das Gespenst des Kapitals*. Zürich: Diaphanes.

Voss, Günter, and Pongratz, Hans J. (1998). 'Der Arbeitskraftunternehmer: Eine neue Grundform der Ware Arbeitskraft?' *Kölner Zeitschrift für Soziologie und Sozialpsychologie* 50(1), 131–158.

Wagner, Falk (1985). *Geld oder Gott? Zur Geldbestimmtheit der kulturellen und religiösen Lebenswelt*. Stuttgart: Klett-Cotta.

Wallerstein, Immanuel (1974). 'The Rise and Future Demise of the World Capitalist System: Concepts for Comparative Analysis'. *Comparative Studies in Society and History* 16(4), 387–415.

Wallerstein, Immanuel (1979). *The Capitalist World Economy*. Cambridge: Cambridge University Press.

Walras, Leon (1954 [1877]). *Elements of Pure Economics, or The Theory of Social Wealth*. Homewood, Ill.: Irwin.

Walzer, Michael (1983). *Spheres of Justice: A Defense of Pluralism and Equality*. New York: Basic Books.

Weber, Max (1972). *Wirtschaft und Gesellschaft*, 5th Edition. Tübingen: Mohr und Siebeck.

Weber, Max (1978). *Gesammelte Aufsätze zur Religionssoziologie, Vol. I*. Tübingen: Mohr.

Weber, Max (1981). *Wirtschaftsgeschichte: Abriss der universalen Sozial- und Wirtschaftsgeschite*. Berlin: Duncker und Humblot.

Weisskopf, Thomas (1993). 'A Democratic-Enterprise Based Market Socialism', in Pranab Bardhan and John E. Roemer, ed., *Market Socialism: The Current Debate*, 120–141. New York: Oxford University Press.

Welskopp, Thomas (2017). 'Zukunft bewirtschaften: Überlegungen zu einer praxistheoretisch informierten Historisierung des Kapitalismus'. *Mittelweg 36: Zeitschrift des Hamburger Instituts für Sozialforschung* 26(1), 81–97.

White, Harrison C. (1981). 'Where Do Markets Come From?' *American Journal of Sociology* 87(3), 517–547.

White, Harrison C. (2005). 'Varieties of Markets', in Richard Swedberg, ed., *New Developments in Economic Sociology Vol. II*, 23–57. Cheltenham: Edward Elgar.

Wilson, Rodney (1997). *Economics, Ethics and Religion: Jewish, Christian and Muslim Economic Thought*. London: Macmillan.

Windeler, Arnold (2003). 'Kreation technologischer Pfade: Ein strukturationstheoretischer Analyseansatz' in Georg Schreyögg and Jörg Sydow, ed., *Strategische Prozesse und Pfade: Managementforschung 13*, 295–328. Wiesbaden: Gabler.

Windolf, Paul (2005). 'Was ist Finanzmarkt-Kapitalismus?' in Paul Windolf, ed., *Finanzmarkt-Kapitalismus: Analysen zum Wandel von Produktionsregimen*, 20–57. Wiesbaden: VS.

Witt, Ulrich (2006). 'Evolutionary Economics'. Papers on Economics and Evolution, No. 0605. Jena: Max Planck Institute of Economics.

Wolf, Martin (1999). 'Why This Hatred of the Market?' in *The Globalization Reader*, ed., Frank J. Lechner and John Boli, 9–11. Malden, MA: Blackwell.

Wright, Erik Olin (2010). *Envisioning Real Utopias*. London: Verso.

WTO (2015). *International Trade Statistics 2015*. Geneva: World Trade Organization.

Zelizer, Viviane A. (1997). *The Social Meaning of Money*. Princeton: Princeton University Press.

Zinser, Hartmut (2006). 'Der verkaufte Gott: Zur Vermarktung der Religion'. *Westend: Neue Zeitschrift für Sozialforschung* 3(1), 109–120.

Zürn, Michael, and de Wilde, Pieter (2016). 'Debating Globalization: Cosmopolitanism and Communitarianism as Political Ideologies'. *Journal of Political Ideologies* 21(3), 280–301.

# Index

For Product Safety Concerns and Information please contact our EU representative GPSR@taylorandfrancis.com Taylor & Francis Verlag GmbH, Kaufingerstraße 24, 80331 München, Germany